Music in the Works of Broch, Mann, and Kafka

The German Romantic critic Friedrich Schlegel saw music as a paradigm of art, and wished to bring the qualities of music to literature. Schopenhauer saw in music a direct manifestation of the Will, and thus considered it the highest form of art. This study examines the ironic influence of these and similar ideas of music's primacy among the arts on three of the most important modern writers of German: Hermann Broch, Thomas Mann, and Franz Kafka. Of the three, Broch takes Schlegel's idea furthest: His novel *The Death of Vergil* uses the constructive techniques and sonorities of music to extend the cognitive reach of his writing to the non- or supraverbal, and Hargraves traces similar concerns across Broch's career. Unlike Broch, Mann saw in musicality a peculiarly German access to the dark forces within the human psyche. Music is the "glass" through which the reader sees the development of the anti-hero Hans Castorp in Mann's *Magic Mountain*. In *Doktor Faustus*, on the other hand, the hero Leverkuhn conjures with demonic powers to create fictional music; his "strict style" is itself an allegory of the political realities of the twentieth century. Kafka admitted that he had little appreciation for music, but two of his important shorter works, "Josefine the Singer" and "Investigations of a Dog," transform this "unmusicality" into an enigmatic essay on the uses and limits of art. Hargraves uncovers surprisingly parallel concerns among these three very different writers.

John Hargraves is assistant professor of German at Connecticut College, New London, Connecticut.

Studies in German Literature, Linguistics, and Culture

Edited by James Hardin
(*South Carolina*)

John A. Hargraves

Music in the Works of Broch, Mann, and Kafka

CAMDEN HOUSE

First published 2002
by Camden House

Camden House is an imprint of Boydell & Brewer Inc.
PO Box 41026, Rochester, NY 14604–4126 USA
and of Boydell & Brewer Limited
PO Box 9, Woodbridge, Suffolk IP12 3DF, UK

ISBN: 1–57113–208–2

Library of Congress Cataloging-in-Publication Data

Hargraves, John.
    Music in the works of Broch, Mann, and Kafka / John A. Hargraves.
        p. cm. — (Studies in German literature, linguistics, and culture).
    Includes bibliographical references and index.
    ISBN 1–57113–208–2 (alk. paper)
        1. German literature—20th century—History and criticism. 2. Music
    in literature.   3. Broch, Hermann, 1886–1951—Knowledge—Music.
    4. Mann, Thomas, 1875–1955—Knowledge—Music.   5. Kafka, Franz,
    1883–1924—Knowledge—Music.   I. Title.   II. Studies in German
    literature, linguistics, and culture (Unnumbered)

    PT405 .H344 2001
    830.9'357—dc21
                                                        2001037868

A catalogue record for this title is available from the British Library.

This publication is printed on acid-free paper.
Printed in the United States of America.

For Nancy

Contents

Abbreviations

A   Adorno, Theodor W. *Philosophie der neuen Musik*. Frankfurt: Suhrkamp Verlag, 1976.

DF   Mann, Thomas. *Doktor Faustus*. Frankfurt: S. Fischer Verlag, 1967.

F   Kafka, Franz. *The Metamorphosis and Other Stories*. Trans. Donna Freed. New York: Barnes and Noble, 1996.

JSU   Broch, Hermann. *The Death of Virgil*. Trans. Jean Starr Untermeyer. San Francisco: North Point Press, 1945.

KW   Broch, Hermann. *Kommentierte Werkausgabe*. Ed. Paul Michael Lützeler. Frankfurt: Suhrkamp Verlag, vols. 1–13, 1974–1981.

MB   Adorno, Theodor W. *Philosophy of Modern Music*. Trans. Anne G. Mitchell and Wesley V. Blomster. New York: Seabury Press, 1973.

SE   Kafka, Franz. *Sämtliche Erzählungen*. Ed. Paul Raabe. Frankfurt: Fischer Taschenbuchverlag, 1987.

W   Mann, Thomas. *The Magic Mountain*. Trans. John E. Woods. New York: Alfred A. Knopf, 1995.

Z   Mann, Thomas. *Der Zauberberg*. Frankfurt: Fischer Bücherei, 1967.

Introduction

Broch, Mann, Kafka, and Musical Modernism

I TRACE MY INTEREST IN GERMAN LITERATURE to the influence of music, specifically, to a revered piano teacher I studied with at college. She was a German refugee and the first person to make German culture, in several of its facets, come alive for me. This woman, now long dead, was a person who had had plenty of reasons to reject her native language and culture, but who instead chose to show us young men (for it was a men's college) who chose to study the piano with her that the richness and greatness of German culture was not to be judged solely by the events of the twentieth century. During this time I began to learn and play the unique body of music which comprises the world of the *lied*, and to become fascinated by that realm where music and words are intertwined in such astounding variety. This inexhaustible variety showed me that music had the ability to heighten, even transform, an indifferent text, or, in other instances, simply to be the background for great poetry; the best case is where music and great words are combined in an art which is truly greater than the sum of its parts.

When I began to study German literature more intensively, I became fascinated by the well-known close association of music and eighteenth- and nineteenth-century German writing; from the age of Goethe to the Romantics, and down through successive literary generations, the affinity of German writing for music has been well documented.[1]

This trend continues just as strongly into the twentieth century, with Thomas Mann (*Doktor Faustus,* 1947) and Hermann Hesse (*Das Glasperlenspiel,* 1943) among the most well-known authors of all those who choose the world of music as the milieu of their novels.

But however obvious the affinity of music and literature within German-language cultures may seem, most scholarship investigating this affinity has had to struggle with the chasm that effectively separates them: the nonmimetic nature of music. When studying the affinity of music and literature in German one is confronted with the history of that philosophical debate in aesthetics as to which art form is the "higher." Some writers have taken a historical approach to this question, tracing the history of literature with regard to its interest in and connection to music. This approach can be a survey of musical characters within the body of literature.[2] Some writers have tried to bridge this gap by looking into the phenomenon of verbal music,[3] where words are made to reproduce the experience of absolute music, such as Thomas Mann did with Wagner's Prelude to Act 3 of *Die Meistersinger*. There are innumerable books and articles on specific writers such as Thomas Mann and E. T. A. Hoffmann, and on writers' interest in various composers, musicians and compositions. There have been conferences on German literature and music, like the one at Champagne-Urbana[4] and compilations of essays on music and literature of a specific period, for example, the 1992 volume by Claus Reschke and Howard Pollack.[5] Most of these attempts at investigating the relationship between words (or literature) and music address specific composers and specific works. They are largely descriptive or historical. While modern sensibilities tend to avoid trying to answer questions on the hierarchic rank of music and the other arts, it is clear that the age in which we live is one in which the effective influence of both sound (the ubiquity of modern popular music in everyday life) and image (popular press, television, Internet) are beginning to rival, if not overtake, that of the written word. This phenomenon was even hinted at in some of the essays of Hermann Broch.[6]

The present study is the first book-length attempt to investigate the importance of music in the writings of Hermann Broch (1886–1951), one of the greatest and best-known writers of the twentieth century. The study will show that music is central to the philosophy, and in some cases, to the structure, of Broch's work. In an attempt to clarify the unique quality of Broch's approach to music, the study will also investigate in depth two works of Thomas Mann, and several of Franz Kafka, two German-language writers together with whom Broch is often discussed. As will be seen, music has a radically different significance for all three writers; and while music is important in Mann (and relatively unimportant in Kafka), it is central to the thinking of Hermann Broch.

Broch's other extraliterary concerns, such as mathematics, sociology, and physics, have received some attention; Ernestine Schlant and Willy Riemer, among others, have examined the question of Broch's mathematical and physical interests;[7] studies on aesthetic considerations such as architecture, kitsch, and ornament exist in profusion. Friedrich Vollhardt's *Hermann Brochs geschichtliche Stellung*[8] investigates the effect of Broch's early philosophical studies on his 1931/32 novel *Die Schlafwandler* (The Sleepwalkers) and on his theories of value and aesthetics. But almost no attention has been paid to the significance of music in his novels and essays.[9] Although Broch's musical training and background were not professional, music came to occupy an important position in his works and philosophy: he tried to expand the reach of literature by bringing to it the aesthetic and epistemological qualities of music. So in light of the many important musical references and the philosophic implications of music throughout his work, the dearth of writing on the subject is surprising. The present study makes a modest start at filling this gap. It examines the most important writings of Hermann Broch that have a strong thematic or philosophical link with music, and it analyzes the relationship of these writings to Broch's essays. While there are musical references in each of the works discussed, they play a much larger role in some works than in others. The longest chapter is devoted to the most musical of Broch's work, *Der Tod des Vergil* (The Death of Virgil, 1945); two sections of that chapter discuss music which the work inspired, and the relationship between music and time.

Broch can be seen as advancing a belief dating back to German Romanticism: the judgment that, of all the arts, music is the highest, most sublime form of expression.[10] In Germany, this subordination of other arts to music[11] was a conscious rejection of the hierarchy outlined in Hegel's *Ästhetik*, where music, while ranked above the plastic arts, is a step below poetry. Broch's philosophical position on music and literature clearly has Romantic antecedents.

Music's shift to the top of aesthetic hierarchy began with Wackenroder, in his portrait of the fictional composer Berglinger in *Herzensergießungen eines kunstliebenden Klosterbruders* (Out-pourings of an Art-Loving Friar, 1797). Here, music's conflation of meaning and form, of signifier and signified, its association with the direct and immediate expression of innermost emotion, are all qualities ascribed to music to justify assigning it primacy among the arts. Its capability of expressing universality[12] echoes throughout Romantic theory, but also in the modernist Hermann Broch.

Music's ability to work miracles, or at least moral improvement (Aristotle's μουσικη παιδεια), is a Romantic topos (cf. Wackenro-der[13] and Kleist[14]) which Broch uses, sometimes ironically, as in *Pasenow* (1931) or *Huguenau* (1932). Even Broch's naïveté about music's technicalities and how music is created has a somewhat Romantic sound, and he sometimes slips into that same kind of *Schwärmerei* which is common in musical description from Wack-enroder to Mann. This attitude is common in Romantic descrip-tions of musicians.[15] But for the most part Broch maintains a cool objectivity in his discussion of music. He is unlike Wackenroder's musician, Berglinger, who is dismayed on discovering the me-chanical, mathematical basis of music composition. Broch is more like Mann's Leverkühn (*Doktor Faustus,* 1947), and Hesse's Knecht (*Das Glasperlenspiel* [The Glass Bead Game], 1943), in that he affirms the mathematical and natural aspects of music, and like Hesse's hero, Broch accords music preeminent artistic status because it is the most abstract of arts.

Significantly, Broch did not write an artist's novel (*Künstlerro-man*) like Mann's Faustus novel; except for the poet Virgil (who at this point is primarily confronting his own mortality, rather than artistic issues), there is only one other sympathetically drawn crea-tive figure in Broch's work — and he is a physicist.[16] But music is a latent protagonist in many passages of the novels discussed in this study, particularly in *Der Tod des Vergil*. It is not just in *Die Schlafwandler*, but throughout the works, that one is reminded of Schopenhauer's comparison of the art of music to sleepwalking: music, "like a magnetic somnambulist, attaining insight into things which one has no idea of when awake."[17]

The French composer Jean Barraqué (1928–1973) read Broch's *The Death of Virgil* in French translation in 1955, and felt that the work was so innately musical that he decided to devote the rest of his creative life to a gigantic musical work based on texts from the novel. This incomplete work, which was to have been "much longer than the *Saint Matthew Passion* and *Parsifal* combined,"[18] envisioned five parts, four of these corresponding to the sections of Broch's novel, with the fifth recapitulating themes from all four. Barraqué, like Broch, wanted to create works "in which technique and aesthetic are perfectly fused."[19] If the writers of modernism share "one tendency that distinguishes them from the poetic tradition celebrating cosmic harmony: [it is] a fascination with dissonance."[20] This fascination with dissonance is reflected in the work of Barraqué, whose work is briefly discussed in the chapter on *The Death of Virgil.*

Another concern Broch has in common with many other German writers is the relationship of time and space in the various arts. With music, of course, time has a special significance. From at least the time of Lessing's *Laokoön* (Laocoön, or On the Limits of Painting and Music, 1776), German writers have been discussing these relationships. Many other writers (Schopenhauer, for example) also viewed the irreversible process of time as the essence of the world's negativity and imperfection. Consequently, annulling time has an ethical and utopian component in the writings of such thinkers. The idea that music is the art that accomplishes this best is not unique to Broch. The concept of music stopping time, turning time to space[21] (and its converse, of architecture being frozen music), has a tradition going back beyond Goethe. The Viennese writer Otto Weininger, whose work Broch knew, has thoughts on time and music which had an obvious influence on his earliest writings.[22] Few if any writers, however, took these ideas as literally, or applied them as conscientiously to their efforts, as Broch.

Like Schopenhauer, Broch emphasizes the immediacy of musical experience. For Schopenhauer, music "expresses completely in its own language the inner essence of the will before it congeals into singular forms."[23] For Broch, on the other hand, the special quality of music is not that it is the manifestation of the will (which in Schopenhauer must ultimately be denied), but that it expresses a unitary, integral cognitive process incapable of expression by the intellect and its faculties. It is for this reason that Broch refers to his work as "musical." George Steiner sees in music a clue to understanding the meaning of existence:

Music *means,* even where, most especially where, there is no way whatever to paraphrase this meaning, to restate it in any alternative way . . . In music, being and meaning are inextricable. They deny paraphrase. But they *are,* and our experience of this "essentiality" is as certain as any in human awareness.[24]

This existential quality of music and its "meaning" is echoed in Broch specifically in certain essays, and implicitly in much of *Vergil,* as will be demonstrated. Contrasting Broch with Mann brings two aspects of Broch's musicality into sharper focus. Mann's musical tastes were Romantic to the core, the sympathetic portraiture of his twelve-tone composer Adrian Leverkühn notwithstanding.[25] Despite the appropriation of Schönberg's (via Adorno) theories of "new music"[26] in *Doktor Faustus,* Mann's most characteristic descriptions of music and its philosophical implications usually take place in the context of Romantic music, from Beethoven to Wagner, for example, in *Buddenbrooks* (1901), in the novellas *Tristan* (1903) and *Wälsungenblut* (The Blood of the Walsungs, 1906) as well as in *Doktor Faustus* itself.[27] Despite the reverence for Schönberg which he shows in his essay on music, Broch actually evinces fairly little interest in music after Beethoven. If Mann's passion for romantic music is most like that of his character Gerda Buddenbrook, Broch's might be more that of the old organ master Pfühl, Gerda's music teacher, with his love of Bachian counterpoint and polyphony.[28] In particular Broch's rejection of opera, and Wagner in particular, distinguishes him from Mann. But if Mann's enthusiasm for Wagner and Romanticism is leavened with irony, Broch's theoretical benediction of modern music and lengthy critiques of Wagner are strangely unconvincing. One must ask: Does Broch protest too much?[29]

Another difference between the two: Mann's writing on music is linked to a negativity which ultimately leads to the demonic extreme of Leverkühn's "music of the abyss." In much of Mann's writing, from *Buddenbrooks* (1901) on, music is associated with decline, aestheticism, disease, and death; characters associated with this decadence abound: from Hanno Buddenbrook in *Buddenbrooks* and Detlev Spinell in *Tristan,* to Rudi Schwerdtfeger and Adrian Leverkühn in *Doktor Faustus.* With Broch, by and large, the opposite applies. Except when choosing to emphasize a debased environment, for which suitably "low" music is used, Broch otherwise usually associates with music the qualities of exaltation, metaphysical progress, apotheosis. Broch ostensibly affirms the progressive quality of "modern" music over a reversion to Romanticism. But this affirmation takes the form of a distanced and theoretical discussion of Schönberg's contribution to the art; nowhere does Broch grapple with the effect of modern music on the listener as Mann does in *Doktor Faustus*. No account is given of the emotional impact of modern music, as Adorno gives, for example (and Mann adapted[30]), in his book *Philosophie der neuen Musik*.[31] In Mann we find music described as basically the expression of pain (Leverkühn's "Lamentation"); in Adorno, twelve-tone music's qualities of autonomy and "indifference" have a correspondence to conditions of modern life. A similar analysis of musical effect in general, or even of an individual musical piece (such as E. T. A. Hoffman or Mann offer, respectively, in analyses of Beethoven's Fifth Symphony or Wagner's *Meistersinger* third act prelude) is not present in Broch's novels or essays. Like Adorno, Broch sees that the historical destiny of music, like that of all art forms, is to change and grow into new forms, to rearrange cognitive properties in such a way that new ones are continually arrived at, then superseded, in an infinite series.

Broch's philosophical positions concerning music have significantly affected his literary output, especially the *Vergil*, and his essayistic work, the essays on Hofmannsthal and Schönberg in particular. Like Hofmannsthal, Broch saw in music a refuge for the artist when language can no longer fulfill the demands placed on it. In his essays he occasionally despairs of the cloudy, dream-like quality of poetry, and of its opaque structure. He admires the rationality of music, its clarity of structure. He regrets that we will never be able to create a "harmonics" or a "counterpoint" of literature.[32] Broch, the *poeta doctus*, envies the composer his theoretical grounding in "rules"; Broch, the *Dichter wider Willen* (poet against his will) as he was termed by Hannah Arendt,[33] ruefully admires the abstract nature of musical cognition.

The present study analyzes those works of Broch that have music as a subject; it also shows in what ways Broch brought to his writing not the forms of music but its cognitive methods. It starts with an investigation of some of the theoretical essays.

xvi   INTRODUCTION

Broch's most important musical method is the attempt to pro-
duce the effect of simultaneity; in this he is a kindred spirit to
Joyce, Proust, and Mann. But unlike Proust and Mann, who aim
for simultaneity but who proceed in more or less traditional narrative forms, Broch directly attacks the reader's sense of narrative
time. Although Joyce's narrative style is also nontraditional, it is
not comparable to Broch's in *Der Tod des Vergil,* where the concept of "eidetic" units is used to construct sentences of great
length and complexity: by attempting a paramusical figuration of
simultaneity, he hoped literature, like music, could have the ethical
effect of temporarily freeing man from the fear of death.

Broch's work does not seem to stop time as well as music does,
nor could *any* extended work of literature. On the contrary, the
style of *Der Tod des Vergil* makes the book seem longer than it actually is. But where the novel is most successful in its figuration of
simultaneity and the use of other quasimusical cognitive methods,
such as the repetition of words and phrases, it is unique. Although
music interests Broch in much of his work, it is in *Der Tod des Vergil* that he puts his ideas to a real test. In a way and to a degree
which no other work has ever achieved, this novel, which is finally
about being, rather than ceasing to be, creates its meaning in the
same way that great music does. What is this meaning? One must
answer the question, as Schumann did when asked the same of one
of his compositions, by playing it again.[34]

Franz Kafka's work can be considered the "control group" of
this study, for when compared to that of Mann and Broch, it is almost devoid of musical references or musical techniques. Although
there are certain repetitive themes in the longer works, Kafka had
so little to say about music that such an analysis would appear to be
far-fetched. But there do exist signs of a concern with music, particularly in his last work, written in part from his deathbed: "Josefine die Sängerin, oder das Volk der Mäuse" (Josephine the Singer,
or the Mouse-Folk). There are notable passages in *Amerika,* and in
the enigmatic "Forschungen eines Hundes" (Investigations of a
Dog), where music plays an anomalous and intriguing role. These
works assign a peculiarly negative role to music: music is an accompaniment to blindness and error, cognitive failure. This is in
marked contrast to the rich and varied role of music in the writing
of Mann and Broch.

The reader will note that the major part of this study is devoted to musicality in the writings of Hermann Broch. As stated above, Kafka and Mann are included for the purpose of contrast and to highlight with particular vividness Broch's unique contribution in the use of musical thematics and musical techniques in the novel of German modernism.

A note on citations: Since all three writers are widely read in English translation, all citations where possible are presented in English translations, and the standard translations are generally used. However, there are a small number of cases where the original German is cited to emphasize a particular point, particularly when dealing with the *Death of Virgil*. Also, there are several works cited which have not yet been translated and published: in these cases my own translations are used. Sometimes where the German is particularly complicated, I give the original in footnote to back up my paraphrase or translation.

Notes

[1] Just a few of the writers of this period interested in music and literature: Wackenroder (*Herzensergießungen*, 1797; *Phantasien über die Kunst*, 1799), E. T. A. Hoffmann (*Kreisleriana*, 1810; *Phantasiestücke*, 1815; *Die Serapionsbrüder*, 1821), Lenau (*Faust*, 1835), Grillparzer (*Der arme Spielmann*, 1844), Keller (*Romeo und Julia auf dem Dorfe*, 1856; *Das Tanzlegendchen*, 1872), Mörike (*Maler Nolten*, 1832; *Mozart auf der Reise nach Prag*, 1856), Nietzsche (*Geburt der Tragödie aus dem Geist der Musik*, 1872), and Schnitzler (*Der Weg ins Freie*, 1908).

[2] George Schoolfield, *The Figure of the Musician in German Literature* (New York: AMS Press, 1966).

[3] Among them most notably, Steven Scher, *Verbal Music in German Literature* (New Haven: Yale UP, 1968).

[4] *Music and German Literature: Their Relationship Since the Middle Ages*, ed. James M. McGlathery (Columbia, SC: Camden House, 1992).

[5] *German Literature and Music. An Aesthetic Fusion: 1890–1989.* (Munich: Wilhelm Fink Verlag, 1992).

[6] For instance, *Das Böse im Wertsystem der Kunst*, KW 9/2, 119–57.

[7] Ernestine Schlant, "Brochs Roman *Die unbekannte Größe (1933)*," 110–34, and Willy Riemer, "Mathematik und Physik bei Hermann Broch, 260–71, in *Hermann Broch*, ed. Paul Michael Lützeler (Frankfurt: Suhrkamp, 1986).

[8] Tübingen: Max Niemeyer Verlag, 1984.

[9] Except for articles by Jean Paul Boyer ("Hermann Broch: auch ein Wagneri-aner wider Willen?" in Kessler/Lützeler, *Hermann Broch: Das dichterische Werk*, 231–38, and Marianne Charriére-Jacquin, "Zum Verhältnis Musik — Literatur im *Tod des Vergil*," in the same work, 7–18.

[10] For a discussion of this idea, see Barbara Naumann, *"Musikalisches Ideen-Instrument." Das Musikalische in Poetik und Sprachtheorie der Frühromantik* (Stuttgart: Metzler, 1990), 1–7.

[11] This ranking is not necessarily made by all Romantics, and certainly not by their chief theorist, Friedrich Schlegel, whose goal was to bring to literature the qualities of musicality. Music was seen as the paradigm for the other arts: in music one saw the completed development of the Romantic ideal still to be achieved in literature. (Naumann 3). Broch's fragment *Ophelia* offers a simi-larly paradigmatic view of music. (Hermann Broch, *Novellen, Prosa, Fragmente,* Kommentierte Werkausgabe, vol. 6 (henceforth: KW 6) (Frankfurt: Suhrkamp, 1980), 32–33.

[12] "Dein ganzes Leben muß *eine* Musik sein": Wilhelm Wackenroder, *Her-zensergießungen eines kunstliebenden Klosterbruders* (1797) (Stuttgart: Re-clam, 1979), 107.

[13] *Die Wunder der Tonkunst,* in *Phantasien über die Kunst* (The Miracles of Music, in Fantasies on Art, 1799).

[14] "Die heilige Cäcilie oder die Gewalt der Musik" (Saint Cecilia, or the Power of Music, 1810).

[15] See George Schoolfield, *The Figure of the Musician in German Literature* (New York: AMS Press, 1966), 13.

[16] The physicist Richard Hieck in *Die unbekannte Größe* (The Unknown Quantity, 1933).

[17] "wie eine magnetische Somnambule gibt Aufschlüsse über Dinge, von de-nen sie wachend keinen Begriff hat." Arthur Schopenhauer, *Die Welt als Wille und Vorstellung (The World as Will and Idea)* (Munich: Piper, 1924) I, 309.

[18] Andre Hodeir, *Since Debussy,* trans. Noel Burch (Grove Press: New York, 1961), 200.

[19] G. W. Hopkins, *Musical Times* 107 (4 Nov 1966), 952.

[20] Susan von Rohr Scaff, *History, Myth and Music. Thomas Mann's Timely Fic-tion* (Columbia, SC: Camden House, 1998), 1.

[21] Hofmannsthal's *Buch der Freunde* (The Friends' Book), a collection of aphorisms he collected over his lifetime (and which Broch quotes in his study), contains the trope as well. Hugo von Hofmannsthal, *Buch der Freun-de. Tagebuch-Aufzeichnungen.* (Leipzig: Insel-Verlag, 1929), 76.

[22] "'Zum Raum wird hier die Zeit': hierin liegt, recht dunkel freilich, der Raum als Symbol der Vollendung" ("Here time becomes space": in this we

can see, if obscurely, space as the symbol of perfect completion). This *Parsifal* citation, from Weininger's essay "Über den Gedankengehalt der Werke Richard Wagners" in: *Über die letzten Dinge (Last Things)* (Vienna: Wilhelm Braumüller, 1930) is discussed by Manfred Durzak (cf. below, chapter 5, note 21). Other similarities between the two writers: Weininger's discussion of the numbers 1 and 3 are very like Broch's early aesthetic sketches, reverence for Beethoven as the greatest composer, and contempt for dance in general (seen in Broch's essay *Hofmannsthal und seine Zeit* (1947/48) and in Part 3 of the trilogy *Die Schlafwandler, Huguenau.*

[23] Georg Simmel, *Schopenhauer and Nietzsche,* trans. Helmut Loiskandl, Deena Weinstein, and Michael Weinstein (Amherst: U of Massachusetts P, 1986), 92.

[24] *Martin Heidegger* (Chicago: U of Chicago P, 1989), 44.

[25] The narrator describes a late, presumably twelve-tone work: "How I love the stormy surge of yearning that is its essential character, the Romanticism of its tone — since, after all, it is handled with the strictest modern methods; a thematic work, to be sure, but with such strong transformations that there are no true 'reprises.'" Thomas Mann, *Doktor Faustus,* trans. John E. Woods (New York: Alfred A. Knopf, 1997), 478.

[26] Schönberg threatened to sue Mann if he did not acknowledge twelve-tone music as his intellectual property (which he did). But beyond the use of Schönberg's terminology, Mann borrowed much more heavily from the ideas and passages in Theodor Adorno's writing.

[27] Even here when describing the serial creations of his friend, Zeitblom's Romantic bias is evident.

[28] Pfühl, of course, is eventually partly won over, but not without resistance!

[29] Or, as Jean Paul Boyer asks in his article in Kessler/Lützeler: *Hermann Broch: Das dichterische Werk,* 231–38, was he a Wagnerian *malgré lui*?

[30] Mann had access to Adorno's manuscript before its final publication in 1949.

[31] Theodor W. Adorno, *Philosophie der neuen Musik* (Frankfurt: Suhrkamp, 1976), 36ff., "Schönberg und der Fortschritt."

[32] Hermann Broch, "Das Weltbild des Romans," in *Hermann Broch: Kommentierte Werkausgabe,* vol. 9/2, ed. Paul Michael Lützeler (Frankfurt: Suhrkamp, 1974–1981), 108.

[33] Hannah Arendt, in *Dichter wider Willen: Einführung in das Werk von Hermann Broch* (Zurich: Rhein-Verlag, 1958), 41.

[34] Steiner 44.

1: Hermann Broch:
Biographical Background; Music Essays

Biographical Background

EARLY MUSICAL INFLUENCES ON BROCH were those typical of a prosperous Viennese Jewish family of the *haute bourgeoisie* at the turn of the century. There is considerable data, in letter form, attesting to these early musical influences. The family engaged as a tutor the journalist and sometime music reviewer David Bach (1874–1947),[1] who was later to become the feuilleton editor of the Vienna journal *Arbeiter-Zeitung*,[2] and was a friend of Arnold Schönberg. Young Hermann attended the Staats-Realschule in Vienna with future composers Alban Berg and Egon Wellesz, both of whom would later study under Schönberg. Broch maintained a correspondence with Alban Berg in later life, exchanging a copy of his *Schlafwandler* for a copy of the last scene of *Wozzeck*.[3] Broch must also have known the much younger Rudolf Bing (b. 1902), later to become general manager of the Metropolitan Opera.[4]

Correspondence between the twenty-one-year-old Hermann Broch and his ardently courted fiancée-to-be, Franziska ("Fanny") de Rothermann, written in the years 1907 to 1909, reveals some of Broch's earliest impressions of music. This unpublished correspondence has a marked erotic component; musical interests shared by the two young people were a significant part of their courtship period. In an early letter of the correspondence (26 November 1907[?])[5] Broch compares their relationship to Wagner's infamous affair with Mathilde Wesendonck, and Franziska's opinion of his (Broch's) "compositions" to Wesendonck's of Wagner's.[6] Evenings at the opera were a feature of the Broch family routine, and Broch's frequent reports on his activities, sent to placate the jealously uneasy Fanny, often include mention of theatrical and musical performances. Operas and operettas mentioned in these letters include *Manon Lescaut, Bohème, Butterfly,*[7] *Samson et Dalila, Bajazzo* (*Pagliacci*), *Il Barbiere di Seviglia,* Oskar Straus's *Ein Walzertraum,* Johann Strauss's *Fledermaus.* Other musical activities of this period comprised sessions of four-hand piano duets with his uncle and his brother. Broch seems to have been a sufficiently accomplished pianist to play opera scores (or portions of them) and various *Albumblätter* of Grieg.[8]

Broch and his family also frequently attended operetta performances at the Karlstheater, where they had a subscription. (Broch refers to "usual" seats). At one point Broch invites Fanny to attend a concert of baroque music on historic instruments (*concert des instruments anciens*). In a letter, Broch associates this concert with his reading of eighteenth-century French literature, finding an elegance and simplicity in both.

In another letter of this period, he refers to his ideas on rhythm, associating with them, one imagines, his romantic feelings for Franziska:

> It is well-known that there is nothing baser than to bore one's fellow men . . . but not being a bore means not to repeat oneself. But real feeling must of necessity repeat itself. This may sound like drivel, but feeling really has a rhythm, and thus the ability either to sweep you up or be monotonous.[9]

The linking of rhythm with emotion which Broch discusses in this letter to his fiancée is consistent with the later music essay. Broch is sensitive to the appeal of rhythmic music, which he tried to explain in theoretical terms in the 1912 essay noted above (*Notizen zu einer systematischen Ästhetik*). During a trip to Budapest in 1908 he complains of being depressed by gypsy music:

> The gypsy music, even though it is incessant, has the decided advantage of conjuring up the great fiddler's elegy. It's really rather sad, this music, for they play the Czardas so well and the Waltz-Dream so poorly.[10]

A week or so later he writes:

> Yes, I slaved away on Grieg for a while. I am terribly fond of him — he has definitely come the closest to the secret of rhythm. By the way, have you ever noticed how everything beautiful in life is rhythmic?[11]

These are not musically sophisticated observations; Grieg, gypsy music, Oskar Straus: all the music mentioned by Broch was widely appreciated by the public at that time. That Broch appreciates the popular, even kitschy, music of the day is less remarkable than the unspoken need to rationalize these tastes — tastes he seems to be defensive about. Broch seems embarrassed about liking Puccini, for example; the quoted letter (see notes to this chapter) attribute this attraction to Franziska's effect on him. An early fragment, "Dirigent Jasper"[12] has an orchestral conductor musing about similar distinctions: "he asked himself why there was a Tchaikovsky when there was already a Beethoven. What were these people here? Tchaikovskys, or even less, much less. He just didn't want to conduct any more."[13]

Broch's ambivalence about popular music, and opera in particular, remains characteristic through his life. In the diary of letters to his lifelong friend Ea von Allesch,[14] Broch put down some thoughts about music. (According to the annotations written by Broch's son, H. F. Broch de Rothermann, Ea von Allesch was very musical and took piano lessons herself almost her entire life.) At one point in the journal, Broch records having taken his son to an evening at the Volksoper: "picked up the boy, went to the theater to see The Tramp; it's funny, one just can't appreciate this so-called music any longer."[15] His ambivalence is shown by the wording: the "so-called" music certainly is a pejorative term; yet Broch finds it strange that he can no longer understand or appreciate it. In another entry in the same journal, Broch sees in Schubert traces of the Viennese operetta to come.

> After supper my brother played Schubert, to rework it into Foxtrots. He [Schubert] doesn't deserve any better: the entire world of Viennese operetta is already present in him. The problem with Schubert, as with all so-called "light" music (with few exceptions) is: it's all been said already—the construct of a relationship to all that exists (die Konstruktion des Gesamtzusammenhanges des Seienden überhaupt) as in Beethoven, for example, is no longer possible.[16]

Did Broch really think Schubert was "light" music? This harsh judgment shows that sometimes Broch's philosophical expectations of music interfere with his ability to see the work on its own terms. Schubert is found wanting, because, unlike Beethoven, whose work

represents a construct of the "total inter-relatedness of all existence" (Gesamtzusammenhang des Seienden), Schubert's work
"says" everything. Is this because it is lyrical? or because it sets poetry, in *Lieder*? At any rate, its mode of cognition is fragmentary
and partial, like natural science ("Einzelurteil und Wissenschaft"),
in Broch's view. He continues with a sort of rear-guard tactic, as if
defending his view against those with more authority:

> Of course, one need not be "musical" to know this; musicality is
> a precarious concept anyway — music is the only art in which re-
> ceptivity is seen as positive, which of course it is not.[17]

Musicality in this passage refers to the auditor, not the composer.
It is a puzzling statement, in that it denigrates receptivity to music,
as compared to the receptor, say of a painting or a play. This is not
a position Broch usually takes with regard to music, as has been
noted.

In the following year (1921), Broch engaged a certain Oswald
Kabasta to teach his son piano; he also secured him a teaching po-
sition at the Traiskirchen school where his son was enrolled, and
Kabasta acted as the conductor of the school orchestra as well.[18]
He later rose to prominence under the Nazis, becoming the head
of the Reichsmusikkammer. He committed suicide in 1945.[19]

Throughout his American years Broch maintained casual relationships with musical figures such as Roger Sessions (who read the
first drafts of the English version of *Der Tod des Vergil*) and the
musicologist Viktor Zuckerkandl. Broch's attendance at concerts
seems to have fallen off greatly in America; the radio was the
source of most of Broch's musical stimulation. Numerous references in the correspondence affirm the fact that he usually wrote
with the radio playing classical music; Broch's financial and physical
ills would have precluded attendance of many live performances.

Musical Background in Broch's Essays

Broch's interest in the philosophical and aesthetic significance of
music is evident in much of his essays, beginning with the earliest
essays on *Kultur* from 1908 and 1909. Continuing on through his
career, many of Broch's essays on aesthetics, translation, myth, and
kitsch are filled with musical references. There is only one essay,

however, which focuses directly on music; this is the 1934 essay, *Gedanken zum Problem der Erkenntnis in der Musik*[20] (Thoughts on the Problem of Musical Cognition). Before looking at this, however, it may be useful to look at some earlier writings, in which Broch first addresses certain concepts that appear in the essay.

"A Systematic Aesthetic"

Broch's earliest attempts to formulate a theory of aesthetics are contained in the fragment *Notizen zu einer systematischen Ästhetik*. The concepts central to his discussion of music are first raised tentatively in this essay. One of these concepts is ornament; ornament fascinated Broch, and he saw it as playing a crucial role in the art and culture of a civilization. Broch sketches the development of ornament, which begins as rhythm, whether in the dimension of time or space.[21] Thus, the artistic analogy to the rhythmic, ecstatic dances of primitive peoples (rhythm proceeding along the time line) is the rhythmic repetition of notches along a line, an edge, a stick. (See illustration #1 at end of chapter.) The most elemental ornament is the tattoo — notched scars in a line on the human body (Broch here is inspired by Adolf Loos[22]). When art frees itself from the body to find other objects, this is the beginning of plastic art (*bildende Kunst*).[23] Ornament progresses in similar fashion from line to surface (circular symmetry, e.g., patterned rugs) and to the third dimension, building (tectonics). Broch employs the vocabulary of music to describe the elaboration of forms of ornament:

> The forms arise like the dimensions of space: first power, rhythm, second, harmony, third, depth . . . and from the combination and spiritualization of the forms arises the edifice of art, proportional and harmonious.[24]

Strikingly, Broch uses musical terms in analogy to the three spatial dimensions; of course, rhythm, harmony (Gleichklang) are not exclusively musical terms. Indeed, coupling *Gleichklang* with *Ebenmaß* (proportion) indicates the extended meaning of "harmony": parts fitting with and balancing other parts of the whole. (*Gleichklang* might be another manifestation of the principle of *Gleichgewicht* (balance), discussed below.) Depth (Tiefenwirkung) is not a musical term in any direct sense (volume or texture?); Broch is outlining an aesthetic theory which encompasses both visual art and music.

Broch continues his use of musical vocabulary in a comparison of a baroque scrolled capital ornament with a baroque musical rondo theme. (See illustration #2 at end of chapter.) A schematic drawing of the architectural ornament is divided into four sections: the musical quotation begins with an "apoggiatura," continuing with "development," "transition," "roll-up," ending with "center circle," which seems to refer to the final curling of the ornament at its lower end.[25] Although Broch's terminology is not musical, the analogy is valid in part: namely, that each portion mirrors or balances some other portion of the musical theme or the architectural ornament. Although Broch specifies that the *speed* of the melody corresponds to the speed of the curve, it is actually the intervals of the melody which do this, and not the tempo changes.[26] Each curve supposedly represents the same "natural equation." "Natural" is undefined (natural shape?), and Broch concedes the arbitrary nature of his example, it being both "transparent" and "incorrect." But he justifies it with the earlier statement: the curve and the musical analogue are shown only two-dimensionally, and the comparison requires three. The curve represented by the musical theme needs another dimension: time, or tempo. If one imagines the melodic dimensions as the x- and y- axes, then the music's spatial curve would be completed in a depth or z-axis measured in time units. With this, Broch repeats his theme of the architectural quality of music: "Is not this curve yet another indication of the spatial, the architectural (quality) of everything musical!"[27]

This comparison is forced. The example confuses ornament with the shape of the melodic line. He does not define "ornament";[28] melody, however, is not ornament, but a component of composition: to compare it with any architectural ornament is an inappropriate analogy. Broch tries to smooth over this confusion: because its origin was the line, ornament has a special ability to reproduce pictorially a musical expression. Broch was influenced by his reading of Wilhelm Worringer's popular treatise *Abstraktion und Einfühlung* (Abstraction and Empathy, 1908).[29] Broch attributes the music and the architecture of an era to a similar ornamental impulse; the architectural ornament and the musical ornament of a culture are a kind of shorthand reduction of the style of that culture. In an effort to be scientifically convincing Broch uses mathematics and geometry. Ornament, he maintains, is the most prominent characteristic of style (this, again, is an appropriation of Worringer's theory). He calls ornament the abbreviation, the signum, the differential of style. As the differential of a function reduces its variability to a formula, ornament reduces the variations of style to a formula. The style is thus the integral of its ornament, the material of the artistic expression being the constants operated upon by the various integral functions. While the metaphors here are somewhat forced, it is significant that Broch wants to see a "natural" (as in "natural science") or mathematical logic in aesthetic phenomena. With Broch as with Worringer, art proceeds from pure ornament to naturalism:

> All art moves from pure rhythm, primitive style, to rationalizing naturalism; fine art proceeds from pure ornament to a free conception of nature, dance-song becomes poetry. The general tendency is toward freer application of the medium, for the old, all-too-well-known becomes a cliché, becomes routine band-leader music (*Kapellmeistermusik*).[30]

This last sentence anticipates Broch's later theories of kitsch. He adapts Worringer's theory of ornament to music as well as to the plastic arts.

A central concern in this early essay (which remains with Broch throughout) is the principle of balance (Gleichgewicht), and its relationship to rhythm and symmetry. Invoking Goethe's phrase *Atmen des Alls* (the breath of the universe) Broch sees simple rhythm as the artistic equivalent to human respiration and circulation. (He notes that the psychology of art attributes artistic emotion to an alternation between feelings of tension and release,[31] also a rhythmic pattern.) Rhythm and life have the same immediate relationship to time; time runs in parallel with both. The principle of balance (Satz vom Gleichgewicht; here primarily a physical principle) expresses itself in life processes in the element of time, that is, rhythmically. Rhythm is thus the simplest image of the essence of life. In rhythm are met two premises of life: the ego tends toward balance, and its life is subject to time. Thus one can appropriately compare rhythm to the strivings of the ego.[32]

The essay purports to explain why rhythm is ecstatic: at base, it is the reason why music seems to overcome time, to be experienced

spatially. The most basic component of rhythm is: energy + coun-
terenergy, connected by a pause.

> Thus while rhythm strives forward in a continuum with life, its
> effect immediate and momentary, to understand its individual
> component would require its reversal or interruption: these two
> poles create together an impression of simultaneity and the
> manifestation of time is changed into that of space — the ele-
> ment of rhythm becomes the balance of symmetry.[33]

This argument is dialectical: rhythm consists of individual elements
of energy in a time continuum; the individual elements, however,
tend themselves toward stasis. These two poles of rhythm (*"Pole"*)
operating at once create in the auditor the impression of "simultaneity." But this does not mean real simultaneity, but instead that
the listener loses *consciousness* of time. As a result of this transformation, that is, the "loss" of time, rhythm is manifest not in time,
but space (die Erscheinungsform der Zeit wandelt sich in die Erscheinungsform des Raumes), the only remaining dimensional possibility. The basic element of rhythm is an expression of the
principle of equilibrium, in its being transformed to spatial symmetry. While symmetry in art and architecture is cyclical or axial,
music's is temporal. Its symmetrical balance is developed from the
repetition of the rhythmic figures; thus (per above) the essence of
musicality is perceived spatially.[34]

The aphoristic, insistent style of Broch's argument does little to
conceal its lack of real coherence. Revealing a scientific concern
with the mechanics of aesthetic principles, the essay also reflects
what was to be Broch's lifelong skepticism about "aesthetic" effect.
Echoes of Nietzsche, Worringer, even Weininger can be detected.
The fragment shows a youthful eagerness to come up with answers,
to relate everything aesthetic to the principle of balance, in a kind
of unified field theory for aesthetics. Nowhere in his later writings
does Broch try so specifically to explain the mechanics of the
transformation of time into space; however, the central importance
of this phenomenon in the effect of art, and most especially music,
remains constant throughout his later writing, both in the novels
and the essays.

Musical Cognition

The essay dedicated to Schönberg, *Gedanken zum Problem der Erkenntnis in der Musik* (Thoughts on the Problem of Musical Cognition, 1934), though more difficult and dense, is written in a clearer, more logical style. Broch is no longer the epigone of the Viennese critic and writer Karl Kraus (1874–1936) and his apocalyptic journalism. The essay is a plausible attempt to incorporate musical cognition into Broch's general theories of cognition. It uses many concepts from the earlier essay.

Musical cognition, it is implied, is rational cognition. Broch defines rational cognition by first defining rational activity, which occurs when one fact or situation (Sachverhalt) can be derived from another, in a series of finite steps. It is perceptible by the senses (im Sinnlich-Wahrnehmbaren) and directed by logic. Rational cognition, as a kind of thought activity, is a special case of general rational activity.

The argument has music in mind, for it says rational cognition is not necessarily identical with linguistic expressibility. To be sure, rational activity is always "understandable" (because "logical") but its communicability is not immediate; it must be interpreted. So also similarly with rational cognition: while communicability is intrinsic to all cognition, this communicability does not necessarily take the form of ordered human speech, nor is it necessarily translatable into such. Every naturalistic representation of an object, be it theatrical, pictorial, or photographic, can be seen as a rational communication, as a nonlinguistic definition, and can only be interpreted by human speech, not duplicated. Another example of this quasi-linguistic function of rationality is the musical leitmotiv. In short, linguistic communicability is just a special case of general rational cognition.

Beyond this, there is also "a generalized, a supra-linguistic, even supra-rational cognition! Herein lies the true worth of the individual who creates value."[35] This kind of intuitive cognition is characterized by *a priori* experiential content, breadth, and immediacy. Nontheoretical, nondeductive, it is the knowledge of an experienced creator or scientist. It is the cognitive richness (Erkenntnisreichtum) of a Beethoven, unrelated to any theoretical knowledge about music. This kind of *a priori* knowledge is crucially important to civilization: the unlimited "progress" of rational activity would only lead to a meaningless vacuum without an *a priori* knowledge of the goal.[36] Broch emphasizes the importance of emotion (Gefühl) in this kind of pre- and super-cognition.[37] It is this feeling which the truly life-engaged person can use to link his individual existence with the totality of existence. Literature is seen as the conscious entry of irrationality into language.[38] Irrational, emotional cognition is communicated, using another mode of expression, namely, linguistic-architectonic form, such as that in poetry. This process is not reversible, it cannot be translated back into actual language: it can only be interpreted.

Irrational cognition can be the "architectural" configuring of certain elements such as sounds, words, figures, musical tones, and objects, in a symbolic way. Rationalizing activity (Rationaliserung) is a dialectical pattern: the ongoing application of these symbolic and architectural expressions is an infinite progression from illumination (Aufhellung) to rigidification (Erstarrung), in which the newly created symbol is repeatedly rigidified into a convention, but within which it gets its actual linguistic meaning. In general, art has the tendency to move from originality to convention. The opposite process, *Irrationalisierung*, occurs in poetry and music. A lyric poem originates in a rational communication, but through *Irrationalisierung* it raises the original emotional content above the level of the finite and rational by use of the architecture of language. This irrationalizing process is more evident when the architecture of a poem is subjected to a second "architecturing," namely, that of music — analogous to the relationship of drama and opera — for now the original rational communication is completely overshadowed by the emotional content, and "irrational interpretation" takes place.

Creating music would thus be the translation of rational into emotional symbols. This translation process (presumably irreversible), this reciprocal "interpretability," mutual "growth out of each other" (Auseinander-Herauswachsen) is by no means restricted to language and music, but is most easily achieved here. Structural similarities are necessarily present: no language would be translatable into another — and all are — were they not all in principle built in the same way. Languages are a product of an all-powerful "Logos" (the rational structure and ordering principle of all systems).[39]

This logicality (basis in the logos), this form, is the form of equilibrium, of balance, an idea which dates to the essays of 1912, but there it had a distinctly physical sense. Here it has become metaphysical, and is central to Broch's value theory. All human formative activity and therefore all value setting — in a sense, then, the form of form itself — consists in establishing and maintaining an equilibrium. For Broch, the principle of equilibrium describes man's need to master the world. The subject needs a predicate. All rational attempts to master the world are at base the equation, "this is." Man constantly and unconsciously seeks to establish this balance in all actions, expressed or not, in everyday situations, or in a great "truth" — efforts to transform onrushing life into a condition of stasis: which as an approximation of the final end of life can give the illusion of canceling out time, of annulling death. This condition of general stasis, of all-encompassing equilibrium, is the end point of Broch's closed system, is the impossible goal of Broch's philosophy. Though unattainable, it is in the striving for such a stasis that Broch locates ethical behavior.

Music represents an area whose level of abstraction from the empirical approximates that of mathematics. In its freedom of form and its ability to create new forms, music, like mathematics, anticipates the advancing knowledge of the empirical physical world.[40] Mathematics thus has "a mystical-irrational foreknowledge of world happenings in their totality,"[41] a characteristic trait of mathematical genius. Music, with its greater richness of form, more closely approximates the infinity of forms of the empirical world than does mathematics. Thus, the musician is more "tuned" to the totality of the world than the mathematician;[42] (this is related to its capability of suspending time, to turn time into space, of which more will be said later). Music has all the freedom of form of mathematics, and like mathematics, logically it must continually seek new form elements, which in fact are constantly made available to it, and so it can offer an infinite number of these combinations of equating. Thus by the addition of every new element, music's complexity approaches the infinite. This self-reproducing system[43] with its ever-richer possibilities of combining and equivalenting is a reflection of the variety and totality of the world. This universal cognition (Welterkenntnisse), peculiar to music, is char-

acterized by the annulment of time.[44] This capability forms the
cognitive center of music.

Music and Time

Throughout his essays Broch repeatedly returns to this theme: music's peculiar ability to transform time into space, into a "spatially
architected structure."[45] This "architecting" of passing time becomes an annulment (Aufhebung) of onrushing time, and thus
cancels death from human consciousness.

This point should be examined carefully, for it is at least paradoxical that music should transform time into space. Any listener
knows that music is the art which most necessarily requires time,
that a work of music, in essence, is not notes on the printed page,
or the recording on which it is registered; rather, music is musical
elements executed in time. Leaving aside the question of how it
does this, why does this matter? Why does music's annulment of
time become a liberating function?

The answer can be found in many of Broch's essays, for example, in *Das Böse im Wertsystem der Kunst* (Evil in the Value System
of Art), namely, that time is equivalent to death.

> Nowhere is this so clearly apparent as in the phenomenon of
> time: not physical time, but that time which is man's most basic
> experience of life, that time which ebbs away in every hour of his
> breathing, conducts him into the future and ends in death. In
> time and its passing the relativity of values is anchored . . .[46]

Here Broch says formative activity aims at re-ordering values from
sequentiality to simultaneity. Simultaneity is a "spatial" arrangement, but the word "spatial" (räumlich) is not to be taken literally,
but in an extended sense:

> It is this transformation of temporal sequence into a construct
> which must be termed "spatial" in an expanded sense, and which,
> to the last detail, reflects the value system of music: the transfor-
> mation of sequential to simultaneous, perceived spatially: this is
> the essence of music.[47]

The Schönberg essay concludes by defining the special mission
of music as just this: "architecting time into space" and thus canceling out death in human imagination. Since in Broch's system all
true cognition is informed by the knowledge of death, then it is re-

served for the cognitive pronouncements of music to perform a special act of liberation (cf. Beethoven), mystical and irrational, yet convincingly rigorous, an act of cognition which brings about in a single art work a perception of the totality of the world, a monadic reflection of an infinite process.

As elsewhere in his essays (for example, in "James Joyce und die Gegenwart"[48]), Broch says literature and art in general convey irrational knowledge of the world's totality in a single defined act: the art-work. In contrast to Friedrich Schlegel's theories of poetry, Broch clearly privileges music here[49] above the other art forms, including literature. Broch's well-known diplomatic talents notwithstanding, this position was not taken just for this *Festschrift* for Arnold Schönberg; Broch's sense of the affinity of music and mathematics increased its appeal to him as a mathematician. Moreover, music's extraverbal communicability seemed more suitable for expressing the ineffable than the written word, as will be seen in the discussion of Broch's *Virgil*.

Concluding the essay Broch speaks not only of music but of art in general. Like science, art can only provide single flashes of insight, but unlike science, its scope is the whole of human existence, while science's goals are more focused.[50] Science moves systematically towards "truth" using already developed forms, whereas in art the cognitive process requires ever new forms, necessitating, not step-by-step progress, but the substitution or alternation of one work for another.[51] Art proceeds from irrational knowledge to irrational knowledge, still subject to the Logos. Importantly, irrational cognition, unlike scientific knowledge, is available to anyone, perhaps especially to the unsophisticated, the unlearned, via the individual work of art, which speaks to the spirit, not the intellect.[52]

The essay is flawed by a vagueness and ill-defined terms; but its speculative daring is admirable, and it avoids the logical shoals of the 1912 *Notizen*, by simply stating that music accomplishes the effect of *Zeitaufhebung* without trying to explain how. Moreover, it is often unclear whether Broch is talking about music or art in general. Broch's conclusion would seem to be applicable to all forms of Art:

> And since the Logos looks toward the divine, and cannot turn
> back, it must want that which is new, to press for new values even

> in irrational cognition: to actualize the Logos is art's holy mission, is the task of irrational cognition.[53]

Dedicated to Schönberg, these ideas might imply wholehearted approval of the explorations of the Second Viennese School (serialism). However, to judge from Broch's correspondence it is not clear that this was actually the case. One wonders, moreover, whether Broch would find the "simple-minded" (*die Einfältigen*) in particular edified by such music.

One must note the consistent stance Broch takes in all the theoretical writings on the "rationality" of music. Its nonverbal nature and "irreversibility" (unlike mathematics, logic, and all verbal language) is in no way a contradiction of its highly rational structure. In the 1933 lecture *Das Weltbild des Romans* (The Novel's View of the World), music's clarity and structure according to a visible plan is held up in contrast to the "dreamlike" quality of poetry:

> And though great music's structure is clear due to its abstractness, this is not so of poetry. Reinforcements from the sphere of emotion and the irrational are diffused throughout poetry much more than in music, which, — strange though this sounds — from this point of view is part of an essentially more rational sphere. Poetry is dream-like, music is not.[54]

In the much later lecture on translation,[55] Broch sees in music the ultimate artistic symbol of an increasingly abstract perception of the world in Western culture:

> The more man develops his ability to comprehend the world through use of abstract logic, and even mathematics — and in this at least up till now the West has been ahead of the East — the more music's formal content comes to symbolize to him his own inner logic.[56]

Here, too, Broch emphasizes music's "natural"-ness; its empty signs (geringe Inhaltsbedeutung) bespeak a formal content whose essential quality is a connection with physical law. In this sense Broch's theories on music are in accord with Aristotle (and Georgiades: see chapter 5).

In "Mythos und Altersstil" (Myth and the Style of Maturity), also from 1947, Broch reiterates the idea that music, though a medium nearly vocabulary-free, nonetheless needs to re-form itself anew each generation, to avoid the paralysis of *Verkitschung* (becoming kitsch). The avatars of the two attributes Broch most venerates in music — its formal content (*der geformte Inhalt*) and constant creative innovation — are Bach and Beethoven, respectively. As mentioned before, this need for constant innovation is hardly unique to music, nor original with Broch.

Finally, it can be said that throughout Broch's theoretical writings the following characteristics of music are constant: (1) its basis in rhythm (like all ornament), therefore natural; (2) rational organization and irrational effect; (3) irreversibility (with language); (4) communication on a higher level than verbal language; (5) its effect of *Todesüberwindung* (vanquishing death) by transforming time into space.

In the novels Broch's use of music in general demonstrates all of these qualities prominently. The following chapters will examine the use of musical ideas and techniques in the chief novels, *Die Verzauberung, Die Schuldlosen, Die Schlafwandler,* and *Der Tod des Vergil.* (The essay *Hofmannsthal und seine Zeit* is given a separate chapter.) The chapters discuss the novels not in chronological order, but rather in an order determined by the relative importance of music in them, ending with the most "musical."

Illustration #1. Notches. Visual representation of rhythm.
Taken from Broch, Notizen zu einer systematischen Ästhetik
(1912), KW 9/2, page 21.

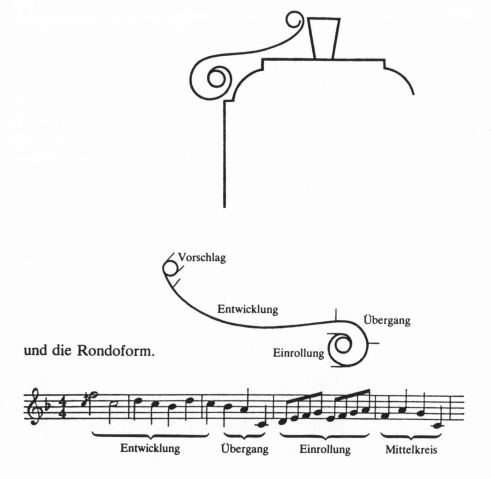

Illustration #2. Baroque Ornament in architecture and musical notation. Taken from Broch, Notizen zu einer systematischen Ästhetik *(1912), KW 9/2, page 25.*

Notes

[1] Henriette Kotlan-Werner, *Kunst und Volk. David Bach* (Vienna: Europa-verlag, 1977). Bach's biographer does not mention this.

[2] Paul Michael Lützeler, *Hermann Broch. Eine Biographie* (Frankfurt: Suhr-kamp Verlag, 1985), 34.

[3] KW 13/1, 211. Letter dated August 27, 1932.

[4] In a letter to Joseph Bunzel dated January 22, 1950, he urges him to seek a position as "Theatersoziolog" with Bing in New York: ("Do you know Rudi Bing from Vienna? I knew him when he was a young boy, and surely he re-members [me], but I don't know if he knows how 'rilly' famous [Broch says 'berihmt'] I am.") Broch Archive, Beinecke Library, Yale University (hence-forth "YUL unpub."). Translations of unpublished materials are mine.

[5] YUL unpub.

[6] "Of course I take your allusion to Wagner-Wesendonck to reflect your high opinion of my compositions; if your antipathy toward the (word) 'lady-friend' is based on the commonly held contrast between *love* and friendship (a view that could easily be applied to the W.-W. relationship), well then, you are just much too enchanting for words, my dear, and besides, we two are people who wouldn't adapt well to such a (word-) change." YUL unpub.

[7] Broch seems to have enjoyed *Madama Butterfly.* "I might have liked the piece; the second act has a lovely, sweet finale, and it is all made very pretty. But without you it brings me no pleasure at all" (December 3, 1907[?]). In another letter of about the same time (Dec. 1907–Jan. 1908[?]) he writes: "They are presenting 'Manon Lescaut' at the Volksoper; I'd enjoy seeing it first with you. Up to now I have always hated Puccini . . . but apparently you draw all my [tastes] over to your viewpoint . . ." (YUL unpub.).

[8] On November 2, 1908[?]: "Hoffmanns came for the evening, the rest of which I spent at the piano with my uncle. I returned here early this morning, loaded with music scores (Samson and Delilah and a whole library of Grieg.)" YUL unpub., f. 38. In a letter dated October 20 (1908) he mentions that his brother's presence will be a nuisance but that he is happy to have someone to play four-hand music with. But: "If only I didn't feel so much the need for you when playing music! Sometimes it just makes me mad with happiness, dear, to enjoy music together with you." YUL unpub., f. 47.

[9] YUL unpub., f. 44.

[10] YUL unpub., f. 45.

[11] YUL unpub., f. 45 (3 Nov 1908).

[12] KW 6, 320–25: a portion of the also fragmentary *Filsmann* novel (1932).

[13] KW 6, 322.

[14] Hermann Broch, *Das Teesdorfer Tagebuch für Ea von Allesch,* ed. P. M. Lützeler (Frankfurt: Suhrkamp, 1995).

[15] Popular folk operetta by Carl Michael Ziehrer (1843–1922). *Teesdorfer Tagebuch,* 115.

[16] *Teesdorfer Tagebuch,* 80–81.

[17] *Teesdorfer Tagebuch,* 81.

[18] A letter from the eleven-year-old boy in spring of 1921 reveals the extent to which music had become a part of his education: "please find out when the Philharmonic is [playing]. I have permission from Lassmann to go, and have gotten a ticket for Saturday for Shakespeare's 'Irrungen' and Goethe's 'Siblings,' and hope to get one for the Konzerthaus for Saturday's 'Manfred' performance, so in any case, whether for the symphony this Saturday or next, I could stay over night with you [i.e., Broch and Ea von Allesch]. Why didn't Mother come yesterday? It was Kabasta's final performance: Ninth Symphony [Beethoven?] and Bruch's Violin Concerto." YUL, unpub., f. 56.

[19] H. F. Broch de Rothermann, notes to the diary of letters to Ea von Allesch, YUL unpub., f. 880, 15c.

[20] KW 10/2, 234–45. This essay was part of a birthday *Festschrift* for Arnold Schönberg. Original title: "*Irrationale Erkenntnis in der Musik*" in *Arnold Schönberg zum 60. Geburtstag, 13.9.1934* (Vienna: Universal-Edition, 1934), 49–60.

[21] KW 9/2, 23.

[22] Adolf Loos, "Ornament und Verbrechen" (1908), in: *Trotzdem* (Innsbruck: Brenner-Verlag, 1931), 79–92. But Loos actually says that a cross was the first ornament (80). As for tattooing, he says, "Der papua tätowiert seine haut, sein boot, sein ruder, kurz alles was ihm erreichbar ist. Er ist kein verbrecher. Der moderne mensch, der sich tätowiert, ist ein verbrecher oder ein degenerierter" (79).

[23] KW 9/2, 2.

[24] Original: "Die Formen heben sich gleich den Dimensionen des Raumes: in erster Potenz — Rhythmik, in zweiter — Harmonie, in dritter — Tiefenwirkung . . . und aus der Verbindung, Kombinierung, Vergeistigung der Formen baut sich in Ebenmaß und Gleichklang das Gebäude der Kunst." KW 9/2, 23. (Translations JAH except where noted.)

[25] Broch uses the German words: Vorschlag, Entwicklung, Übergang, Einrollung, Mittelkreis.

[26] Here the writer is more concerned with making a point than with the niceties of argument!

[27] KW 9/2, 26.

[28] But see "Ornamente (Der Fall Loos)," KW 10/1, 32–33: "Ornament, however, was the musical expression of the type and the spirit of *all* art, the quintessence of culture, the symbol of life, clearer and more concise than all reason."

[29] "It could be ornament's origin in the linear figure which gives it, more than other features of style, the ability to reproduce musical expression: it is the "square root" of the essence." KW 9/2, 26. A quotation from Wilhelm Worringer's chapter on ornamentation, from his work *Abstraktion und Einfühlung*, might illuminate the origin of Broch's thought: Worringer's thesis is that ornament in art has its origin in the abstract-linear impulses of the artist, and not in any naturalistic, mimetic impulse; "es kann auch hier nicht die Rede sein von einer Stilisierung eines Naturvorbildes, sondern auch hier wird ein abstrakt-lineares Gebilde allmählich naturalisiert. Der Ausgangspunkt des künstlerischen Prozesses ist also die lineare Abstraktion, die zwar in einem gewissen Zusammenhang mit dem Naturvorbild steht, aber mit irgendwelchen Nachahmungstendenzen nichts zu tun hat." Wilhelm Worringer, *Abstraktion und Einfühlung* (Munich: Piper, 1976), 99.

[30] KW 9/2, 29.

[31] P. M. Lützeler traces this to Broch's reading of Worringer. See KW 9/2, 33, f. 17.

[32] Lützeler refers to Schopenhauer for comparison: *Die Welt als Wille und Vorstellung, Bd. 2, 387 and 390.* "Die Heftigkeit des Triebes . . . lehrt uns, daß in diesem Akt sich die entschiedenste Bejahung des Willens zum Leben, rein und ohne weiteren Zusatz . . . ausspricht . . ." KW 9/2, 33, f. 20.

[33] KW 9/2, 17.

[34] Like Schopenhauer and Goethe, Broch unwittingly quotes Schelling's mot: the musical composition becomes architecture, while architecture can be seen as "frozen music."

[35] KW 10/2, 237.

[36] KW 10/2, 238.

[37] "That cognitive knowledge, that pre-cognition, which is both pre- and supra- knowledge, inconceivable but present everywhere, and because it is beyond conceiving, man can only access it as emotion, and precisely as emotion it is the most valuable thing in life." I give the German here: Das erkennende Wissen, dieses Vor-Wissen, das zugleich Über-Wissen ist, Vor-Erkenntnis und zugleich Über-Erkenntnis, unfaßbar und doch allüberall, wird in seiner Un-

faßbarkeit dem Menschen als Gefühl habhaft: nur als Gefühl, und eben als Gefühl jedem einzelnen das Wertvollste seines Lebens. KW 10/2, 238.

[38] "diese Irrationalität des Sprachlichen wird sich selbst bewußt, tritt sozusagen in den Bereich des Rationalen, wenn die Sprache zum Instrument des Dichterischen wird." KW 10/2, 239. "This irrational quality of language self-consciously enters the realm of the rational when language becomes the instrument of literature."

[39] See Ernestine Schlant, Ernestine, *Die Philosophie Hermann Brochs,* (Bern: Francke Verlag, 1971), 12. Broch sees a general logical form underneath all things, a logicity which applies equally for things rational and irrational, which he dubs the general "value logic" (*allgemeine Wertlogik*) and which is at base simply the logic of symbols in general.

[40] "wenn die Mathematik in ihrem Formenfortschritt stets der empirischen Erkenntnis vorauseilt, wenn sie die Formen vorbereitet, in welche die physikalische Erkenntnis oft erst viele Jahre später eingegossen wird . . ." KW 10/2, 242.

[41] ". . . ein mystisch-irrationales Erfassen des Weltgeschehens in seiner Gesamtheit . . ." KW 10/2, 242.

[42] "Der Musiker jener Totalitätsstimmung noch viel stärker unterworfen ist . . ." KW 10/2, 242.

[43] Broch unconsciously anticipates in this theory of *Formenreichtum* the "proliferating series" of Barraqué's serial composition technique. Cf. chapter 5.

[44] "Music attains its peculiarly sublime level through universal cognition . . . which is clearly under the sign of annulling time." The original German: "Welterkenntnisse, die nun freilich — und damit erreicht die Musik die ihr eigentümliche klar-erhabene Sphäre — . . . im Zeichen der Zeitaufhebung stehen." KW 10/2, 243.

[45] KW 10/2, 242.

[46] KW 9/2, 128 ("Das Böse im Wertsystem der Kunst") (translation mine).

[47] KW 9/2, 128.

[48] . . . die Totalität einer Welterfassung, wie sie das Kunstwerk, zumindest das im Goetheschen Sinne, anstrebt, drängt alles Wissen der unendlichen Menschheitsentwicklung in einen einzigen simultanen Erkenntnisakt zusammen: in einem einzigen Dasein, in einem einzigen Kunstwerk und seiner Totalität soll die Ewigkeit eingeschlossen werden, und je näher das Kunstwerk an die Grenze der Totalität vorstößt, desto zeitraubender erweist es sich. KW 9/1, 86. Here Broch emphasizes the quality of "undoing" time with the word "zeitraubend." This last phrase is translated by Eugene Jolas, in "Joyce and the Present Age" (Transition: Paris, 1949), 101, as: "eternity must be comprised in a single existence, in the totality of a single work of art, and the

nearer the work of art comes to the frontiers of totality, the greater its possibility of survival." Jolas ignores the effect of simultaneity with this translation.

[49] The original reads: "es ist der Musik vorbehalten, mit jeder Erkenntnis, die sie ausspricht — nochmals sei Beethoven erwähnt —, einen Befreiungsakt auszulösen, irrational und mystisch, dennoch von überzeugender Strenge, einen Akt der Erkenntnis, der in einem einzigen Kunstwerk die Totalität der Welt erstehen läßt, monadischer Spiegel des unendlichen Vorganges." KW 10/2, 243.

[50] KW 10/2, 243.

[51] "wenn es sich also hier auch nicht um einen System-Fortschritt handelt, sondern um den Wechsel einzelner kunst-werklicher Monaden." KW 10/2, 244–45.

[52] "Wo immer ein konservatives Lebensgefühl auftritt, gründet es sich letztlich in dem Wissen um das ruhende, irrationale Weltgefühl, das den Tod und das Leben umspannt, gründet es sich in dem Geist, *dessen auch der Einfältige — und vielleicht gerade dieser im allerreichsten Maße,* [emphasis mine] teilhaftig werden kann, es gründet sich im Vorhandensein des Kunstwerkes, des Gedichtes und des Liedes, das die Erkenntnis des Einfältigen ist. . . ." KW 10/2, 243. Wherever a conservative feeling for life appears, it is finally grounded in knowing a calm, irrational universal feeling spanning life and death, in that spirit accessible even to the simplest, perhaps most especially to them, grounded in the existence of the work of art, the poem, the song, which is the insight of the simple-minded."

[53] KW 10/2, 245. The idea of art freely transforming itself through time, without regard to the time, or its content, is Hegelian: Adorno's *Philosophie der neuen Musik,* page 22, quotes Hegel's *Ästhetik:* "Dieß müssen wir jedoch als kein bloßes zufälliges Unglück ansehen, von welchem die Kunst von Außen her durch die Noth der Zeit, den prosaischen Sinn, den Mangel an Interesse u. s. f. betroffen wurde, sondern es ist die Wirkung und der Fortgang der Kunst selber, welche, indem sie den ihr selbst innewohnenden Stoff zur gegenständlichen Anschauung bringt, auf diesem Weg selbst durch jeden Fortschritt einen Beitrag liefert, sich selber von dem dargestellten Inhalt zu befreien." Hegel (Duncker und Humblot: Berlin, 1837), S. 231. v. 10(b).

[54] KW 9/2, 108.

[55] "Einige Bemerkungen zur Philosophie und Technik des Übersetzens" (1947), KW 9/2, 61–86.

[56] KW 9/2, 67.

2: *The Spell* and *The Guiltless*

The Spell

THERE ARE THREE ORIGINAL VERSIONS of Broch's *Bergroman* (Mountain Novel), of which only the first was completed by Broch, in 1934/35. This first version is the version selected for inclusion in the *Kommentierte Werkausgabe*, and has the title *Die Verzauberung*, which was eventually translated into English as *The Spell*.[1] Broch stopped work on the second version of the *Bergroman* in 1938, and was working on completing the third version at his death in 1951 (this fragment was published in the Bibliothek Suhrkamp under the title *Demeter* in 1967). Typescripts of the three versions (with variants — Broch made several carbons of each version, which over time varied from each other) are held in the Broch Archive of Beinecke Library at Yale.[2] Although only the first version is complete, Broch had distinct and different intentions for each of the three, with the last most influenced by his study of mass psychology. Since Broch's intentions were cut short by his premature death, and since the incomplete later versions have significant musical references lacking in the first (KW 3) version, the present chapter will consider the later variants as well.[3] (Moreover, the first edition of Broch's work, that of the Rhein-Verlag in Zürich, included the novel (called *Der Versucher*) as an aggregate of all three versions, considerably longer than the first version.)[4]

To varying degrees music is portrayed as both good and bad art in the novel, but as in *The Sleepwalkers*, it is presented primarily in debased form. This accords with the setting: an isolated mountain village which becomes infected with prefascist cultural and racist ideas; music also becomes politicized and popularized as kitsch. A few examples will suffice: In version 2 (37), the youngest daughter at home (Zäzilie)[5] turns on a radio and performs a primitive little dance to a jazz tune.[6] Zäzilie's response to the music is direct and authentic, the primitive dance response to rhythm, which Broch sees as the beginning of ornament and decoration. When the demagogue Marius Ratti enters the inn and abruptly switches off the radio, he does this because to him jazz is a symbolically decadent and urbanized form of art; the local radio retailer is the Calvinist Wetchy, who, for various reasons, becomes the scapegoat for the perceived and real problems of the villagers, and thus could be seen as representing the Jew. Even Ratti is initially beguiled by the music and dance, but he resists its "decadent" appeal. However, in turning off the music, he paradoxically illustrates the effect of "good" music; Zäzilie's motionless figure is symbolic of her awakening consciousness:

> ... one leg slightly bent, so that she almost stood on one leg, one arm raised with the palm of the hand turned toward the ceiling as if trying to snatch back from there the vanished strains, and her face, not yet aware of its awakening, awakening forever, could not yet slip back into the restraint of the flesh ...[7]

The "awakening" of Zäzilie is the increase in cognition afforded by music, symbolized spatially by her dance-position. Although the music is called "city" music, not fit for a child or a peasant, Marius is manipulating both music and technology (the radio) for his own purposes.[8]

The most strikingly positive reference to music is found in the interior monologue of the country doctor during the church service.[9] In version 1, there is a brief mention of music before the narration proceeds to observations of the various parishioners.[10] However, in version 2, there appears at this point an extended meditation on the philosophy and aesthetics of music. Several of the themes from the early essays already mentioned appear in the first sentence of the passage from *Bergroman* (version 2):

> Und so hob das Orgelspiel an: es faßte den Wind der Wolken und den der Berge, es faßte den Wind des Frühlingshimmels, es faßte den Wind der Frühlingserde und den ihrer gekräuselten Wellen, es faßte den Wind der Weltvielfalt und diese mit ihm zu einem einzigen maßvoll singenden Sturm zusammen, in dessen strömenden Brausen, gelenkt von der musizierenden Einfalt eines Dorfschulmeisters, all die wehende verwehte Vielfalt zur tönenden Gestalt wurde und sich als solche dem Jetzt des Zeitlichen vermählte, sich dem Raum vermählte, der zwar nur der einer dürftigen und leider schon recht schadhaften Dorfkirche war, der

aber dennoch in seinen gotischen Mauern unverlierbar die Töne von Jahrhunderten umfangen hielt.[11]

Here the most noticeable theme is that of the architecturing of music, the transformation of time into space. The organ physically forms the music into a palpable shape, congruent with the interior of the little village church. The unifying effect of the work of music on the variety of the world is also emphasized. The simple village's schoolmaster's unconscious access to this irrational cognition is consistent with the essay on musical cognition.[12] Form is given to an amorphous world, and its immanent tendency to degrade and disintegrate is halted by melding the sounding shape ("tönende Gestalt") with the timeless Now. Later in the passage, just as music gives shape to the shapeless world, so also religious belief is said to unify and shape existence:

> da sang es weiter, . . . denn was die Welt strömend und brausend und allerfüllend durchweht ist Glaube, unerfaßlich allerdings in seiner Gestaltlosigkeit, ungläubig wie der Wind, wie die Wolken, wie das Sein, welches bloß dahinlebt, ungläubig wie alles, das in Ungeformtheit und Unbewußtheit kaum an sich selbst zu glauben imstande ist, trotzdem so glaubensschwanger und zur Form drängend, ja, diese Form aus eigner Kraft schaffend, daß allzeit das Wunder nahe ist, allzeit bereit, den Glauben als gestaltetes Sein, wundertauschend Seele und Welt, in Welt und Seele schöpferisch erstehen zu lassen.[13]

Music is called the echo of completeness ("Echo der Ganzheit"), it is a mirror reflecting infinity, it is the tangible or sensible model of all order, of shaped form in the world and its systems ("Solch gestaltete Form, geahnt in allen Ordnungen des Menschen, ist das Tönende"). This restates music's formal content ("geformter Inhalt," mentioned in Broch's essay *Mythos und Altersstil*).

Not only the content, but also the form of the prior paragraph is strikingly musical. It begins with a "downbeat," a marker: "Und so hob das Orgelspiel an." The words "es faßte" repeat four times in quick succession, each time with a more complicated object, but always a variation of the previous object, until the result becomes itself a single measured singing storm, rounded off by the caesura-like "zusammen," completing the meaning of the four preceding "es faßte" phrases. Other quasimusical devices are typical of Broch's style: oppositional phrases, employing active/passive forms of a word, or positive/negative version, e.g., "wehende verwehte," "dem Jetzt des Zeitlichen" vs. "die Töne von Jahrhunderten." (This stylistic device is used much more in *Der Tod des Vergil*.) A form of recapitulation is also employed: "denn was die Welt strömend und brausend und allerfüllend durchweht," for example, repeats the musical concepts of the first part, as the emphasis changes from music to faith. Most importantly in this passage, music is shown to be a system which brings form to the formlessness of sound, just as belief brings systemic order to the chaos of existence. Paraphrasing Goethe's "Urworte: Orphisch" ("geprägte Form, die lebend sich entwickelt"), Broch's doctor-narrator describes music as "gestaltete Form":

> Solch gestaltete Form . . . ist das Tönende, in das die Unge-
> formtheit des Seins einzugehen vermag, das maßvoll strömende,
> das brausende Wunder, das in unausschöpflichen Maßen sich der
> Orgel entlöst, und das All in der Musik spiegelnd, gleichwie Mu-
> sik im Worte gespielt wird, versammelt zu stets erneuerter und
> eindringlicherer Gestalt . . .[14]

The telling change from "spiegelnd" (mirroring) to "gespielt" (played) demonstrates what Broch is attempting to do with language; here it is basically a kind of music of words instead of tones. As the tones are gathered together and repeated in ever newer, more forceful shapes, Broch's words also gather into repetitions, recapitulations, and take more of their significance from the musical effect they create than their semantic meanings. There is another thematic impetus to this passage, and it is of a gathering together of tones, of people, of systems: "Versammelt zu stets erneuerter und eindringlicherer Gestalt"; "sie zu ihrem Glauben zu versammeln"; "die Menschen aus ihrer Verstreutheit zusammenzurufen"; "auf daß sie . . . sich zur Einheit der Gemeinde und Gemeinschaft scharen mögen." This side of Broch's utopian vision, this aspect of the dialectic view of history, represents the conserving, the physical spatializing of a dynamic process, and finally, the upending and annulling of time, is the desired effect of art, especially of music. As the parishioners gather in the church, they are a symbol of their reverence and belief in something beyond their own lives; they are:

the reflection of the word, the reflection of the music and the reflection of the visible and invisible universe and its completeness,
reflection of faith, borne by the sounds and mastered by the
gesture of prayer.[15]

This use of music as a metaphor for the totality of the universe and
its knowledge, inexpressible in literal or cognitive terms, is central
to all the novels.

Ritualistic and mythological aspects of music appear in the
Steinsegen ceremony (version 2, chapter 4). The parish priest, the
sexton, and various others from the village climb in procession up
to the little chapel (dedicated to St. George) at the top of the
mountain each spring (a lunar holiday), to participate in a semi-
pagan rite of consecration. The mood of these annual pilgrimages
is jovial, but with an underlay of urgency. The object of this ritual
veneration are some lumps of ore from the the so-called "Dwarves'
Tunnel" mine which opens at the top of the mountain. These
"stones," as they are called, are kept in the chapel, and represent
chthonic forces within the mountain which for obscure reasons require periodic appeasement. As the procession winds up the
mountainside, various traditional texts are sung or chanted. As this
year's *Bergbraut*, Irmgard must greet the parish priest with a curious little verse:

> Gelobt sei Jesus Christ
> Was im Berg gefangen ist
> Durch ihn befreit werden solle
> Vertrieben Satan und Unholde
> Alles Böse weiche von dannen
> In Jesu und Marien Namen.[16]

This primitive chant is almost a parody of an archaic church hymn
lyric with its clumsy rhythm and its use of assonance.[17] Immediately
after Irmgard repeats this little ditty in her "village schoolmaid"
voice, almost in fulfillment of its prediction "alles Böse weiche von
dannen" a fusillage of cannonfire occurs — another custom of the
"Steinsegen" festivities, which nonetheless quite paralyzes the parish priest with astonishment — the narrator almost fears he will
have to come to his aid.[18] Such pagan racket is contrasted with the

metaphorical music of the flowers and the wind, which the priest, after regaining his composure, can hear nonetheless:

> als horchte er durch all die heidnische Böllerei hindurch auf das Singen der Blumen, auf das unhörbare Echo, mit dem sie den silbersäuselnden Alpenwind spiegelten, die Blumen gleichfalls den Wind vernehmend . . . und er lauschend dem Winde, in dem der große silberne Atem der Erde weht, Echo jenes noch größeren Atems, von dem das Meer kündet und singt, Echo-Atem der Ewigkeit . . .[19]

As so often in Broch, the text suddenly digresses into the contemplative and speculative; here it starts with auditory stimuli: the chant, the shooting, and the sounds of nature, all combined in a musical composition whose sounds are themselves metaphors of sound: singing flowers, inaudible echoes, silver-sighing wind, etc. Broch's primal symbol here for music and the provenance of its cognition is the rhythm of life itself, that is, breathing. As in the Schönberg essay, the expansion and contraction of the respiratory cycle (*Atmen des Alls*) is the quintessential musical pattern.

In the climactic twelfth chapter of the first version (there exist only fragmentary sketches for this chapter in the later versions) music is an accompanying theme to the events leading to Irmgard's ritual murder. From this point in the novel, music is presented as *völkisch* and kitsch, or in Broch's terms, the fitting aesthetic accompaniment to ethical evil. When the lackey Wenzel calls his tipsy troops together into marching formation, one of them beats a drum as the young men sing their marching tune. The songs seem to echo Nazi rally music, but with a pathetic, even clownish quality: "We are men, not boys . . ."[20] Nonetheless, even this has some appeal to the not quite impartial narrator: "I suddenly felt a strange and childish urge to be allowed to march among them, for is it not as if the uniform cadence of man's steps could save him at least temporarily from the helplessness of his dream?"[21]

The following Friday, the day of the mountain church consecration, which will culminate with Irmgard's death, the narrator hears accordion music accompanying the procession to the ceremony. He ironically calls it a "serenade," which lures him to his balcony — the seduction of the doctor by primal forces he does not completely acknowledge is anticipated in the ironic image of this "*Ständchen*." The likewise ironically named "Musik-Christian" is the instrumentalist; a strange figure with literary antecedents in Keller's "Schwarzer Geiger," or Lenau's *Faust*, he is a musical conjurer of unhealthy passion. The narrator, almost willingly, conspires with this music:

> The sky . . . was without a cloud, and the firs sang their dark, sharp-pointed chant into the blueness above. But it was not that which I had heard, even though it was quite audible, but the chords of an accordion . . ."[22]

It is music of and for the mob which is played at the wild dance which follows: a Breughel-like scene of dangerously excited yokels dancing to Christian's tune follows Mutter Gisson's ominous statements: "There'll be time for dancing before it [the storm] comes," "The world is dancing," and "When the trees are dancing, you, too, are allowed to dance."[23] While Mutter Gisson and the narrator tread a stately oldster's measure, around them the peasants get down to lustier rhythmic pleasures. An even more negative description than in *Huguenau* (see *Schlafwandler* chapter) is given of the private ecstasies and peculiarly indecent character of public dancing:

> They were moving without a pause and apparently without tiring, they struggled for their rapture with the grim determination of people possessed, with a grim passion that no longer had anything in common with the usual carnival merriment, driven by a magic tide which irresistibly rose and tore with it everything in its path a tide generated in the twilight of mankind and ascending to the twilight of the starts, all to the accompaniment of the accordion.[24]

The madness which follows is of course not caused by, but merely accompanied by, this relentlessly lowbrow folk music. The ecstatic workings of rhythm and music are noticeable on the narrator: "under the spell of the dance, under the spell of my own blood in which I felt birth and death so close together that they seemed to have become one and the same,"[25] continues the doctor. As a silent, yet musical and contrastive commentary on the proceedings, the Mignon-like figure of Zäzilie appears, singing the "texts of her own life" to the tunes of the accordion-player, gliding hither and thither in a cool wash of moonlight. Innocent, she too is affected by the music, but she projects stasis, thus *Zeitaufhebung*: ". . . at times stopping like a trout that stands still against the current and letting the coolness and the music ebb away from her . . .[26]

But on the whole the atmosphere created by the music and dance is sinister, colored, as in *Huguenau* (see chapter 4), by the murder that is to come. The *niveau* of the music, as of the dancers, is similarly in contrast with the narrative flights of speculation. Even the insects are a chorus of mistuned falsetto voices (see *Schuldlosen* discussion below) and the acetylene torches, like the gas jets in *Pasenow*, hiss unpleasantly in the "singing swarms of gnats."[27]

With the appearance of the straw-clad, horned and bearded *Geister* (spirits) the evening becomes a sort of homespun *Walpurgisnacht*. The accordion is joined by two ill-tuned violins, the spirit figures themselves shaking cowbells and chains and other objects.[28] The spirit chorus (*"Unholde"*) sing in quatrains a semicomic story of a dragon and a virgin; the symbolic scourging of a "witch" follows. Then a kind of antiphonal ballad begins, with the refrain ("syncopated rhythm") sung by the crowd: this ballad (the narrator calls it a "mining song") itself describes a ritual sacrifice very like the one about to occur ("ins Herz traf sie der steinerne Speer") as one by one the torches extinguish, a classical death emblem (as in the final sequence of *The Death of Virgil*).

As it becomes ever clearer that something dreadful is about to take place, a silence descends on the crowd,[29] who seem at first to reject Marius and his call for this sacrifice, and to side with Mutter Gisson.[30] But Wenzel bellows for music: "Music! Music! Play on! The commanding voice of Wenzel drowned all other sounds."[31] The call proves crucial: the sinister Musik-Christian takes up his *Ländler* again, and the mad dance begins anew, Wenzel beating time, while the last lamp is extinguished. Sabest (the butcher) dispatches Irmgard with one knife stroke, to the accompaniment of a "jämmerlicher Ländler" ("wretched little dance-tune.")[32] The music of this sequence seems in some way accountable for sustaining the atmosphere of mass hysteria which makes the killing possible. Broch's very negative conception of folk music (cf. his comments on Schubert's *Ländler* in the letters in the second chapter) is extensively drawn in this novel. That the same musicians play the very same music[33] at the near lynching of Wetchy only underscores the negative attributes Broch ascribes to folk music. Ratti, for example, sings as he tries to promote his version of "die neue Zeit."[34] The scene of the mine accident has the rescuers singing an obscene work song: "Fair little Mary, now we ram it in."[35]

Only at the conclusion does music once more gain its extra-human cosmic quality: before Mutter Gisson dies, she becomes "singing":

> And as the sun plays on the stones, an infinite playing on the earthly lyre, it is as if we heard a singing, a singing ordering our fear to join in it . . . And yet in truth it is a singing. For it is Mother Gisson.[36]

On the whole, though, *The Spell* makes little use of the philosophical affinities of music. Aside from the scene in the church, music is used as stage setting, as an attempt to provide authenticity and color to Broch's "anti-*Heimat* novel."[37]

The Guiltless and Mozart's *Don Giovanni*

In Broch's library of some 2,000 volumes, the only work specifically dealing with music is Hermann Cohen's[38] 1915 study, *Die dramatische Idee in Mozarts Operntexten*.[39] Since Broch's library[40] held virtually no books on topics other than philosophy, mathematics and physics, Cohen's little book filled a unique place in Broch's otherwise scientifically oriented holdings; the present study will consider it in an examination of Broch's *Die Schuldlosen* (1949, translated as *The Guiltless*), a novella cycle based in part on the story of Don Juan.

Zerline's Tale

> Giovinette che fate all'amore,
> Non lasciate che passi l'etá[41]

The central novella of the *The Guiltless* sequence is *Zerline's Tale* (*Die Erzählung der Magd Zerline*), a very free adaptation of the Don Juan story. So free, in fact, that one might not see the resemblance to Mozart/DaPonte's work were it not for the names of the characters and Broch's own commentaries on *Die Schuldlosen*.[42] In these commentaries, Broch remarks that, having completed the

Vergil, he reverted to the narrative mode of the *Schlafwandler,* abbreviating and concentrating the characters so that they represent the world views of an epoch: here, 1913, 1923, and 1933.[43] Accordingly, characters are presented in a truncated, yet exaggerated form, and their dialogues and speeches are often highly unnatural, expressing their inner thoughts more clearly than they could in actuality. The characters are in turn caricatures (Zacharias, Zerline), fairy tale-like (Melitta), or surreal (Hildegarde and A. at the end).[44] For the sake of compactness Broch sees events leading to "mythic" and "operatic" situations (309); because opera is a form now associated with the bourgeois, an opera-like format for his novel is a fitting form for a contemporary bourgeois audience, says Broch. Accordingly, the principal character names are taken directly from Mozart: the erotomane von Juna (an anagram of Juan), the maid Zerline, the Baroness Elvire; two other characters are appropriated without their names: the magistrate Baron W., Elvire's cuckolded husband (Don Ottavio), and the beekeeper (the Stone Guest).

The structure of the novella *Zerline's Tale* accords with Broch's reference to "operatic" situations. It is set in a frame, with A., the narrator,[45] reclining on a daybed on a warm summer afternoon, musing on his past life abroad. (This is similar to E. T. A. Hoffmann's *Don Juan,* with a drowsy narrator in the loge relating his dream-like conversation with Donna Anna.) As in Hoffmann, it is unclear whether the story is real or a dream. The narrative begins on Sunday afternoon at two o'clock, introduced by the clanging of church bells. The room is deeply shaded and A. is in a drowsy funk when he hears a knock at the door: it is the ancient housemaid, Zerline, who lets herself in. From this point on, Zerline is the prime mover of the tale and A.'s role is limited to responses, as Zerline tells him the history of the house, of her mistress the Baroness Elvire, and the lover they shared, Herr von Juna. Her speeches are exactly as Broch describes them in the commentaries, exhibiting an operatic quality: long monologues, archaic turns of phrase and a nonconversational, oracular style, like certain libretti of Wagner[46] or Strauss.[47] She chants her memories like a seer. Juna, to be sure, is not larger than life like Don Juan — Broch describes him somewhat disparagingly as a "fin-de-siècle Erotiker,"[48] but his effect on Zerline is powerful. The passion he awakens in her creates the real insights of Zerline's narrative. Unlike the naïve, susceptible maid of Mozart's opera, Broch's Zerline has an astonishing grasp of the nature of sensual passion, its limits and possibilities, and she literally sings the praises of her lover.[49] She knows also the limits of her Don Juan: he can "serve" her, but not love her, exemplifying the difference between the aesthetic and the ethic in Broch's moral philosophy, seen from an erotic standpoint.[50]

Cohen and Broch share some insights into the Don Juan story. Cohen's study is an elucidation of his "Ästhetik des reinen Gefühls" (esthetics of pure emotion). He maintains that Mozart brings "the problem of love into the passion of a superman,"[51] that passion is a "serious" matter. Cohen agrees with Hoffmann's hypothesis that Donna Anna too was seduced by Don Juan, although she avenges not her lost honor but the murder of her father. Whatever took place between Don Juan and Donna Anna, Cohen maintains that she did not confront him with obdurate inaccessibility.[52] In his view, all three women are attracted by and yield to the superhuman aesthetic charms of the *Übermensch* Don Juan.[53] In Broch, the women are likewise helpless before Juna's erotic attraction, but only Zerline becomes fully conscious of her situation. In the end, despite her innately sensual nature, Broch's Zerline, like Hoffmann's Donna Anna, and possibly like Mozart's, sees the "abyss" before which they stand, and pulls back. She sees that the passion she feels is ultimately only partial knowledge, is aesthetic, and therefore insufficient.[54]

Broch's Zerline, although no moralist, sees more clearly than any of the other characters what is wrong with her affair with Juna — namely, his inability to love. Juna is not merely decadent, he represents an extreme case of what Broch sees as a disintegration of values. In this sense he is Broch's answer to Mozart's Don Juan, who was himself an idealized case of one value system (the erotic) exhaustively incorporated in one figure. Juna is eventually tried for murder and acquitted by Elvire's magistrate husband, whose meek acceptance of his cuckoldry and pallid sexuality remind us of Mozart's Ottavio. Broch's Don Juan, unlike Mozart's, escapes destruction (he would have been guillotined), eventually sets himself up in Spain (naturally enough) and, in the end, it is the abandoned women who are damned to a hell on earth. As Zerline relates in her final "strophe" (she calls it an *Abgesang*) of the story, it is the Baron, not Juna, who dies (of a broken heart), and then she herself takes over his family, by psychologically manipulating the Baroness and her illegitimate daughter Hildegarde. The latter has inherited the wantonness of her father Juna, while Zerline must seek love from ever younger men and finally boys, before a celibate old age. Zerline's *Abgesang* concludes with the admission that she had really loved the Baron, and not Juna, all along. This curiously arbitrary statement seems to retract her great love for Juna; might it perhaps be a correpondence to Donna Anna's rejection of Don Ottavio in the final quartet, where she puts him off for one more year (a year which Hoffmann says she will not survive)? Or perhaps it is her belated recognition of love beyond sensuality, the attenuated love Donna Anna feels for Don Ottavio. The correspondences with Mozart's opera and Hoffman's story are tantalizing, but Broch's main aim is the incorporation of the theme of Don Juanism into his polyhistoric novel on indifference and the evil it causes.

Zerline's narrative is framed by A.'s ruminations on money and commerce. At the beginning of the story, the town bell towers are striking two, at the end, four; at both points A. muses on his colonial past and his passive, apparently inadvertent success in the world of commerce, which in reality is an escape from responsibility.[55] Various themes are introduced to A. by Zerline in her tale, but the whole has such a dream-like context that A. need not pay it much attention. A. falls back to sleep and Zerline's tale for the moment disappears. It is as if the little *opera seria* which she has sung for him is just an interlude, forgotten as soon as it is over; but the themes she sounds continue throughout much of *Die Schuldlosen*. The Don Juan theme is woven through the lives of other characters introduced in the next novella, *Eine leichte Enttäuschung*.

Interlude

The reader will note conspicuous musical elements in the lyric "Stimmen — 1913" introducing the first section of the novel. While the title "Stimmen" is not necessarily a musical reference, the original name given them was "Cantos," implying singing. The beginning of "Stimmen 1913" is unmistakably musical: what German ear can fail to hear in its galloping tetrameter Schubert's "Erl-König"?[56] The poem is *Zeitkritik* in the Karl Kraus manner, a parody of a beloved popular cultural icon. A later section of the poem is a hexametric parody of *Faust II*:

Und neunzehnhundertdreizehn hat sich's so vollzogen
mit leerem Seelenlärm und opernhafter Geste,
und doch war's immer noch der leichte schöne Bogen,
des Liebesritus Hauch, der Nachklang einst'ger Feste,
Steifkragen, Mieder, Spitzen, ob Reiz des Glockenrocks:
Oh letztes sanftes Jahr im Abschied des Barocks![57]

As usual, the word "operatic" (*opernhaft*) has negative connotations; vacuous "soul-noise" (*leerem Seelenlärm*) (translated as "empty sound") produces operatic gesture, and the characters' actions in *Zerline's Tale* parody conventions of late Wilhelmine society. Broch finishes his pessimistic précis of European intellectual history with an extensive musical metaphor, in which the outmoded resolutions and unisons of traditional (Bachian) music represents the old order of things, now broken. The triad (*Dreiklang*), the number three has special dialectical significance for Broch. The "line of music" is the old polyphonic fugal tone-row, which, like a dialectic, led one somewhere, along a progressive path (*Fortschreiten*). Music is also the symbol of the Platonic idea, which man cannot see; music is just the "eye" of the here and now. But now, the triad is "intolerable and absurd," an art form which is decadent, disconnected (*verbindungslos*). Old musical and artistic values must not be either perverted or resuscitated, but replaced by new, unknown forms. Old values as well as futile attempts to recombine old forms, "motionless in their rapidity" (*unbeweglich vor Raschheit,* a reference to Futurism) are done for. The lyric ends with a parody of a soldier's song: "Kling klang Gloria, Wir ziehen in die Schlacht," itself evocative of certain Mahler songs, and a fittingly military finish to the era which the First World War brought to an end.

Ballad of the Beekeeper: Broch's Idealized Artist

Immediately preceding *Zerline's Tale* in the cycle is the *Ballade vom Imker*. In the mythic figure of the beekeeper Broch shows a perfect artist; a minute sketch of the successful artist, as opposed to the extensive portrayal of a failed artist in the *Vergil*. The tale is brief: the nameless protagonist is a skilled craftsman, who after a series of personal misfortunes adopts a little girl whom he names Melitta (bee). Economic forces cause him to give up his craft and become a factory worker. After the war, the old man is able to eke out their living by teaching beekeeping as an itinerant instructor and finally becomes a kind of force of nature himself, sleeping in the open fields and striding across the countryside, "bienengefeit, lebensgefeit, todesgefeit."[58]

This beekeeper figure returns later in the cycle, as an avenging Commendatore, but in this story he has the characteristics of the idealized artist, and the art associated with him is music: while his wife was still alive, the beekeeper sang with her as they tended the hives. After her death, he sings to Melitta. As the economic environment became "handwerksfeindlich" (inimical to fine craftsmanship), he loses his enthusiasm for his work. Beekeeping, too, no longer is enough. Just as he regrets having become a technician in a factory, he begins to see the bees as anonymous factory workers like himself; a former craftsman, he has contempt for this kind of work (87). He often thinks that perhaps it is only the handcraftsman who is really free, not farmers, or businessmen or factory workers, but those who, in emulation of God on the sixth day of Creation, can create something totally new. (This medieval conservatism is presented quite negatively in *Die Verzauberung*.) He even imagines that God created the inflation to wipe out commerce and to reposition the creative worker as the central focus of the economy. While he is developing these thoughts, he becomes increasingly allied with and interested in the natural world around him ("Schöpferwelt"), and in music. He sings again now, but with a change. No longer folksongs from the time of his marriage, no popular songs, jazz or arias from opera. These are not what the artist should concern himself with: he says, only the blind sing songs they know already. In a crucial passage (quoted below) the artist receives insight (*Erkenntnis*) through the faculty of sight, and music is its immediate expression, unverbalizable and otherwise inexpressible. Music as true art, rather than the creation of kitsch, is not reproducing the songs of composers, or recreating the sounds of nature—Broch uses synaesthetic metaphors to present this insight:

> Those who see . . . sing their vision, the perpetually renewed vision of life; they sing what is new in it, hence themselves.[59]

The Platonic ideal is hidden beyond the veil of perception, perhaps not accessible, but reflected in sound.[60]

The ability of music to express the inexpressible, a consistent theme in Broch, is found in a great many other writers, particularly of the late nineteenth century. Nietzsche's *Geburt der Tragödie aus dem Geiste der Musik*, a work which Broch undoubtedly knew, assigns to music the Dionysian moment of art.

> Singend und tanzend äußert sich der Mensch als Mitglied einer höheren Gemeinsamkeit, er hat das Gehen und das Sprechen verlernt und ist auf dem Wege, tanzend in die Luft emporzufliegen. Aus seinen Gebärden spricht die Verzauberung.[61]

The *unio mystica* of art and artist, brought about most clearly in the Dionysian realm of music is the same for Broch's singer as for Nietzsche's. The artist is a kind of imitation of God, and like Broch's beekeeper himself becomes a work of art ("darum singt er sich selber"):

> ... so tönt auch aus ihm etwas Übernatürliches: als Gott fühlt er sich, er selbst wandelt jetzt so verzückt und erhoben, wie er die Götter im Traum wandeln sah. Der Mensch ist nicht mehr Künstler, er ist Kunstwerk geworden.[62]

Broch sees the artist and the artisan in similar, but not identical, functions. Unlike Goethe's ironical narrative pose in Broch's favorite novel *Wilhelm Meisters Wanderjahre*, Broch does not find the artisan's utility to society greater than the artist's; but both bring dead material to life, artistic ability being termed *ein spürendes Sehen* (intuitive seeing, 82). Broch sees the artisan's hand guided by this gift, but with the artist, it is his "whole person" under this direction (88). It is left, however, to music to purify and deliquesce that form, that truth, which the eye has seen.[63]

The artist, unlike the artisan, is always running the risk of producing kitsch, by repeating the acts of creativity. Broch attaches a kind of inadvertent, unwilled and unreplicable quality to the creation of art. The beekeeper can distinguish without effort between *Kunst* and *Schund* (art and trash), his access to art is immediate and unreflected. Thus, no longer can he find pleasure in organ music and church choirs. Using singing as a metaphor, Broch has the beekeeper reject all mediated forms of art. He no longer listens, because he sings now only for himself. This is a music that is not even audible now, it is a knowledge, of death, a secret he may not, cannot reveal or communicate. He does not possess the ability to write down his music in notation, and if he could, he wouldn't. It is clear this is a superauditory music, not really music at all.

> Was immer im Lied des Wanderers mitklingt, das Summen der Biene bis herab zum Brummeln der Hummeln und hinauf bis zum weichklirrenden Jauchzen der Lerche, es ist niemals Nachahmung der Töne . . .[64]

This music is not representational, imitative or mimetic. It is metamusic, metaphorical in message, and its theme is the knowledge of death.[65]

The sound of buzzing bees, humming insects, etc. has a leitmotiv character which is present in several stories.[66] The bees are presented as a kind of debased form of artisan, and their sounds, marginally perceptible as music, are frequently alluded to. In the passage quoted above, for example, the rhymes are musical in themselves (*Summen, Brummeln, Hummeln*). A. later has a kind of auditory premonition of "Summen" in *Eine leichte Enttäuschung* before he finds Melitta.[67] The beekeeper's earlier craft, the making of drafting instruments, is presented as a stage of artisanship through which he has progressed. In that he now tends bees and teaches this skill to others, he is closer to the natural forces which drive the world, but also ethically more effective, because he is bringing this closeness to others. He is an intermediary between life and death, having knowledge of both, expressed by his singing. The artist is also believed to have healing powers, through his knowledge of death.[68]

Broch continues the development of the Don Juan material into the 1923 section of the novel with the ninth chapter, *Erkaufte Mutter* (The Bought Mother). The preceding chapters, *Eine leichte Enttäuschung* (A Slight Disappointment), *Die vier Reden des Studienrats Zacharias* (Studienrat Zacharias's Four Speeches), and *Die Ballade von der Kupplerin* (Ballad of the Procuress), do not utilize the musical or dramatic materials of Don Juan in any significant way.[69] In *Erkaufte Mutter,* A. becomes a present-day successor to von Juna, having seduced the Baroness away from her house in town by buying up the rights to the old hunting lodge, the scene of von Juna's conquests. In an "operatic" conspiracy between Zerline and the malignant Hildegarde (daughter of the Baroness) Melitta meets an untimely death, Hildegarde seduces and unsexes A. metaphorically, partly by her role in the death of Melitta, and partly by causing A.'s permanent impotence: thus she avenges the Baroness, using A. as a proxy for the departed von Juna. Other musical motivs are employed in the chapter, but are not directly related to the Don Juan story. There is one scene at a garden party held by the Baroness, in which A. has a hallucination: a chorus of voices, partly human, partly insects, is a stimulus for an auditory trance in which the present, particular, and individual dissolve into the general, timeless, and multiple. In a metaphor characteristic of Broch, the choral component of this musical experience symbolizes the simultaneity and multiplicity of all creation. At one particularly gruesome point in the narrative, as A. receives the proof of Melitta's death — the bloodstained handbag he had once given her — he imagines that he is in the final scene of an opera: a "tragic, or at least tragicomic" opera. To him the irreality of the situation is like that of opera (again the use of opera representing "aesthetic" or inauthentic art), yet A. imagines that the point of opera, of every opera scene, even, is: "at the moment of perception to become nonbeing and yet to persist in being,"[70] a negative comment on the aesthetic effect of opera. A.'s life is ethically wanting because he aspires to a state of escape, of irreality, of which the retreat to the hunting lodge is a physical symbol, and of which the entire operatic construct of the story is the overriding metaphor.

Finale: *The Stone Guest*

As noted before, the characters of the novel inhabit a symbolic, opera-like world; they are grotesques, incomplete exaggerations of certain features only. So the Don Juan narrative of *The Guiltless* appropriately concludes with another opera fragment: *The Stone Guest.*

Ten years have passed with Zerline and the Baroness living from the largesse of A., who shares the hunting lodge with them. The lodge is a kind of Calypso's island, and its inhabitants are in a trancelike amnesiac state, purposefully closing out all memories of the past. (A. cannot even quite remember Melitta's name.) This acceptance, or indifference to recent events is what constitutes the guilt of the "guiltless."

This idyllic, ethically ambivalent retreat is not destined to last, however. As in the Mozart opera, a supernatural authority appears on the scene to exact retribution and expiation; but the theme of the avenging commendatore/Beekeeper figure is not announced by ominous blasts of brass and woodwinds, as in Mozart. As the figure of Melitta is often associated with the leitmotiv of insect sounds (*Summen, Hummeln,* etc.) so the figure of the Beekeeper is also linked with the sounds of nature, and most explicitly with song. Unconsciously adopting the beekeeper's habit, A. begins to take long walks through the forest, picking seasonal flowers for the Baroness. Inverting the Beekeeper's return to nature, A. lets nature return to him; he retires to his room, throws open the windows and swaddles himself in winter clothing. His closeness to the elemental forest, to nature and its forces, is metaphorically presented as wind, and as song.[71] The arrival of the mysterious visitor is signalled by bird and human song, and by the ominous sounds of an axe felling trees. Unusual natural events accompany the approach of the stone guest—bird-song, bee-song, human song, and an ominous rainbow of snow crystals. As the rainbow is dispelled, footsteps are heard at the door, like the knocking on Don Giovanni's door. This is the beekeeper, analogous to Mozart's Commendatore, returned to avenge the death of Melitta, his daughter. Now blind, as if to emphasize further the primacy of the auditory over the visual, the old man (Lebrecht Endegut ("live right, end well": *nomen est omen*)) has "business" with A. As A. listens, the singing he heard has stopped, but the sounds of the axe-blows continue. He wonders if he had not imagined the singing—he is, after all, inexplicably drowsy (as he was in Zerline's tale: A's state of semiconscious sleepwalking is the sign of his indifference, and thus his guilt).

The "Wanderer" (like Wagner's Wotan-Wanderer, he carries a staff) is not hampered by his blindness; he can read the expressions on A.'s face. A. is confused, imagines he is seeing a ghost, an old school examiner, or perhaps tax auditor; he unconsciously slips into the archaic (operatic?) Ihr-address form, as did Zerline. Eventually he remembers Melitta and her suicide and realizes that this is her grandfather, or father, or a ghost, he is not sure. In a scene with Faustian echoes, A. learns that he is guilty and may (should), freely, commit suicide. He and his accuser discuss the concept of will, which, A. is assured, is infallible. A. fears that he may make a wrong decision in killing himself, but the Wanderer reassures him that his will has already decided for him. A. (from the Beekeeper we learn the A. is for "Andreas," or Man — the name is derived from Greek ανηρ, man) begins his long confession. He finally comes to understand his guilt as stemming from his indifference to his own human individuality, and thus to that of all other men. A. comes to realize that in the new age men have lost their sense of their own individuality, are merely part of a mass organism:

> Man has shattered his limits and has entered into multidimensionality, into the new dwelling place of his self, and in it he wanders about lost, lost in immensity. We are a We, not because we form a community, but because our limits coalesce. (KW 5, 266; Manheim 260)[72]

This loss of one's individuality was symbolized in the humiliating encounter with Hildegarde by A.'s impotence. Here A. must expiate his original "sin" of indifference, which is caused by his failed sense of himself as an individual, by in fact ceasing to exist, by killing himself. Now one hears a reprise of the music which signalled the entrance of the beekeeper. A. touches the hand of the Beekeeper/Commendatore, which is indeed hard and cold like that of a statue. The old man then leaves, with the final comment, "he who acknowledges his guilt is called" (267). As he leaves, however, the "Song" begins again, accompanied by the rhythmic axe-blows. In an audible reminiscence of Leporello's panic at the Commendatore's heavy tread, the axe-blows are mimicked by the description of the "Song": "Hölzfällerlied, Márschchoral, Psálm und Trósteshymne." The motive of music is combined with the concept of collapsing boundaries, of the blurring of individual consciousness, which makes possible A.'s expiation: he attains insights, ineffable and inexpressible, which are only made possible by the dissolution of his conscious perception of the three-dimensional world. These insights are hinted at with images of heavenly bodies, snow, and music. As lightly falling snow joins heaven and earth in one indistinguishable whiteness,[73] so also the song, which metaphorically accompanies the approach to knowledge of all reality — this song disappears, is absorbed into the totality of the world:

> ... in the softness of the snow the sky vanished, the song van-
> ished, the this-worldly and the other-worldly vanished, yet re-
> mained inescapably present, present in the starry harmony of the
> all, resounding in the now inescapable common center.[74]

He shoots himself through the temple, falling into an x-shaped
cross (Andreaskreuz, or Cross of St. Andrew) on the floor, an ex-
culpatory suicide for the guilty "Guiltless."

Epilogue: *A Passing Cloud*

In the final chapter, *A Passing Cloud,* Hildegarde walks to church
clutching her hymnal, and in the final sentence, as she enters the
church, "filled with sweet hopelessness," she opens her hymnal to
sing. The implication of the text is lightly ironic: though utterly
self-absorbed (here in comic sexual anxiety), the woman is described as "in perfect harmony" with herself, and hardly able to
think of herself. For this final view of another "guilty" protagonist,
the power of music is presented negatively, as superficial, a cultural
inheritance of conservative society.

Here in Broch's last completed work of fiction, as in all the
others, music is presented in association with nonverbal, thus superior, forms of cognition. The linking of music, however, with the
breakdown of individual boundaries, as seen in the garden party
scene, and at the end of the Commendatore chapter, makes clear
another connection of music and cognition: this cognition must
include death. It is this knowledge towards which the "Song" is
pointing, which A. feels drawn towards, which brings him to suicide. Life and true cognition are, it appears, not compatible. The
inaccessible "meaning" of music symbolizes this incompatibility.

Notes

[1] Hermann Broch, *The Spell,* H. F. Broch de Rothermann, trans. (San Francisco: North Point Press, 1989).

[2] The three versions have been published together as: *Hermann Broch, Bergroman. Die drei Originalfassungen textkritisch herausgegeben von Frank Kress
and Hans Albert Maier* (Frankfurt: Suhrkamp, 1969).

³ This chapter will refer to versions 1, 2, or 3, as indicated by Kress/Maier. Since version 1 was used in the *Kommentierte Werkausgabe*, page references to it come from KW 3. Other references use Kress/Maier page numbers.

⁴ Hermann Broch, *Gesammelte Werke, v. 1–10* (Zurich: Rhein-Verlag), *Der Versucher*, 1952, ed. Felix Stössinger.

⁵ Saint Cecilia, music's patron saint. But here Zäzilie represents innocence and naïveté, rather than music itself. Later she provides an example of musical propaganda, singing a quasi-fascist ditty, unconscious of its anti-Semitic implications.

⁶ A similar passage from Version 1 in *The Spell*: "She jumped from one leg to the other, raised one little arm and then the other, and a grave and holy awakening could be seen on her face, soundless was her dance, a hushed skipping on heavy gray woolen socks, nor did she stop her angelic dancing as the jazz rhythms now switched to that of a tango." 24.

⁷ *The Spell*, 24–25.

⁸ "Er stand da, die Finger am Apparat, als handle es sich darum seinen Willen durchzusetzen." Version 2/1, 40. (Kress/Maier page numbers include a section as well — thus, here: version 2, section 1, page 40.)

⁹ Kress/Maier: Version 2/2, 93–97; Version 3/2, 65–69.

¹⁰ KW 3, 49–50.

¹¹ Version 2/1, 93: "And so the sound of the organ rose up: it gathered together the wind of the clouds, the wind of the hills, and the wind of the earth, the wind of its rippling waves, it gathered the wind of the world's diverseness, gathered all these together into a single, measured singing storm, and in its rushing roar, led by the simple musicality of a village schoolmaster, all the windswept sweeping complexity of the world takes on the form of sound, uniting all with the Now of temporality, uniting with the room, which to be sure was only that of a shabby, sadly derelict village church, but one which still held fast within its Gothic walls the sounds of centuries" (except where noted, trans. JAH).

¹² "In diesem Gefühl . . . ist auch der einfältige Mensch des Geistes voll" (KW 10/2, 239, and similarly, 243).

¹³ Version 2/2, 93–94: "And so it continued singing . . . for that which streaming and roaring wafts through all the world is faith, indeed incomprehensible in its formlessness, nonbelieving like the wind, the clouds, like existence itself, which just goes on, nonbelieving as everything unformed and unconscious is barely capable of believing in itself, yet nonetheless so pregnant with belief and urging towards form, even to the point of creating its own form, so that the miracle is always at hand, always ready to have faith arise and creatively take its place in the world and in the soul."

[14] Version 2/2, 94. "Such configured form . . . is that of music, in which the amorphousness of Being can dissolve, the measured rushing, roaring miracle which looses itself from the organ in inexhaustible measure, mirroring the universe in music, just as music is played in words, re-gathered to ever-renewing, more penetrating form."

[15] "Spiegel des Wortes, Spiegel der Musik, Spiegel des sichtbaren und unsichtbaren Alls und der Ganzheit, Spiegel des Glaubens, getragen von den Klängen, bezwungen von der Geste des Gebetes . . ." Version 2/2, 94.

[16] KW 3, 90. "Blessed be Jesus our Lord / Whatever's in the mountain hoard / Will be set free by His grace / Satan and monsters he will chase / All evil return from whence it came / In Jesus' and in Mary's name. *The Spell*, 86.

[17] Broch's thematic borrowings from the writings of Peter Rosegger (Austrian novelist of provincial life, 1843–1918) have been persuasively pointed out (George Schoolfield, "Notes on Broch's *Der Versucher.*" *Monatshefte* 48, 1956, 2–5.) Rosegger's embedded lyrics in *Wanderung durch Steiermark* and *Der Gottsucher* may well have inspired Broch to invent *völkisch* lyrics of his own.

[18] Version 2/4, 203.

[19] "As if he were listening, despite the heathen cannonade, to the singing of the flowers, to the inaudible echo with which they reflected the silver-murmuring alpine wind, the flowers in their turn hearing the wind . . . and he, attending the wind, in which the great silver breath of earth moves, an echo of that still greater breath, of which the sea tells and sings, the breath and echo of eternity . . ." Version 2/4, 203.

[20] KW 3, 164.

[21] KW 3, 247; *The Spell*, 254.

[22] *The Spell*, 257. KW 3, 250: "wolkenlos war der Himmel . . . und die Tannen sangen ihr dunkles spitzes Lied in die Bläue hinauf. Aber nicht dieses hörte ich so eigentlich, obschon es gleichfalls recht vernehmbar war, sondern die Klänge einer Ziehharmonika waren es . . ."

[23] *The Spell*, 258–59; KW 3, 252.

[24] *The Spell*, 262; KW 3, 255.

[25] *The Spell*, 263.

[26] *The Spell*, 263; KW 3, 256.

[27] *The Spell*, 266; KW 3, 259. Broch de Rothermann translates *singen* here as "buzzing."

[28] The scene is reminiscent of (Mann's) Aschenbach's dream of Panic frenzy, with acetylene torches instead of *phalloi*; "Männer, Hörner über den Stirnen, mit Pelzwerk geschürzt und zottig von Haut . . . ließen eherne Becken er-

dröhnen und schlugen wütend auf die Pauken . . ." Thomas Mann, *Der Tod in Venedig* (Frankfurt: Fischer Bücherei, 1954), 60.

[29] Broch's 1934 essay "Geist und Zeitgeist" describes the murderous climate of Europe as "Stummheit," the denial of the word and the Spirit.

[30] KW 3, 277.

[31] *The Spell*, 285.

[32] *The Spell*, 285.

[33] KW 3, 287.

[34] KW 3, 148.

[35] *The Spell, 336.* KW 3, 326.

[36] *The Spell,* 363. KW 3, 353.

[37] This phrase is from Carole Duebbert's essay of the same name in: *Broch's Verzauberung. Materialien,* ed. P. M. Lützeler (Frankfurt: Suhrkamp, 1983), 226.

[38] The neo-Kantian philosophy professor (1842–1918) taught and wrote as Broch was coming of age. Broch possessed several of his works.

[39] Cohen, Hermann: *Die dramatische Idee in Mozarts Operntexten* (Berlin: Cassirer, 1915).

[40] The so-called "Wiener Bibliothek." Klaus Amann and Helmut Grote: *Die Wiener Bibliothek Hermann Brochs. Kommentiertes Verzeichnis des rekonstruierten Bestandes* (Cologne: Böhlau, 1990). Although Broch's library obviously contained many works of literature as well, there is no listing of these.

[41] Lorenzo DaPonte, *Don Giovanni* I/7, "You maidens made for love, don't let time pass you by."

[42] KW 5, 301 ff. In the article "Brochs Roman in elf Erzählungen: *Die Schuldlosen,*" Michael Winkler takes the view that the Don Giovanni myth underlies much of Broch's writing before this work; in a comparison of Broch's text with DaPonte's book, Winkler discovers many subliminal references to *Don Giovanni,* among them the themes of gluttony, thunder, alienation, parasitism, justice and Final Judgment. In *Hermann Broch: Materialien.* ed. Paul Michael Lützeler (Frankfurt: Suhrkamp, 1986), 183–98.

[43] KW 5, 304.

[44] KW 5, 309.

[45] Is it a coincidence that the writer of Kierkegaard's paean to Mozart's *Don Giovanni,* "Immediate Stages of the Erotic," also uses the signum A.?

[46] For a discussion of similarities in Wagner's and Broch's use of poetical language see Jean Paul Boyer, "Hermann Broch: Auch ein Wagnerianer wider

Willen?" in *Hermann Broch. Das dichterische Werk*, ed. Michael Kessler and Paul Michael Lützeler (Tübingen: Stauffenburg, 1987), 231–38.

[47] For example, KW 5, 103.

[48] KW 5, 302: "Inhalt und Darstellungsmethode der *Schuldlosen*."

[49] KW 5, 110: "der psalmodierende Singsang."

[50] Kierkegaard has an interesting discussion of the paradox that the object of erotic feeling is itself devoid of eroticism, the "Greek" consciousness holding that "that which constitutes the power of the god is not in the god, but in all the other individuals, who refer it to him; he is himself, as it were, powerless and impotent, because he communicates his power to the whole world." Søren Kierkegaard, "Immediate Stages of the Erotic," in *Either/Or*, vol. 1, (Princeton: Princeton UP, 1971), 62.

[51] Cohen, 83: "das Problem der Liebe in die Leidenschaft des Übermenschen."

[52] Cohen, 86: "daß Donna Anna dem Jupiterblicke nicht harte Unnahbarkeit entgegengesetzt . . ."

[53] Donna Anna: "It is the innocence of grace, which, through the dimension and power of passion, achieves solemnity, life and truth," (88). Elvira: "In this Faust-poem one must see Elvira as Gretchen; she becomes a penitent at the very momen she yields herself," (90; trans. JAH).

[54] Cohen says of Mozart's Zerlina: "It is the superior force of personality and the magic of masculine beauty to which grace in its innocence must be subject. There is no aesthetic defense against it; of course, morality has defenses," (88; trans. JAH).

[55] Like Wagner's *Holländer*, A. is Dutch, and has wandered over the world; he too is in search of redemption.

[56] For example:

> Darauf der Vater: "In herrlichstem Führen
> Ging der Fortschritt voran. Wer wagt dran zu rühren!
> Du störst ihn mit Zweifeln und ängstlichem Schaun;
> drum schließe die Augen zu blindem Vertraun!"
> Drauf sagt der Sohn: "Kalt faßt es mich an —,
> hat's dir noch immer kein Leid getan?" (KW 5, 15)

[57] KW 5, 18–19:

> "And so the year thirteen has passed away
> with empty sound and operatic stance.
> The light-slung arch, however, still holds sway
> recalling festivals and rites of high romance,
> lace, corsets, crinolines, and stand-up collars that choke,
> last gentle farewell year of the Baroque."

Hermann Broch, *The Guiltless,* trans. Ralph Manheim (North Point Press: San Francisco, 1987), 10. All translations from the German in this chapter are Manheim's.

[58] KW 5, 93: "proof against bees, proof against life, proof against death."

[59] KW 5, 87; *The Guiltless,* 82.

[60] KW 5, 88. "It is the unseen within the seen, transposed into sound. Such was the old man's singing; his singing was himself, for he sang everything he saw and had ever seen." Mannheim 82.

[61] Nietzsche, Friedrich, *Werke* (Kritische Gesamtausgabe, 3. Abtlg. 1. Band) (Berlin: Walter de Gruyter, 1972), 26: "In song and in dance man expresses himself as a member of a higher community; he has forgotten how to walk and speak and is on the way towards flying into the air, dancing. His very gestures express enchantment." Walter Kaufmann, *Basic Writings of Nietzsche* (New York: Modern Library, 1968), 37.

[62] Nietzsche, 26:

"Just as the animals now talk, and the earth yields milk and honey, supernatural sounds emanate from him, too: he feels himself a god, he himself now walks about enchanted, in ecstasy, like the gods he saw walking in his dreams. No longer an artist, he has become a work of art." Kaufmann 37.

[63] KW 5, 88:

"For that very reason song, music, can do still more; it can and must encompass that which has already been formed and made visible, free it from the last trace of dead slag, and transpose it into purest life, into visible song transcending the audible." Manheim 82.

[64] KW 5, 88:

"And whatever sound may chime with the wanderer's song, from the buzzing of the honey-bees down to the droning of the bumble-bees and up to the softly-strident rejoicing of the lark, it is never an imitation of sounds . . ." Manheim 82.

[65] KW 5, 90.

[66] But there is also music in the very name Melitta: μελισσα, Attic μελιττα ("bee") is one letter removed from μελισμα: song.

[67] KW 5, 125 and 128.

[68] KW 5, 90.

[69] Zacharias, a comic figure, delivers an unsubtly anti-Semitic lecture in a small chamber-music auditorium, and is described as having never attended a serious concert. His nonmusicality is associated with his narrowness and outsider status among the better-educated citizenry. (KW 5, 143). Michael Win-

kler sees in the *"methodisch konstruierte Erotik"* of Zacharias and Philippine an implicit parody of Wagner's *Tristan*. Michael Winkler, "Brochs Roman in elf Erzählungen," in: *Hermann Broch Materialien,* ed. Paul Michael Lützeler (Frankfurt: Suhrkamp, 1986), 187.

[70] "im Augenblick der Konstatierung nicht-seiend zu werden, und doch im Seienden zu verharren!" KW 5, 222; Manheim 224.

[71] "the breath of the forest . . . was an intimation of the infinitely remote and almost weightless reality which is order. And sometimes it was like song, the distant song of weightlessness. And one day it was real song." 245.

[72] Broch was working on the *Massenwahntheorie* at this period.

[73] Conflation of heaven and earth is a utopian trope in much of Broch's writing.

[74] KW 5, 274. Mannheim 268.

3: Musical Ideas in
Hugo von Hofmannsthal and His Time

Introduction

IN *HOFMANNSTHAL UND SEINE ZEIT*,[1] Broch examines at length the politics, art and values of late nineteenth and early twentieth century Europe; he devotes considerable analysis to music and its related arts, drama and dance, and to painting. In this work he concludes that the genre of opera was the representative art form of the time.[2] He supports this conclusion with an argument based on the nineteenth century's impulse to misuse the aesthetic sense to deny or ignore reality. This denial is at the root of what Broch calls decoration:[3] the misuse of art to mask, select, adorn, and thus deny reality.

Music Among the Arts

But the nineteenth century was highly realistic in its literary and artistic vocabulary; it rejected the decorative, saccharine, and sentimental: it tended to portray social relationships realistically. While painting's vocabulary was strongly naturalistic, the genre had a necessarily limited scope; in contrast, the novel with its great length was particularly well suited to capture the totality of the nineteenth century. Yet, strangely, it was the theater, and not the novel, which became the representative genre of the epoch. How did this come about? Just as theater architecture remained baroque, so the influence of the eighteenth century extended (in theater) into the nineteenth. The novel, with its gritty naturalism, was not read by a public searching for "something beautiful,"[4] was certainly not read by the common people (though perhaps by certain conscience-stricken bourgeois readers); at most it provided a summer entertainment. The theater, on the other hand, satisfied

the need both of the *Bürger* and the *Volk* to see a spectacle, to experience decorative beauty, and to enjoy life. As Broch puts it:
"Theater is makeup."[5] In the main, theater could not afford to take
the naturalistic turn of the nineteenth-century novel.[6]

However, the baroque tradition of theater and its nineteenth-
century materials were in conflict: whereas formerly it had treated
with ever-increasing elegance and simplicity the fate of kings and
gods, with profoundly moral implications, in the nineteenth century this baroque machinery, to remain "modern," had to become
more involved in psychological and social motivations of the bourgeois classes: the repertoire had changed from victory and defeat,
the ethical situation of the hero, to the presentation and explica-
tion of bourgeois psychological and social principles. This transition led inevitably to an excessive and overblown treatment of
bourgeois tragic materials; inevitably, since the theatrical machinery
in place, schooled as it was on Racine and Corneille, was inherently
conservative in technique: and from this point (Broch maintains) it
is not far to a dialectic turn — the marginally genuine (echt) tends
to the decoratively spurious — (das dekorativ Unechte) and operatic. No wonder that the period, in its insatiable love of decoration
found its "high culture" in the opera.[7]

More important than this "*Unstil*" (nonstyle), perhaps, were
two countermovements of the period — the new French literature
inaugurated by Baudelaire, and French Impressionism in painting,
an outgrowth of naturalism.

Broch never really defines *Unstil*, but he says the style of an
epoch is an "interference" pattern (once again, Broch's fondness
for metaphors from the natural sciences) created by the meeting of
the various "wave movements" in cultures. Thus, the style, or nonstyle, of the nineteenth century is the confluence of various cultural
trends, interconnected, yet in a curious "purity" remaining distinct
from one another: rationalism, individualism, historicism, romanticism, eclecticism, skepticism: the strains intertwining, but not
combining.

Broch proposes that it is the task of art to ask the question:
what is reality? Since only art "produces reality," only the artist can
ask the question.[8] Literature and painting do this via a medium in
which there is a substantial gap between the signified (das Ge-
meinte) and the signifier (das Meinende), whereas in music the

layer of symbol (the language of tone) and the musical "reality" (sound) which it is trying to create, are the same thing. In music, the medium is the message, so to speak, whereas in literature the reality is mediated in countless layers of words and their meanings and sounds.

Music of the "Value Vacuum"

Broch's account continues: Germany entered a period of literary and artistic sterility after the time of Goethe and Hölderlin.[9] With the single exception of Franz Grillparzer (1791–1872), whom Broch considers the sole worthy dramatic successor to Schiller and Kleist, the literature of the period is marked by triviality and provinciality. This period culminated in the "value vacuum" of 1870 to 1890, the period which produced Hofmannsthal. During this period, Germany, land of poets and philosophers, cast off its poets' mantle and became, in Broch's words, if not exclusively the land of philosophers, also a land of scientists, and of musicians. Broch attributes this change to German radicalism, here defined as rationalism taken to the point of extreme abstractness: in extreme abstractness, only science and music remain as justifiable modes of expression. Broch argues similarly in his 1934 music essay, saying that music alone among the arts has claim to the abstractness and "exactness" of science.[10] Like mathematics, and unlike painting and literature, music is not intentional, mimetic, or representational: it only represents itself.

To be sure, Germany was certainly the greatest contributor to advances in science, but it was in music that Germany made its most characteristic contribution. The period of 1870 to 1890, the economic boom, was an intellectual void (Öde) in painting and literature. Art must, by nature, be revolutionary or it is not art. In contrast to science, which is progressive, art is impatient (ungeduldig): it does not supplement or progress towards anything. "Rather, it must strive with each and even the slightest work — if it is to become a genuine work of art — for an immediate grasp of the world totality. For this reason its development proceeds exclusively in revolutionary thrusts."[11]

Since the period was a value vacuum, its art reflects this. The most eminent "reflector" of this emptiness was Wagner, the "unmusical music genius" and the "unpoetical poetical genius" (St, 55), in whose music one can most clearly see the *Unstil* of the time. His nonstyle is painfully evident when he is less than inspired: the "Faust" overture: empty bombast; the Wesendonck-Lieder: empty sentimentality. Broch summarily dismisses these works as too characteristic of the age. But Broch detects Wagner's genius in the discovery of the "architecture" of the vacuum, the *Gesamt-kunstwerk*, Wagner's elaboration of the existing operatic apparatus. It would seem here that since the *Unstil* of the vacuum is really the layering of many styles over one another, that the architecture of this vacuum is indeed reflected in a type of art which is a hodge-podge of many genres. Broch sees Wagner's contribution as "major art" (großes Kunstwerk). Broch maintains a distinction between major and minor art which is crucial to his understanding of Wagner: a major work is that which attempts to sum up and contain the epochal totality of its time, and a minor work does not and cannot do this. Thus a minor work is appreciable within its time, while a great work is only understood and appreciated after the epoch which gave it birth has passed.[12]

Broch's esteem for Wagner is ambivalent:[13] despite the fact that the *Gesamtkunstwerk* is "major art," Broch takes a swipe at Wagner's intentions: he knew his work would satisfy an immediate needs (Bedürfnis) of the time. But it was "far less clear" to him (Wagner) that a project which aimed at immediate success would necessarily have all the characteristics of "minor" art, thus be fated to be in the style of its time — that is, here, in the nonstyle, the "false truthfulness" which, Broch says, did indeed mark Wagner's life and work.[14]

So the "architecture" of the vacuum is to be found in the *Ge-samtkunstwerk*, that is, in opera. How does this most reflect the vacuum of the time? Most of all, Broch suggests, through its complete lack of humor (even, or perhaps most especially, in *Meister-singer*). Wagner's work was both rational and romantic; naturalistic and pompous; sentimental and gloomy; catholicizing and mytholo-gizing. Broch finds it nonetheless to be major art[15] because it brewed together the disparate elements of the nonstyle into a specific Wagner style which radically and shamelessly exposed the "na-kedness" of the vacuum. There is a problem with this Wagner critique: if signifier and signified in music are identical, how does

Wagner's music, or anyone's, reflect on the age? But opera is more than music, and a Wagnerian "collective work of art" is more than just opera.

Not surprisingly, Broch admires Nietzsche's critique of Wagner: he calls Nietzsche a heroic figure of the age of the value vacuum, a figure who saw the vacuum and deplored it. Nietzsche alone retained the European scope which German literature had lost: he saw through Wagner and his opportunism.[16] Nietzsche had contempt for Wagner's production because it was the exact opposite of his own: accommodating, not opposing, the odious tendencies of the day: particularly that peculiarly German "hollowness"[17] (*Dumpfheit*) which was really a theatrical prerequisite for a Wagner audience. For Nietzsche, Wagner was not the spokesman for his age, but rather its minion, a minor artiste who dared break with the operatic tradition of his age because he lacked the basic skill to continue it. For this reason Nietzsche felt he had to compare him to "little" Bizet. But this preference may have unintentionally aided the philistines, who could now reject Wagner and his new music for the wrong reasons, just as Nietzsche himself, fifty years after his death, was appropriated for the wrong reasons by the Nazi philistines.

While Nietzsche and Wagner both had genius,[18] Nietzsche had the vision to see and react against the value vacuum and its potential for evil consequences. Nonetheless Broch concedes Wagner's genius and his place in history, partly because of his instinct for self-promotion, his naive genius, and his "special feeling for the epoch."[19] Wagner knew the bourgeoisie would replace the cathedral with an opera house, would choose opera as its form. The public may have preferred Verdi, a "*Vollmusiker*,"[20] to Wagner (*Antimusiker!*), but there are still Wagnerian influences in *Falstaff*. The styles of Wolf and Bruckner are "unthinkable" without Wagner, and Broch calls them the "two most genuine and profoundest music geniuses of the epoch."[21] The public, and even Nietzsche, could not see the revolution in music which Wagner began; Wagner was the catalyst for the new age of music.

On the whole, then, Broch assesses Wagner, if not his operas, positively. Wagner was a visionary whose greatest works embodied the negatively charged spirit of the age. The *Gesamtkunstwerk* as represented by, say, *Götterdämmerung* (a "glorification" of German being and German fate), accurately reflected the valueless center of culture which was Germany in 1880.

Music in *"museal"* Vienna

Broch makes more musical observations about Vienna and the Viennese in "Vienna's Gay Apocalypse of 1880."[22] Events such as discoveries in physics and medicine in Berlin and Vienna made it possible to ignore the still, empty center of the value vacuum. But Vienna was essentially different from Germany because of its *museal* quality, that is, its devotion to museum art, and thus, artistic conservatism; it was less a city of art than a city of "decoration par excellence."[23] Germany, on the other hand, despite Weimar, never set itself up as a literary institution, and not even Munich, that "Athens on the Isar," and the center of painting, thought of itself this way. The idea of being a living museum was something Vienna reserved for itself, was thus a sign of its decline, its "cheerful vegetation," in short, its *museal* quality.

Vienna, proud of its commonalities with Paris, is a theater city nearly on a par with Paris, and a music city second to none. Broch sees the Burgtheater and the Comédie Francaise as parallel institutions, and both cities have not just opera but *Volkstheater* and *Singspiel* too, which are in the main influenced by the "higher" legitimate stages (Burgtheater and Opera). The theater and opera traditions of Bourbon Paris and Habsburg Vienna provide a solution to a political power problem: aligning the ascendant bourgeois class with the Court, rather than the nobility: while in Protestant countries the tendency to greater intimacy, privacy and smaller scale occasioned by the inward turn of religion in the Reformation had its secular counterpart in the bourgeois culture of chamber music and still-life painting; in Catholic countries, the secular counterparts to the mass were theater, symphony, and opera, which bore the insignia of the Court, and allowed the growing bourgeois to come into the immediate proximity of the monarchy. The great theater tradition of the Bourbon and Habsburg residence cities springs from their royal court theaters.[24]

The growing gap between Paris or London, world cities, and provincial, *museal* Vienna is also seen in the popular theater. Broch compares the operettas of Offenbach and Sullivan with Johann

Strauss's work. Where once the Viennese stage had its ironic note (romantic in Raimund, biting in Nestroy), it has by now become degraded to the point where all that remains is an "idiotic" imitation of comic opera. Broch laments the "flat cynicism" of purely "decorative amusement"[25] and judges the Strauss waltz to be a suitable token of this "immorality."[26] The cynicism of the French and English operettas stem from their cosmopolitan nature and political intentions, and thus have a moral underpinning. All this is missing from the Viennese scene from 1848 on — Broch remarks "operetta form . . . became a specific vacuum product; yet as a vacuum decoration it proved itself all too durable,"[27] and he see its later world popularity as the sign of a world decline into a value-vacuum.[28] Broch finally sees the Austrian society as "stateless" and its main purpose as a collective to be aesthetic, not ethical; it is an audience, not a body politic; it sees the player, not the play; hears the virtuoso, not the music. Vienna, as the capital of this unethical society, is a "metropolis of Kitsch."[29]

Hofmannsthal, Language and Music

At this point Broch (finally) comes to deal with Hofmannsthal. He compares the education of the two prodigies, Mozart and Hofmannsthal. While Leopold Mozart strove to educate his son to be a craftsman first, assuming that the rest of his life would sort itself out from there, Hofmannsthal's father took the reverse tack: he had no interest in choosing his son's vocation, but wanted his son to follow him philosophically (*im Weltanschaulichen*); namely, in the pursuit of aesthetic pleasure. Broch views this attitude with predictable distaste.[30] Indeed, Broch finds the figure of Hofmannsthal troubling, if interesting: he is conservative, backward-looking, fixated on the dream world of Imperial Austria. But because Hofmannsthal was so sensitive to the mediacy of verbal language, he was open to the communicative power of musical language.[31] For Broch (speaking of Novalis), poetry and mathematics have a "Pythagorean relation," but for the unmathematical Hofmannsthal, music took the place of mathematics in that relation, and this was the reason for his eventual attraction to the musical stage. Broch admires his overcoming the language crisis so famously expressed in the Chandos letter,[32] by allowing language first to become mute, and only then to refind its voice through "magical means."[33] Broch quotes Hofmannsthal's *Buch der Freunde* repeatedly: "Finer and spiritually richer than language critique would be the attempt to wrest oneself free of language and into a magical mode, as is the case with love."[34] This rejection of language alone leads Hofmannsthal, in Broch's analysis, inexorably to the realm of music. "True love of language is not possible without the denial of language."[35] And it is precisely with this denial of language "that the power (Magie) of music is invoked and called to aid . . ."[36]

Hofmannsthal's significant step from theater to opera was "a step from linguistic skepticism to linguistic despair and the love of language, yet also one that still includes self-transcendence . . ." It is the "final stylistic intensification of the theater."[37] Hofmannsthal's concept of style made this final "radical conclusion" (radikale Abrundung), that is, the turn to music, a necessity.[38]

Broch's special affinity for the problem of Lord Chandos can be adduced from his statements here and in other writings, where music becomes the medium in which cognition operates and is operated upon in nonverbal form, representing the secret, unreachable reality beyond language. Hofmannsthal's move to operatic theater is his solution to the "language-desperation" of which his proxy Chandos complains. Hofmannsthal's use of music allows "mute" words to gain the quality of interpretability (Ausdeutbarkeit).

Did Hofmannsthal not create his own kind of *Gesamtkunstwerk*, like Wagner? Yes, but Wagner is the revolutionary and Hofmannsthal the reactionary. Wagner embraced the value vacuum, while Hofmannsthal, in his assimilation of the entire tradition represented by the Burgtheater, tried, in vain, to escape this vacuum. One sees in Hofmannsthal's collaborations with Strauss a conservative poet allied with a conservative musical sensibility, a clinging to a musical theatrical structure which in Vienna had always been a given. Vienna, even in Hofmannsthal's time, had always harbored a strong anti-Wagnerian faction, sensing correctly that Wagner stood for a removal of the "rules." Hofmannsthal at some level sensed this too, and that he would finally also be absorbed into the vacuum. Finally Broch sees in Hofmannsthal's work a pathetic, yet admirable, attempt to preserve and enliven the inheritance of imperial Vienna of the eighteenth century by reviving the splendor of its baroque grand opera, "the self-affirmation of a true destiny, Hofmannsthal's existence, his high style and his high art."[39]

So, as with Wagner, Broch is ambivalent about Hofmannsthal's contribution to his time. In an artistic sense, Hofmannsthal is the equivalent of Pasenow, a perhaps admirable character whose value system obsolesces during his lifetime, in short, a Romantic; the opportunist Wagner is a kindred spirit to cynical and value-free visionary, Huguenau.

In the essay Broch discusses different kinds of *Gesamtkunstwerk*. The dreamlike, mood-driven theater works of symbolists such as Maeterlinck, as set to music by Debussy, become a new type of this genre. Not opera, a new type of total art work is formed of music, dance, pantomime, ballet, all originally inspired by a verbal text — but one which has become attenuated from the theatrical performance. The ballet works of Stravinsky and Debussy revitalized a genre which (in the West, at least) had more or less "run aground," and given it new significance and seriousness. This new ballet is associated with the new music; thus, ballet comes to overshadow opera, insofar as its connection to musical advances is concerned. Since ballet is, by this definition, a "modern" genre, the new ballet finds a predictably cool reception in Vienna. In Vienna the advent of popular forms of dance as found in waltzes and operettas destroyed the old ballet tradition, and when modern ballet arose to challenge these platitudes, Vienna rejected it. Broch maintains that the Russian ballet was revitalized by the inclusion of folk materials (Glinka and Stravinsky). In this Broch characteristically emphasizes the importance of mythic and symbolic materials. Apparently Broch's esteem for Stravinsky as an innovator was high (unlike Adorno's[40]). Debussy and Stravinsky differ from Wagner: Wagner is an innovator who prepares the way, culturally speaking, by embracing the value vacuum, while Debussy and Stravinsky are forerunners of the new (unspecified) value system, but are denied success in Vienna, which has no use for the symbolistic or impressionistic in music.[41] While Hofmannsthal did not reject dance,[42] for him there could be no *Gesamtkunstwerk* without the word.[43] Hofmannsthal reacted to Debussy's *Afternoon of a Faun* in Viennese fashion: he ignored those features of the ballet which were new, the musical, and emphasized the old, that is, the theatrical and balletic.[44]

Broch notes the "productive misunderstanding"[45] which gave musical impressionism its name, borrowing the term from painting: painting deals with light and shadow, creating the forms of the picture out of the atmosphere; music, of course, does not deal with light and shadow: this impressionistic music captures and records "atmospheric moods," emphasizing clarity and brightness, thus resembling rococo, rather than romantic music. Noting that even Wagnerian music has an element of this type of "atmospheric mood," its mood painting contained in the technique of the unending melody, Broch nonetheless sees a significant difference in luminosity (Helligkeitsdifferenz) between Wagner and the impressionists. "It's a long way from beer to absinthe."[46] Broch sensibly points out the difficulty of maintaining an "atmosphere" with just melody, that polyphony is necessary for the maintenance of mood, but that even this is really a somewhat inferior type of musical expression: for impressionistic music, when not part of theater, almost always requires some sort of verbal tag to give the "bourgeois, in his absence of thought,"[47] something to think about (e.g., "Ride of the Valkyries," "The Sea," etc.). Since music and symbol both operate on a super-rational level, according to Broch, the idea of music which needs the word to complete its meaning is inevitably negative.[48] Broch consistently favors absolute over programmatic music for its greater cognitive content (Erkenntnisinhalt). Where the word is necessary for complete expression, then the increase of cognition through music alone has been insufficient.

In a discussion of Hofmannsthal's opera librettos, Broch concludes that while Hofmannsthal rejected *fin de siècle* art, in his Strauss collaborations he presented the Viennese a "farewell festival" to the Austrian millennium. These operas and their symbolism coincided with the end of an age.[49]

Music and the Avant-Garde

Broch notes the "prank of destiny"[50] which placed the birth of avant-garde music in the city of the *Rosenkavalier*. But Romanticism was still strong in Vienna's musical world in the first decade of the twentieth century; as even Schönberg's *Verklärte Nacht* shows.

Britain and France as well are in transition, though slow: Hindemith, Delius, Du Parc, Fauré and Ravel typify this change. While Broch does not specifically mention the musical avant-garde, he develops a theory of the avant-garde in the other arts: he finds that in the fine arts, the avant-garde usually attains an appropriate (*adäquat*) critical response, quickly enough pushing "salon" art into semi-oblivion. This is not the case in the literary arts, where writers of the salon remain in vogue until the next generation can appreciate the new literature. Why does the acceptance of the avant-garde take place more slowly in literature? Radical artists, Broch conjectures, typically spring from proletarian backgrounds, while radical writers are generally from bourgeois or higher social groups. However, it would be a mistake to assume that radical artists are interested in social revolution, despite their class origins. A true revolutionary would not take the indirect route (through art) to his aims. Moreover, Broch maintains, one can only depict social-revolutionary aims in art through the use of a conventional, naturalistic medium like salon art, not abstraction or Impressionism, where form came dangerously close to dissolving into medium. So conservatism characterizes both socialist and fascist art; Marxism and Fascism alike condemn abstract art as bourgeois and degenerate.[51] Missing in this analysis is any comment on the musical avant-garde and social change. Since for Broch, music's "immediacy" precludes any agenda or intention, music (presumably) could not be social-revolutionary in intent. Why, then, does the writer lag so much behind the artist in achieving breakthroughs? What prevents him from creating new world realities with the unconditionality of the painter? Broch asks. It is the innately conservative medium of language which the writer is not free to recreate, as is the painter. In fact, the painter is almost freer than the musician, writes Broch. The writer with his intransigently rational tool, language, can only express irrational reality through the *un*said (tensions between words, lines) but can avail himself only sparingly of invention and novelty. (Broch maintains that Dada artists do not use language.)

Painting's formal changes have nothing to do with content as such; painting is guided and determined by an interest in technical problems: problems uncovered but unsolved by Impressionism and Postimpressionism, especially Cézanne. Broch describes these formal changes equivocally: the effect of their "ruthless unconditionality"[52] is uncanny (unheimlich), almost "demonic." The reductive quality of such painting makes "useless" all knowledge of and about men. Is this a criticism of painting gone too far in the direction of *l'art pour l'art*? Broch does not come out and say this. On the contrary, it seems he is using the example of painting's reductiveness to compare it to writing, which is inherently more "conditional" and bourgeois in its origin, medium, and intent: even so radical a writer as Joyce shows interest in "beauty," while artists who have no fear of "smashing convention" are unconcerned with beauty. Broch mentions Picasso's *Guernica*; to call its uncompromising (unbedingt) quality beautiful would would be a blasphemous denigration of the human suffering and horror it depicts and predicts. But he also says "he who could not tolerate such dehumanization was forced to recoil from the unconditionality of the new."[53] James, Mann, Proust: all three in various degrees conscious of this new age, pulled back from its "ruthless unconditionality," remaining, for all their mastery, devoted to the styles and outlook of the nineteenth century in which the novel had its finest flower.

So the twentieth-century novel, despite all "hypertrophied artistic exertions,"[54] remained mired in its psychological-naturalistic origins; it remained a salon product, for the most part, and where it avoided the esoteric (by which Broch means a kind of artiness), the novel, like any art form which does not continue to progress, often turned to kitsch. The mass-produced films and novels of the twentieth century are the limiting cases of what becomes of an art form whose success becomes fixed by popularity as a folk art. This kitsch-form has an equivalent in the theater, namely, the operetta. Broch notes the continuity of theater's outward form through centuries of stylistic changes; further, since actors are human beings, the theater must remain naturalistic to some extent, no matter how experimental it gets. Thus, theater cannot be just for aesthetes or elitists — it must appeal to at least a segment of the theatergoing public in order to exist at all; yet this public does not expect always to see mere kitsch, but will tolerate or even welcome challenging works. In theater, the two dynamics of "art" and naturalism meet.

Ethical Art

Broch summarizes: by 1910 the novel had only evolved as far as naturalism, while art was avant-gardist and deeply anti-naturalist. In this continuum, music is different from painting and sculpture — in art, representational work is analogous to setting a text to music, and abstraction is the equivalent of "absolute music." Broch implies that music in combination with a text is somehow less free, because it must complete something outside itself.[55] Music and painting are also different mimetically; painting must "symbolize" the three-dimensional world in two dimensions, and this raises it to the artistic level of absolute music.[56] For sculpture this is impossible, for it represents the three-dimensional world in three dimensions — even granting that sculpture can deal with a variety of shapes and forms greater than nature's. Music's "non-natural" quality raises it above painting and sculpture.[57]

Broch now offers a definition for art: No matter what symbol sets a system of art manipulates, and regardless of what (or whether) a work-external content is concerned:

> Structures in which the human spirit sees its own totality reflected, and which in this manner convey to it a piece of self-knowledge, it places under the rubric of art. And this is most clearly manifest in the phenomenon of music, which in turn, resonates in this very way within the structure of every work of art.[58]

What does this mean? First, that art reflects the totality of the human spirit in each of its manifestations, that is, in the work. Second, it increases man's knowledge of himself in so doing. While Broch passes over how this is done, he sets music up as paradigmatic of this cognitive reflection and increase. This generality and vagueness is characteristic of Broch's style. If, however, we grant Broch's categorization of music as the most abstract of the arts, then what is "most clearly manifest" in the musical phenomenon is the self-cognition it affords, simply because it has no other, work-external content, such as an image, a plot, etc. More importantly, however, music undergoes organic change: the "developmental" aspect of music is also clearly manifest in history. All art, like music, must change through time according to its own internal necessity.[59] Music "resonates" (mitschwingt), for that very reason, in the structure of every work of art because its evolutionary nature is, for Broch, the model of all art.

The concluding paragraphs of the Hofmannsthal essay revisit this concept of resonance. Karl Kraus's *Absolut-Satire* is "ethical art *par excellence.*" Although progress does not exist in art (only further development, but not leading to "higher" levels), ethical progress *is* possible, even probable. The "secret hope" of ethical progress "resonates" within every ethical deed.[60] Furthermore, the development of art, although in itself nonethical, and nonprogressive, serves the cause of ethical progress, and participates in the mystical hope that progress does exist, and that it will finally overcome the world's evil. It is only granting this hope, and this "serving" role of art in the cause of ethical progress, that makes understandable the internal ethic of art itself, its isolation from any external *"Tendenz."* This rigor, this internal objectivity, is most clearly exemplified in the area of music, and so the vocabulary of musical harmony, resonance, is appropriate to describe the ameliorative, utopian function of art.

Notes

[1] Broch wrote this between 1947 and 1950; the publication history is complex.

[2] Broch had said this earlier (1933) in the essay on Kitsch, *Das Böse im Wertsystem der Kunst,* KW 9/2, 119: "Even the previous era, that prewar period we call the 'bourgeois' era, surely did not find its expression in the eclectic styles which it produced, and if it had any kind of representative art, it was that of grand opera only" (trans. JAH). ("Schon die vorhergegangene Periode, jene Vorkriegsperiode, welche wir die bürgerliche nennen, hat ihren Lebensausdruck sicherlich nicht mehr in den eklektischen Stilen gefunden, die sie hervorgebracht hat, und wenn es auch für sie eine Art repräsentativer Kunst gegeben hat, so war es doch nur die der großen Oper . . .").

[3] KW 9/1, 111.

[4] Hermann Broch, *Hugo von Hofmannsthal and His Time, the European Imagination, 1860–1920,* trans. Michael P. Steinberg (Chicago: UP Chicago, 1984), 38. All English translations are Steinberg's.

[5] KW 9/1, 117.

[6] Eventually, Naturalism made a late debut in the theater with Hauptmann's *Vor Sonnenaufgang* in 1890.

[7] KW 9/1, 114–19. Broch distinguishes between the naturalism and realism of painting and literature and the artifice of theater. Regrettably, he gives no reason for this distinction.

[8] KW 9/1, 122; Steinberg (St) 42.

[9] KW 9/1, 135: "Das Wert-Vakuum der deutschen Kunst," the Value Vacuum of German Art.

[10] KW 9/1, 136. Jean Paul Boyer, "Hermann Broch: Auch ein Wagnerianer wider Willen?" *Hermann Broch: das dichterische Werk,* ed. M. Kessler and P. M. Lützeler (Tübingen: Stauffenburg Verlag, 1987), 231–38. Boyer observes that Broch rejects much of the music of the nineteenth century because it was not abstract, too programmatic. Broch associates music with logic, not emotion, according to Boyer. Hence his preference for Bach, late Beethoven, the Vienna School. (However, there are places where Broch specifically links music and emotion, e.g., the essay "Einige Bemerkungen zur Philosophie und Technik des Übersetzens (1946), KW 9/2, 61–86.)

[11] KW 9/1, 138; St, 53.

[12] Curiously, Broch seems to think that Wagner was underappreciated in his lifetime — an opinion at odds with the crowds of the faithful at Bayreuth.

[13] Boyer discusses this ambivalence in the previously cited article, "HB: Auch ein Wagnerianer wider Willen?."

[14] KW 9/1, 141; St, 56.

[15] KW 9/1, 141; St, 56.

[16] KW 9/1, 141; St, 56.

[17] St, 56. A better translation for *Dumpfheit* here is "stupor."

[18] Broch calls Nietzsche a *"nicht-musikalisches Genie"* and Wagner a *"Musikgenie, wenn auch unmusikalisch"* (KW 9/1, 142). Nietzsche (who did compose) was a writing genius, while Wagner, though perhaps not innately talented as a composer, successfully made his music the medium for his theatrical genius.

[19] KW 9/1, 140; St, 54.

[20] KW 9/1, 142.

[21] KW 9/1, 143; St, 57.

[22] KW 9/1, 145–53; St, 59–65.

[23] KW 9/1, 146; St, 60.

[24] But Broch ignores the vital role in the musical life of Vienna played by chamber and intimate gatherings such as "Schubertiades" — these not being

connected to his theme of theater, which ultimately connects with Hofmannsthal.

[25] KW 9/1, 152; St, 64.

[26] It is difficult now to agree with this harsh judgment of operetta, just as Broch's contempt for the architecture of the generation prior to his own seems overwrought. See Karsten Harries' "Decoration, Death, and Devil" in *Hermann Broch: Literature, Philosophy, Politics* (Columbia, SC: Camden House, 1988), 280: "The same architecture that to Broch seemed so full of lies, a cynical attempt to cover up a spiritual emptiness, speaks to us of possibilities of a more humane dwelling. The age that built Vienna's Ringstraße, this age of opera, or rather of operetta, of the waltz and of the *Backhendl* . . . seems once again quite wonderful."

[27] KW 9/1, 153; St, 65.

[28] Broch places a heavy burden on the back of the Viennese operetta! For depth (or shallowness) of social commentary, it is surely the equal of Gilbert and Sullivan.

[29] KW 9/1, 175; St, 81.

[30] KW 9/1, 183. "Both . . . acted 'morally,' each in his way; yet it was the difference between the ethical and the aesthetic that proclaimed itself in the goals of their education, the difference between the Mozartean, active and production-directed 'ethical morality' on one hand, the bourgeois 'aesthetic morality,' as it can best be called, on the other; for the latter in essence remains directed toward passive 'appreciation,' even when it revolves around an appreciation as noble as that of Hofmannsthal." St, 88.

[31] KW 9/1, 217. "Hofmannsthal, an unmathematical spirit, heard . . . the architectonic of music, the penetration of the musical into the linguistic, the ubiquitous resonance of the musical world of expression in the word, reaching beyond the word, yet contained within it and conferring on it the cognitive content of 'visible invisibility.'" St, 113.

[32] In his "Ein Brief" (1902), a fictional epistle of the historical English figure Lord Chandos (1673–1744) (usually called the "Chandos-Brief"), Hofmannsthal expresses frustration at the inadequacy of words to express real emotions.

[33] KW 9/1, 217–18; St, 113.

[34] Hugo von Hofmannsthal, *Buch der Freunde* (Leipzig: Insel-Verlag, 1929), 95. Elsewhere in this work Hofmannsthal also writes: "Painting transforms space into time, music time into space." 76.

[35] Hofmannsthal: *Buch der Freunde*, 89.

[36] Broch: 9/1, 218; St, 114.

[37] KW 9/1, 218; St, 114.

[38] KW 9/1, 219; St, 114.

[39] KW 9/1, 221; St, 116.

[40] See, e.g., "Strawinsky: Ein dialektisches Bild," in: Theodor Adorno: *Gesammelte Schriften*: Band 16 (Frankfurt: Suhrkamp, 1978), 382–409.

[41] KW 9/1, 229. Here Broch's argument is inconsistent: conservative Vienna may have been, but how was it that Wagner's admittedly symbolic operas succeeded there? Broch combines the terms "symbolism" and "impressionism," confusingly. It would have to have been another quality, perhaps the absence of the verbal, which made the new forms uncongenial to the Viennese.

[42] Broch mentions sketches for two ballets from 1901, *Amor und Psyche* and *Das fremde Mädchen*, the 1914 *Josephslegende*, and the 1925 *Achilles auf Skyros*. KW 9/1, 233 (notes).

[43] KW 9/1, 233; St, 152.

[44] KW 9/1, 231.

[45] KW 9/1, 224.

[46] KW 9/1, 225; St, 146.

[47] KW 9/1, 224.

[48] KW 9/1, 225.

[49] KW 9/1, 234; St, 152.

[50] KW 9/1, 235; St, 153.

[51] Broch does not analyze the art of the revolutionary artist (as against the social revolutionary); interested as he is in the relationship of art to ethics, the situation of the artist who wants to make radical change in art (only) does not attract him.

[52] KW 9/1, 243 ("erbarmungslose Unbedingtheit"); St, 159.

[53] KW 9/1, 244; St, 159. *"hypertrophische Kunstanstrengung."*

[54] KW 9/1, 246; St, 161.

[55] While this analogy is not novel, neither is it completely correct, as anyone with an acquaintance of Schubert lieder knows. And if it is less "free," this in no way makes the music at any level "less" than absolute music. Nor is absolute music free of its own self-imposed strictures of form.

[56] All painting, of course, deals with this reduction of dimension. The argument is that reducing the dimensions reduces the "naturalism" of art (positive, for Broch).

[57] KW 9/1, 254; St, 167. Broch's premise, that the dimensional aspect of a medium has anything really to do with the matter of naturalism versus abstractness, is arbitrary. The intensification or concentration resulting from a change in dimensions increases the cognitive content of the art work for Broch, by making it more abstract. However, Broch's point that music is necessarily "unnatural" is inconsistent with the early essays and their discussions of rhythm and ornament. However, one could grant that music's origins may be "natural," but that the art form as it has developed is not. Is "unnatural" a reference to serial music? No, it is simply a loose synonym for "abstract." Music is the most abstract of the arts, which for Broch makes it "unnatural."

[58] KW 9/1, 256; St, 169.

[59] This inexorably organic process of change Broch described more fully in the 1934 essay "Gedanken zum Problem der Erkenntnis in der Musik," KW 10/2, 244–45.

[60] KW 9/1, 275.

4: Music in *The Sleepwalkers*

B ROCH'S TRILOGY, *THE SLEEPWALKERS,* treats music and musical ideas in three ways:

(1) it weaves musical themes and events into the plot in all three novels;

(2) it occasionally interrupts the narration with sometimes lengthy digressions which associate music with utopian or verbally inexpressible aims and values;

(3) some lyrical passages in the set of chapters devoted to Marie, a Salvation Army worker, employ verbal music by using leitmotiv epithets associated with certain characters.

Overall, the musical treatment of *The Sleepwalkers* has much in common with the *Mountain Novel,* for on the whole, the musical episodes parody or negatively reflect the debased and particularized worlds which each novel portrays, while the narrative voice retains a positive, or utopian, frame of reference for music.

Pasenow or the Romantic

Pasenow, the "exposition" of the trilogy, uses a more conventional narrative voice than *Esch* and *Huguenau*: an external narrator,[1] who nonetheless sometimes assumes the thoughts and emotions of Pasenow himself.

The first instance of music in *Pasenow* occurs in the context of Pasenow's visit to his fiancée's villa in the west end of Berlin. The neighborhood is a comfortable island of 1870's prosperity during the economic boom following the Franco-Prussian War. Pasenow hears echoes of this security and insularity in the music which "rings" from the windows: Clementi[2] and Heller[3] études. Both favorites of the salon, Stephen Heller and Muzio Clementi wrote keyboard music often used as exercises for amateur pianists. This music is tame, accessible, and often dull. But, to Pasenow's neurotic sensibility, this respectable music really just veils a scandalous secret at the core of these houses: sexuality. And in the same flash "he saw clearly that every house in the long row of villas which he had passed had as its central point a similar bedroom, and that the sonatinas and the études sent out through the open windows . . . were only intended to veil the actual facts."[4]

Here music is used to display the neurotic split in Pasenow's view of his world: music represents an upper-class veneer of culture camouflaging a base and shameful secret: sexual dependency. The étude form, a strict and rigorous form masking a minimal content, is somehow a musical metaphor of Pasenow's uniform fetish: Pasenow's obsessive thoughts on the function of uniforms are an *idée fixe* of the novel.

Later Pasenow goes to the opera, Gounod's *Faust*. During the intermission, Pasenow's gaze is drawn to two dark, obviously foreign young men; one has a flamboyant mustache. There is a hint of Thomas Mann here: an air of decadence in the young man's far too curly hair, too-small mouth, and delicately chiseled nose, and a "challenging" smile. Pasenow, one suspects, is briefly sexually attracted, for when he discovers with a start that they are speaking Czech,[5] he inexplicably feels that he has betrayed Elisabeth, his fiancée. Is it because his mistress Ruzena's language is Czech? It happens that the young man is Ruzena's brother. Pasenow struggles to recall Ruzena's face, and in his fancy he sees her in the young man's face.[6] Pasenow thinks this thought is "safe"[7] (gefahrlos), but it lingers in his mind even after intermission. That he thinks he is "safe" (that his thought won't be discovered) hints at his repressed homosexuality. He finds the opera, the backdrop to these thoughts, "sugary" and "fatuous," and Pasenow interprets Margarete's sacrifice as a result of gender confusion: operatic convention ensures no one on stage, not even Faust, notices that in Margaret's features are hidden those of Valentin, and for this reason Margarete must suffer.[8]

As Pasenow confuses Ruzena with her brother, he sees Faust confusing Margarete with Valentin, and thus purges his guilt by punishing both the male and female objects of his desire. Pasenow is relieved that Elisabeth has no brothers, and thus that his attraction to her is untainted by other motivations. He leaves the opera house with his feelings of being "faithful" to Elisabeth reinforced (oddly, since Ruzena is still his mistress).

In a curious reading of the opera, Pasenow projects his unconscious fears onto its characters, thus misinterpreting it. But Pasenow's real life imitates the opera: like Margarete's brother Valentin, Pasenow's brother Helmuth is killed in a duel. The text makes clear that Pasenow has unconsciously wished for his brother's death since childhood, and now that it has come about, he must repress his guilt feelings.[9] Helmuth's catafalque in the parlor temporarily displaces the family piano; death has thus displaced music, but in Pasenow's efforts to "rationalize" the death of his brother, death is transformed into a mere matter of drapery and flowers, and Helmuth's coffin seems only like a new piece of furniture, "thus once more reducing the incomprehensible so radically to the comprehensible . . ."[10]

Music and death continue to be linked as Joachim proposes marriage to Elisabeth in her family's funereal music room, upholstered in black silk. This musical center of the Baddensen household is depressingly still and void, and the couple's frigid courtship and wedding night are epitomized by the decor. The black lacquer piano reflecting the gas chandelier above it recalls Helmuth's coffin at Stolpin — even the low seat on which Pasenow sits is called a "catafalque."[11]

Here are more echoes of Thomas Mann, similarities with *The Magic Mountain* which are hard to ignore: Joachim Ziemssen (Hans Castorp's cousin), Joachim Pasenow and his brother Helmuth are all military officers. Both Ziemssen and Helmuth Pasenow die untimely deaths (tuberculosis, and a duel, respectively). As with Pasenow, there is a hint of suppressed homoeroticism in the relationship between the cousins, and both Castorp and Pasenow are interested in "exotic" Slav women. Moreover, both Joachims have confused ideas about characters in Gounod's *Faust*. As Faust does not recognize Valentin as Margaret's brother, Pasenow confuses Ruzena and her brother, and Castorp identifies with Gretchen when he hears Valentin's aria, because he thinks of his cousin as his protector. So Broch seems consciously or unconsciously to be doing what Mann did before him (and would do again later in *Doktor Faustus*).

Later, Bertrand and Joachim attend a musical tea at Elisabeth's family estate, and hear her at the keyboard in Spohr's piano trio;[12] Joachim imagines the piano part as "silvery crystalline drops" falling into the "brown stream of the two stringed instruments."[13] He thinks this is the essence of music: "it was pure and clear and hovered high above like a cloud at a celestial height dropping its pure cold water on the earth below.[14] This description is later used for Elisabeth herself. As Joachim observed earlier in Berlin, however, this music is highly domesticated; like the études of Clementi and Heller, Spohr is *Hausmusik* for the upper bourgeoisie.[15] The absence of Mozart and Beethoven, the "total" musicians of the classical era, is negatively charged. Even the outlaw Bertrand thinks so: "If only she would play something else than that horribly boring Spohr!" Somewhat later, the narration describes his fading love for Ruzena as like a melody he is learning to forget: a symbol of his outmoded romantic and sentimental world.[16]

Two other sequences in *Pasenow* associate a more utopian philosophical message with music. The first is a digression on hunting in the description of the guest bedroom at Stolpin, the second the church service which Pasenow must preside over. In the first passage,[17] two hunters have a metaphysical epiphany which is compared to a musical experience:

> . . . something awoke that rang like music, and the lives they had lived and had still to live were concentrated so intensely into one moment that they could still feel the touch of their mother's hand on their hair as if for eternity, while another shape already stood before them, separated from them no longer by any span of time, any span of space, the shape which they did not fear: Death.[18]

Life is compressed into a single moment, in which childhood stands timelessly next to death, and this annulment of time rings "like music," as it takes the fear from death. The hunter's quest alludes to the legend of St. Hubert, who saw the Cross in the antlers of the deer, and is described in medieval-mystical language fitting the spirit of this "romantic" section.

This passage should be read alongside the "Snow" scene and the "Fullness of Harmony" episode in *Magic Mountain* to indicate how differently both writers employ the ideas of death, of simultaneity, and of Romanticism. The hunters' vision is Romantic like Pasenow's, and the hunter views death as a transcendent moment; he identifies his own death with that of the animal before him, and without fear or negativity. In the "Snow" chapter, Castorp learns to reject death's romantic allure: one cannot, must not, live one's life constantly aware of death's dominion: so death is given a negative cast. Later, in the "Fullness of Harmony" episode, Castorp realizes that the peculiar fascination he has with Schubert's "Der Lindenbaum" is connected with the allure of death. The romantically "German" attraction of the song for him, which beckons back to a reverie of youth, has a component which, the narrator tells us, "is Death." Castorp is aware of the negative aspect of his "death-devoted" attraction to this song.

Later Pasenow must preside over a military church service,[19] where a choral hymn occasions in Pasenow a reverie which takes him back to his childhood, and triggers a confused sequence of images in his memory.[20] He hears his family's Polish cook singing, he sees a religious picture she once gave him, a print of the Holy Family poised on a silver cloud; he remembers how he yearned to take the place of the Holy Infant in the arms of the Virgin, a delightful yet fearful sensation for the young Lutheran boy, for he feared the wrath of his Protestant father at such a heretical wish. Pasenow sees the picture floating, just beginning to break up, on the surface of the melody of the hymn. As it dissolves, the Catholic image becomes Protestant, even secular, allegorizing the breakup of the theocentric medieval Catholic world which is the start of the disintegration of values, the main philosophical theme of *The Sleepwalkers*. He sees an apotheosis of Elisabeth as a blond, Protestant Virgin Mary, suspended in the melody of the choral anthems sung by the soldiers. Inspired by this music, Pasenow sees in the imagined icon the true image behind the earthly forms which are in constant flux; he sees it as a "crystalline drop that falls singing from the cloud."[21] As the chorale ends, Pasenow imagines his fellows to be as fired with religious fervor as he is himself. In Pasenow's Platonist hallucination, musical cognition hints at the idea behind all reality. The recurrent image[22] of a face deconstructed into a landscape of features hints at the imminent disintegration of his world, both necessary and welcome. In the religious fervor which the music has inspired, Pasenow feels he has taken the first "painful" step towards his goal,[23] and, though incomplete, Pasenow's growth through musical cognition is the greatest of all the characters in the trilogy.

Esch or The Anarchist

The world of *Esch* has hardly any music at all. The characters of the novel are for the most part insensible to art in any form beyond their immediate frame of reference. Allusions to music are casual and fragmentary. Instead of *Pasenow's* bourgeois musical forms, the music in *Esch* is vulgar, "low," played by machines, dance bands, tambourines. One instrument, an "orchestrion," is from America, and it is a large music box in a bar run by Esch's lover Mutter Hentje. At the touch of a lever, it plays "March of the Gladiators,"[24] a piece often heard in circuses, and it turns out to be the music which accompanies a group of female wrestlers in their act. The fact that the machine is made in America is not accidental: it is mechanical, technical, and soulless.[25] Broch's treatment of mechanically produced music is predictably negative; the "deadness" of Ilona's exclusively sexual relationship to Korn, and of Mutter Hentje's to Esch, is compared to the Orchestrion's mechanical quality.[26]

While Pasenow goes to opera, Esch and friends attend a Varieté, where the prima donna is just the curtain raiser for the main event, a knife-throwing act. Ilona is the target, and the orchestra plays a waltz preceding her act: as she comes on for her nightly "crucifixion," the orchestra is silenced.[27]

In *Huguenau* as in *The Spell*, religious and political fanaticism include songs, and there is some of this fanaticism in *Esch*: in a moment of enthusiasm both Esch and Lohberg the tobacconist nearly break into song while watching Salvation Army workers sing "Herr Gott Zebaoth, rett', o rett' uns vor dem Tod."[28] The novel features the Army's music, not its social activism; the Army's philosophical significance to the narration is contained in its music. When Esch and Lohberg are driven away by the constable,[29] the silence of the evening reminds him of the hushed orchestra, and he has a vision of existential loneliness; as Pasenow sees Elisabeth as the Virgin Mary, Esch has a vision of Ilona in the Salvation Army uniform, waiting for his signal to play and sing.[30] Esch's confused yearning to save Ilona and thus symbolically to right the wrongs of the world is imbued with music, drawing him to meta-rational experience, to breaking the frontier's of one's own experience.

Another example of the association of music with "frontier"-breaking experiences is a passage on ocean travel,[31] where Esch fantasizes about emigrating to America, and this fantasy is accompanied by folksy band music (*"Muß i denn"*). Since this is quite literally a *"Grenz-Erfahrung"* in the finite world, the act of emigration is appropriately set to banal music. The reader hears this very same music at Lohberg's and Erna's engagement party: Esch hopes to emigrate, and he starts to sing *"Muß i denn"* to celebrate his farewell to the world of the day laborer.[32]

The longest and most significant treatment of musical themes occurs when Esch meets Alfons, the orchestra musician, and Harry Köhler, lover of the shadowy figure Bertrand. Esch is still searching for Bertrand, and in a homosexual nightclub, Harry tells Esch what love is for him: spatial and temporal simultaneity ("And then suddenly distance is annihilated and time is annihilated, and they have flown together . . .").[33] A later meeting takes place after Esch's surreal visit to Bertrand in Badenweiler, and the suicides of Bertrand and Harry. Esch visits Alfons in the gay bar again; Alfons is "thoughtless," a "poor devil," "stupid."[34] But Alfons is also repeatedly described as a musician with special insights,[35] for despite his many perceived defects, Alfons's knowledge of music gives him a special insight into love, women, and the "absolute" that other men lack. He scorns the heterosexual's drive to "possess" women, men chasing after "a bit of infinity" (confusing this with sexual love) to palliate their fear of death: Alfons knows this,[36] and he also can play classical sonatas from memory, "versed in all kinds of knowledge."[37] His neutrality enables him to sympathize with women, whose heightened sense of life's complex relation to the infinite through death is signaled by their sympathy for music. Music, the finite and accessible organ of the language of the infinite, "divines" this complexity:

> Oh, those whose hearts thirsted for possession did not know the rapturous chaos of life, and the others knew little more of it; yet music divined it, music the melodious symbol of all that could be thought, music that annulled time so that it might be preserved in rhythm, that annulled death so that it might rise anew in sound.[38]

This wording is repeated almost verbatim in the dance scene in *Huguenau*[39] (see below). Death, like time, is "aufgehoben" in both senses of the German (that is, both canceled and preserved). Time and death are not overcome, but transfigured by music.

Huguenau or the Realist

This longest and most complex novel of the trilogy has several musical episodes, as well as continuations of motivs from the prior books. Of its eighty-eight chapters, sixty-two make up the many-stranded "story" itself; ten others comprise a series of essays on the "Disintegration of Values"; and sixteen other chapters loosely treat the activities of a Salvation Army singer named Marie, a small group of Orthodox Jews, and the ostensible narrator, Bertrand Müller (sometimes read as a *persona* of the defunct Eduard von Bertrand in *Esch*).[40] These sixteen chapters, like the "Values" essays, were not part of the original plan of the novel, and are interwoven throughout it with only a loose connection to the story. The next-to-last chapter originally had a musicological title: "*Engführung der Gesamtkonstruktion*,"[41] a compact recapitulation of themes from the entire novel. (This was the only poem in the original *Huguenau*-fragment of 1928.[42] Broch dropped the title in the final version, but the poetic "stretto" remains.)

The salient musical figure of *Huguenau* is the Salvation Army singer Marie. She plays the tambourine, and is introduced as a rather pathetic figure:

Die Uniform des Heils saß schlecht, der Strohhut tat nicht passen,
Sie war ein Mädchen und sie tat verblühn
Und wenn sie sang, so war's ein dünnes Singen
Und sinnlos war's, und dennoch trug sie Schwingen.[43]

The prose narrative treats Marie ironically, but the verse hints at her special quality:

Gar manches läßt sich bloß in Versen sagen
So sinnlos scheint es dem, der bloß in Prosa spricht.[44]
Und singend läßt sich manches sagen, klagen
Vom Leide, das in nachtgetränkten Tagen
Gleich Taggespenstern aus dem Herzen bricht,
Gleich Heilsarmeegesängen: und man lächelt nicht,
Wenn sie auf Tamburins und ihre Trommeln schlagen.[45]

Marie has the mystic's immediacy to God. Müller says later to her: "You are a brave but a thoughtless people! You believe that you need only be good and strike up music in order to draw God near."[46] Even banging the tambourine brings musical cognition. Improbably, it is the Orthodox Jew Nuchem Sussin who is first attracted by Marie. This is partly the result of his interest in the Salvation Army's music, for which he has "some feeling."[47] Nuchem's immediacy and directness shows in his feeling for music and for the zealots. He laughs at Müller's complex Hegelian explanation of magic,[48] but is amazed he cannot play the lute hanging on his wall — each time he enters the room, he says, "play." The seemingly comical spectacle of Nuchem's infatuation with Marie and her hymns demonstrates his wish to enter, through music, directly into Zion, as Marie's hymns promise him.[49] He sees in Marie and her music a way to escape his own particularised being, his limitations, through *Grenzerfahrung* (boundary experience).

Müller parodies this pathetic devotion in the ninth episode.[50] While the three sing a hymn set to the *Andreas-Hofer-Lied*,[51] Müller substitutes the real political words — he parodies and ridicules their music to distance himself from their enthusiasms and their forbidden relationship. Using a political melody as a hymn tune perfectly deflates the Army's pathetic attempts at the "earthly absolute" — Müller, outside of Nuchem's and Marie's different value systems, can only satirize them, as Huguenau satirizes the beliefs of Esch and Pasenow.

Musical parody continues in the "Symposium" chapter, itself a dramatic parody of Plato's symposium on love. The main characters of this playlet are the trilogy's eponymous heroes, Esch, Pasenow and Huguenau: they sing a trio at the end, a version of Marie's Salvation Army hymn, first in alternation, then together. Huguenau does not join in till the words "Schütze uns vor Beil und Rade, Schütze uns vor Henkers Hand,"[52] punishments he has good reason to fear. Afterwards Huguenau visits a brothel, allegedly continuing his investigations of Esch, and on emerging is heard humming bits from the Salvation Army hymn as he walks home.

Later, music accompanies Pasenow's religious conversion, as he attends a Bible reading with Esch; Pasenow hears/sees the Pauline epistle Esch reads as frozen drops,[53] as he did with Elisabeth's music and the apotheosis in the church. He sings unconsciously the

Salvation Army hymn with Esch, and feels the singing within him-self, "a singing behind his closed eyes, like a crystalline drop that falls singing from a cloud."[54]

Later, a party is held to celebrate a victory on the Moselle river. This dance scene gathers together all the various characters of the novel. A band plays the German national anthem, to which the soldier Jaretzki, alcoholic and schizophrenic from the effects of war, shouts, "Long live the war!"[55] to point out that the war can-not be won. As dancing begins, a digression on the form ensues: dancing, like music, entails sacrificing freedom, and rediscovering it on a higher level in the strictures of form.[56] As in the nightclub, ab-struse philosophy contrasts markedly with the "low" atmosphere of the setting.[57] The band is playing a medley of German patriotic tunes, waltzes, as well as dances from enemy countries such as the tango, cakewalk, one-step and machiche, degraded forms of music suited to the occasion, for music which is *vaterländisch* or *feindlich* loses its utopian quality, for it aims at esthetic rather than ethical effect; it is kitsch. The "catlike, soft and pliable" tango is like Hu-guenau himself.[58] He is vain of his dancing ability and can do all the dances equally well: connected to nothing, he is as anonymous as his partner and his musical internationalism is shown as inau-thentic and corrupt.

The ecstatic effect of music[59] is discussed; it is more pro-nounced with women[60] and it enables the realist Huguenau to pos-sess a woman without desiring her, just the trait Alfons despised. Instinctively, Huguenau takes advantage of woman's greater sus-ceptibility to music; but he also has another object in mind: Major Pasenow. He wants to be the center of attention, the "warrior dancing before his chieftain,"[61] but Pasenow is disgusted by the "shameless" display, his reaction to the dance a reminder of his "romantic" clinging to outmoded ideologies.

Another character, Dr. Kessel, is a gifted amateur cellist who has lost his wife, is able to overcome and transform the "nonstyle" of the revolution, its "clamorous and terrifying silence" of the age through music.[62]

The chapter called "Keiner sieht den andern im Dunkeln" contains a scene which is a parody of Beethoven's *Fidelio*.[63] Hu-guenau springs open a prison filled with political inmates who raise a chorus of "Hoch soll er leben!" followed by a confused singing of the "Marseillaise" and "Internationale," two opposing anthems summarizing the coming end of all value systems in preparation for a new era.

Finally, just at the end, the novel trilogy "passes through" the *stretto* previously mentioned, a sonnet about a boat like that of Wagner's Dutchman, a ship which can land nowhere. The ship is a metaphor of the isolated unconscious, and the poem is a fugal recombination of epistemological themes from the whole trilogy, an optimistic wish to find redemption at a higher level of human history.

Notes

[1] The first chapter, "Modes of Narration," in Dorrit Cohn's discussion of the trilogy, *The Sleepwalkers: Elucidations of Hermann Broch's Trilogy* (The Hague: Mouton & Co., 1966), offers convincing descriptions of the varied narrative voices of the different novels.

[2] Muzio Clementi (1752–1832) Italian keyboard composer known (in part) for didactic works such as the *Gradus ad Parnassum*.

[3] Stephen Heller (1813–1888), French pianist and composer of Hungarian birth. An early ally ("Davidsbündler") of Schumann. Although "typed" as a composer of études, he was a transitional composer with a foretaste of Impressionism, and of Medtner and Rachmaninov, in his later piano works. (Grove Dictionary of Music).

[4] . . . [es] wurde ihm klar, daß in jedem der Häuser der langen Villenreihe, die er durchschritten hatte, ein ebensolches Schlafzimmer Mittelpunkt ist und daß die Sonatinen und Etüden . . . bloß den wahren Sachverhalt verschleiern sollen. SW 1, 38.

[5] This paragraph contains two leitmotivs which recur throughout the trilogy: wavy hair as a sign of decadence and homosexuality (mostly applied to Bertrand), the compulsive correction of "Czech" with "Bohemian," originally at Ruzena's behest.

[6] This is often a problem for Pasenow (cf. below).

[7] English translations are from *The Sleepwalkers*, trans. Willa and Edwin Muir (San Francisco: North Point Press, 1985).

[8] KW 1, 40.

[9] E.g., KW 1, 46; Muir 40: "He had no feeling of guilt, yet it was as if his brother's death had come about for his sake; yes, as if he had been the cause of it." Dorrit Cohn points out that Joachim's curious surprise that the coffin is not that of a child indicates that this wish dates from their childhood. Cohn 32–34.

[10] Muir 42; KW 1, 48.

[11] KW 1, 159.

[12] Ludwig Spohr (1784–1859), German composer of instrumental music of the early Romantic period. The work cited is the E minor Trio for Piano, Violin and Violoncello, op. 119 (1841).

[13] KW 1, 104; Muir 92.

[14] KW 1, 104; Muir 92.

[15] Spohr was treasured by the Biedermeier public, who were "not concerned with accomplishing new ideals but merely preserving traditional values" (Grove Dictionary).

[16] KW 1, 114. This musical phrase symbolizes the faded love of Joachim for Ruzena. Cf. the "little phrase" of the Vinteuil sonata, the "national anthem" of Swann's love for Odette, in Proust's *Remembrance of Things Past*, vol. 1, trans. C. K. Scott Moncrieff (New York: Random House, 1981), 227–28, 238, and elsewhere. Swann associates Platonic ideas with musical motivs as well. Proust 1, 378–79.

[17] KW 1, 93.

[18] Muir 82; KW 1, 93.

[19] KW 1, 128.

[20] In the seventh *Zerfall der Werte* essay (538–39), Calvinism and its epistemological "asceticism" is discussed. Calvin excluded music from religious services as a sensual distraction. (Perhaps Pasenow's reverie bears this out.)

[21] KW 1, 116, 130.

[22] E.g., KW 1, 157, 171, 174.

[23] KW 1, 130.

[24] KW 1, 185. Composer: The Czech bandmaster Julius Fučik (1872–1916).

[25] There are numerous references to America as the "finite" utopia, which is seen to be negative in character.

[26] KW 1, 352.

[27] Teltscher's knives whistle (pfeifend) as they fly towards their human target (KW 1, 203). The gas lights in the Baddensen's music room also whistle "obscenely" (unanständig) and "poisonously" (giftig) (160). Whistling is antimusical. (Cf. below on Kafka's *Josefine die Sängerin* for more on *pfeifen*.) The whistling of the "poisonous" gas lights anticipates later references to gas, the *unritterliche Waffe*.

[28] KW 1, 216: "Lord God of Sabaoth, save, Oh, save our souls from Hell!" Muir 192.

[29] KW 1, 217.

[30] KW 1, 217.

[31] KW 1, 252.

[32] KW 1, 346.

[33] KW 1, 296; Muir 263–64.

[34] KW 1, 364; Muir 324.

[35] Alfons is described four times as "der Musiker Alfons"; other epithets: "a poor devil of an orchestra player," "a stupid and thoughtless orchestra player," "a fat homosexual orchestra player." KW 1, 364–65; Muir 325–26.

[36] KW 1, 364; Muir 325: "And he forgave the malignant rage of men, for he saw quite well that it sprang from fear and disappointment, saw that these passionate and evil men hid themselves behind a remnant of eternity to shield themselves from the fear that was always at their backs, telling them they must die."

[37] "vielerlei wissend," KW 1, 364. Muir 325.

[38] Muir 326; KW 1, 365. Dorrit Cohn, in the chapter on "Modes of Narration," says: "As a motif, the mystic experience of arrested time appears in connection with almost all the major and minor figures in the book. (. . .) But most persistently it appears in musical surroundings." 54–55.

[39] KW 1, 568.

[40] E.g., John J. White, "The Identity and Function of Bertrand in Hermann Broch's *Die Schlafwandler*," *German Life and Letters*, New Series, Jg. 24, Nr. 2 (Jan 1971), 135–44.

[41] *Engführung*: thematic imitation at a short time interval, in such a way that the statements of the theme overlap. In fugue and other contrapuntal forms it is called stretto. (*Grove Dictionary of Music*.)

[42] KW 6, 121. Dorrit Cohn notes that this poem has four versions in manuscript form; this poem is important due to its placement at the end of the novel. Cohn 156n. 27.

[43] KW 1, 429. (German retained to show the rhyme.)
  "Her girlhood was in flower, and yet upon it / the ugly uniform like a blight was laid; / her singing, when she sang before the Lord, / was a thin, empty piping — yet it soared." Muir 383.
  "There's much that can't be said except in verse/despite the sneers of men who stick to prose." Muir 383.

[45] KW 1, 429. ". . . song is fitter for a curse / or a lament, when day like a dark hearse/ out-glooms the night, summoning ghastly woes, / and in a

hymn the sad heart overflows/ even at a loud Salvation Army Meeting, / nor smiles when drums and tambourines are beating." Muir 383.

[46] Muir 559; KW 1, 617.

[47] KW 1, 489; Muir 439.

[48] KW 1, 489.

[49] "Und Raum ist auch für dich" ("and room is there for you too). KW 1, 514.

[50] KW 1, 549f.

[51] Tirolese national anthem.

[52] KW 1, 559. "Keep us safe from axe and halter, Keep us safe from wheel and brand." Muir 504.

[53] KW 1, 586. "But for the Major the words he had heard were like drops which turned to ice while they fell." Muir 530.

[54] Muir 531.

[55] Muir 512.

[56] KW 1, 568. "Wrapped in the music, he has renounced his freedom of action, and yet acts in accordance with a higher and more lucid freedom of action. In the rigorous security of the rhythm that guides him he is safely sheltered, and a great relief comes to him from that security . . ." Muir 513.

[57] KW 1, 568: "Die Zeit aufhebend, hebt sie den Tod auf und läßt ihn trotzdem in jedem Takte neu erstehen, selbst in den Takten jenes öden und langen Potpourris . . ." [Cancelling Time it cancels death, and yet resurrects it anew in every beat of the rhythm, even in the rhythm of that dreary and endless potpourri . . .] (Muir 513). This wording is similar to that in *Esch*, KW 1, 365.

[58] When Huguenau murders Esch, "he reached Esch with a few feline (katzig) tango-like leaps, and ran his bayonet into his angular back." Muir 614.

[59] A theme since the early essay, "Notizen zu einer systematischen Ästhetik," KW 9/2, 11–35.

[60] KW 1, 569; Muir 514.

[61] KW 1, 569; Muir 514.

[62] Muir 572.

[63] Hans Mayer discusses the Utopian echoes of *Fidelio* in Ernst Bloch's *Das Prinzip Hoffnung*, in "Beethoven und das Prinzip Hoffnung" in *Ein Denkmal für Johannes Brahms* (Frankfurt am Main: Suhrkamp, 1983), 40–59.

5: Music, Silence, and Time: The Architectonics of *The Death of Virgil*

Introduction

Wie? Es wäre nicht erlaubt und möglich, in Tönen zu denken und in Worten und Gedanken zu musizieren? O wie schlecht wäre es dann mit uns Künstlern bestellt! Wie arme Sprache, wie ärmere Musik! (Tieck: *Der gestiefelte Kater*)

BROCH'S *DER TOD DES VERGIL* IS the most well known, and perhaps the most successful, example in German of using musical techniques in a novel. Like the other works dealt with in this study, *Der Tod des Vergil* also has music as one of its themes, but it is the "musicality" of the text which has attracted the attention of many commentators, beginning with Hermann Weigand.[1] He noted that its "four movements constitute a verbal symphony of overwhelming proportions." *Der Tod des Vergil* is not an attempt to present a musical experience, even if some of the narrative techniques are described as "musical," and Weigand's term "verbal symphony" is not identical with the term "verbal music" as used by Steven Scher.[2] With Broch, musicality does not mean "like music," nor does it mean "euphonious."[3] For Broch, as for many German writers from the Romantic movement on, music held a special rank among the arts; he assigned to music a unique epistemological quality (see above, introduction and chapter 1.) So literature is said to be "musical" when it effects cognitive growth in a fashion similar to the way music does. Broch's essay on music attempts to describe how musical cognition differs from strictly verbal communication, and *Der Tod des Vergil* employs verbal language in a similar fashion. Broch's own commentaries show that he considered *Vergil* his most musical work (KW 4, 474–75), but these commentaries should be read with caution. This chapter will examine Broch's novel to determine the extent to which the project he set out for music and musicality is successful.

Origin of Broch's Concept of Musicality

In his "Bemerkungen zum *Tod des Vergil*"[4] Broch terms his method of composition "musikalisch" (474), though commentators note this is only vaguely defined.[5] He implies that musicality is a kind of lyrical self-commentary; while coyly warning readers not to compare his interior monologue with Joyce (which it in no way resembles), Broch nonetheless places himself on the same level as Joyce, Proust and Mann:

> Broch's interior monologue should not be compared with that of Joyce . . . nor is it related to the Proustian recall method, still less with the efforts of Thomas Mann, which run in a similar direction. No, here something completely new is being tried, which one could call a lyrical self-commentary: beginning with the outermost level of reality, going deeper layer by layer, each layer taking the content of the previous one, using it as its lyrical material and in turn being re-processed by the next.

Broch's interest in music in prose dates far back, as early as 1913, in an article on Thomas Mann's novella *Der Tod in Venedig* (Death in Venice, 1912): "Philostrosität: Realismus, Idealismus der Kunst,"[6] where Broch gives an analysis in musical metaphors:[7] the introduction is "the prelude, or upbeat"; the old man character is "the main theme with variations"; Tadzio is the "counter-leitmotiv," and so on.[8] In his essays Broch discusses music in the context of general aesthetic philosophy, and at other times merely metaphorically. In the former view, he emphasizes music's central role in the arts, the origin of cultural forms in rhythm,[9] music's capacity to cancel time (Zeitaufhebung),[10] the significance of the aesthetic principle of simultaneity;[11] but in the latter, as in the review of Thomas Mann, he uses musical terminology metaphorically in describing literary devices.

This second view explains his use of the term "Leitmotiv," a term he used only uneasily to describe his own work. For Broch, leitmotiv is the "least musical" of all musical aids, and he viewed it as more a literary than a musical construct, which Wagner had borrowed from literature and used for his own purposes musically. Broch saw his *Vergil* as one unified lyric work, lyric being the literary form most saturated with musical elements.[12] But he still felt "leitmotivs" in his work had musical importance, and he feared his translator, Jean Starr Untermeyer, was not rendering the German leitmotivic repetitions faithfully into English.[13] However, what he termed a leitmotiv in his writing was often verbal repetition, to foster the impression of simultaneity, and not a true leitmotiv, which would suggest an extraverbal significance, as musical leitmotivs suggest an extramusical one.

Although Broch himself compared *Vergil's* four chapters to the movements of a string quartet or a symphony,[14] its musicality (he says) comes from the lyricism,[15] the self-commentary, and the "through-composed" quality of the work. Most importantly, the musicality of the work provides a new solution to the problem of simultaneity, one of the "most difficult problems of the epic form" (KW 4, 475), for it is only in an *Einheitserlebnis* (experiencing something as a unity) that the aesthetic goal of simultaneity can be attained, that is, that the perception of time can be turned from temporal to spatial.[16] As we have seen (ch. 1), Broch sees music as the paradigm of simultaneity in art:

> In time and its passing the relativity of values is anchored . . .
> Thus, the goal of all formative activity is to create simultaneity
> out of the sequentiality of values . . . It is this transformation . . .
> which . . . reflects the value system of music: the transformation
> of sequential to simultaneous, perceived spatially: this is the essence of music.[17]

Inverting Eckermann's Goethe quote, that architecture is "frozen music,"[18] Broch says that successful music is a kind of architected (spatialized) time. This literary interest in music is not new with Broch.

While nineteenth-century German and English criticism differed on the hierarchy of the arts regarding poetry and music, and while both had come to see music as "the weak spot in the theory of imitation,"[19] as separated from the mimetic principle, in Germany this very indeterminacy was positive[20] — "melomania" came increasingly to replace the neoclassic normative of Horace's *ut pic-*

tura poesis: German literature's ambition more and more was to aspire to the condition of music.

So Broch's interest in a literature which would have the aesthetic effect of music was in the German theoretical mainstream,
alongside Schopenhauer and Otto Weininger. Weininger's widely
read *Geschlecht und Charakter* (Sex and Character, 1904), for one,
may have been an early influence on Broch in this regard, affecting
Broch's thought on value and time.[21] Schopenhauer was an early
influence on Broch's Platonism, and on his theory of rhythm as it
relates to simultaneity.[22] While Schopenhauer does not discuss simultaneity,[23] music for him is uniquely important, for it is the unmediated objectification and image of the will. Unlike the other
arts, which must work through the medium of the Platonic idea,
the will expresses itself directly through music.[24] Schopenhauer's
cognitive goal, the denial of the will, is echoed in Broch's work: it
is analogous to the spatializing of time.[25] Since music cannot exist
except in time, and if music is our only direct view of the will, then
music's undoing of time is the goal of cognition: the negation of
the will.[26]

Simultaneity and Musicality in *Der Tod des Vergil*:
A Textual Example

How does Broch propose to solve the "most difficult problem of
the epic form," namely, simultaneity, and how does this solution
affect the construction of *Der Tod des Vergil?* Broch outlines his answer to this in several of his commentaries.[27] In these essays,[28]
Broch essentially says that one sentence equates with one thought
or instant: "Ein Gedanke, ein Satz — ein Satz, ein Gedanke." A
sentence cannot be ended until the unitary thought (cognitive
unit) which it is trying to express is complete. This requirement results in *Vergil's* monster sentences, sometimes several pages long.

As with some others of Broch's self-commentaries, the explanation of cognitive units is labored, complicated, and ultimately
unsatisfying; Broch struggles to define "thought," but can't. The
"eidetic unit (that is, thought) corresponds to a particular external
or internal segment of the world, located in a particular place in
time and space and perceived for the duration of its existence as a

whole."[29] It is (explicitly) static, unchanging, and elementary; implicitly, an eidetic unit has no real duration, it is more or less instantaneous (KW 4, 481). Thus, simultaneity: a sentence can take a whole chapter, but only an instant of real time (as does Molly Bloom's soliloquy in *Ulysses*) (483, 486). Of course, intention is not effect; with his long sentences, Broch could not achieve the *effect* of simultaneity, since a novel, no less than a symphony, is experienced over time, not in an instant. What Broch means is that his technique aims at the *figuration* of simultaneity.[30] The syntax of a Broch sentence is the representation of a thought removed from the context of time, but this representation is not *perceived* outside time. Like music, the end is in the beginning, and vice-versa. "A properly constructed sentence connects all its parts in a simultaneous relationship; this simultaneity comprises both that which is fleeting and that which is static."[31] So each sentence (Satz)[32] is to represent an instant in time, and a thought (Gedanke). Broch states that the thought is only expressible in terms of syntactic units, which are controlled and selected by "ideal" units of cognition.[33] But as the following text clearly shows, a "thought" is not necessarily a simple, unitary statement; on the contrary, a thought, or a *Kognitiv-Gebilde* (cognitive object) can be extraordinarily complex and extended, while occurring nearly instantaneously.

An examination of the first four pages of the second section, *Feuer — Der Abstieg* (71–74) will show the variability and flexibility of Broch's concept of *Gedanke*.

There are nine complete sentences in this extract, which, as it is a paragraph, could be considered an *Absatz* (section). The first statement is: "Er lag und lauschte." (He lay and listened.) Such short sentences are rare exceptions in *Vergil*. The end of the final sentence of the *Absatz* is: "er lauschte dem Sterben." (He was listening to dying.) The intervening four pages bring in a variety of other themes, but this is the main theme, the *Gedanke*. This demonstrates the cyclic structure of Broch's prose:

> Every action contains its end in its beginning, and every problem
> contains it own solution. Similarly the end of every paragraph or
> chapter must return to its start, even if at a logically higher stage.
> In this sense every paragraph and chapter has a cyclic structure.[34]

In the previously quoted article, Charriére-Jacquin points out the crescendo-like significance of the motiv "Lauschen," with which this section begins, "inconspicuously."[35] It is truly a "statement" in a musical sense (i.e., the statement of a theme). *Lauschen* and its several compounds invoke both sound and silence (the last sentence of the prior chapter ends with *Schweigen:* silence), since it implies a silent, listening subject, waiting to hear a sound. Further, the sound need not be verbal: and the sound might never be heard. *Lauschen* makes no limitation on what might be heard; it has a musical component, both in its meaning, and in its thematically formal repetition within the text. The motiv of *lauschen* mingles two kinds of aural/musical techniques in the novel: it directly invokes the idea of sound/silence, by its content or meaning; and it indirectly invokes musical techniques by its formal arrangement at the beginning, throughout, and at the end of the section in an intensified restatement. Furthermore, it unites this *Absatz* with later ones through repetition of the word.

To continue looking at the nine sentences bound by the theme of *lauschen*: Virgil, though desperately ill, needs solitude even more than care, for he needs to "listen." As he lies, he reflects: the awareness of his lifelong self-absorption mortifies him. This brings a page-long one-sentence reverie: of Virgil the boy in bed in Cremona,[36] the wind, the drafty door; and now, as then, a flickering light outside brings him to question his own existence; the physical sensations of his recumbence remind him of his passage through life; awareness that tonight of all nights he need concern himself with something more essential, something more conclusive (Wesentlicheres und Endgültigeres) than any poetic or childish memory. He reflects on memory, and its reality and its irreality, and then come images, timeless, the image of his body as a ship, as a landscape; Virgil is acutely aware of his body, its vulnerability, its connection to infinity, undescribable image of reality. There is a confusion of reality and images: which is more real? Finally: he recalls his lifelong wish for dissolution of the body, the recognition that his entire life has been a listening to (*lauschen*) death.

This condensation of four lyrical pages shows the essential unity and cyclic quality of thought in the passage. The theme is set in the first sentence: *er lag und lauschte*; digressions, though long, involve only Virgil's memory of his body, his illness, his epistemological search — all well within the compass of *er lauschte dem Sterben*. Like a musical movement, this *Absatz* treats a small number of closely related themes: to reread this section several times yields that experience of unity and timelessness which Broch likens to music.

The next passage reveals further musical characteristics: It begins with *Konnte es anders sein?* (Could it be anything else?) as Virgil notes that man alone stands erect, yet must be prone for sleep, love, and death: these three nouns introduce a triadic theme which can be vertically arranged in a chord form (as with the gods Vulcan-Poseidon, Saturn, and Apollo representing three levels of cognition), or rhythmically (horizontal, as with "Schlaf, Liebe, Tod") effect. Triads[37] are one of the most conspicuous stylistic features of the work, as can be seen in this sentence alone: "Schlaf, Liebe, Tod" is repeated in various ways four times; "unendliches Lauschen" introduces a triad of "unendlich";[38] even the reference to the two-faced Janus is triadic;[39] triadic, too, the motiv of eternal recurrence in the same sentence.[40] These triads have the effect of forward motion, emphatic rhythmically, and stand in contrast to the interweaving duple rhythms of opposites:

> "Himmelslichtes/Erddunkelheit"
> "Sphärentrennende/Sphärenverbindende"
> "Sternschweben/Sternschwere"
> "Oben/Unten"
> "Beglückung/Beschwernis"
> "Ein-/Ausatmen"
> "Keimen/Reifen"
> "Ernten/Fehlernten"
> "Vergehen/Auferstehen"
> "Sterbensenthobenen/Sterbens"
> "golden/erzen"

These word pairs have a retarding effect, work against forward motion, and this is appropriate in the sentence, which discusses stasis as "die Verkerkerung der Seele ins Irdische." The long sentence ends with a reference (back) to "Lauschen," and the next sentence completes the thought: "Er lauschte dem Sterben; es konnte nicht anders sein"(76), the thought with which the passage began.

Of course, triads and duple rhythms alone do not create music out of words. Repetitive and motiv-like devices are as much the domain of poetry as words themselves. However, Broch carries these devices to the point that their semantic meanings are blurred, both heightening and obscuring the normal effect of such words: in the same way that Broch concedes the nontranslatability of music into words,[41] his use of language comes close to the creation of a meta-language, not directly paraphrasable by other words of like meaning, and no longer dependent for its understanding on the content of its form (*inhaltliche Formung*), but rather on the form of its content (*geformter Inhalt*). It is this quasimusical quality of Broch's language that goes beyond any metaphorical "musicality."

A striking example of *geformter Inhalt* (formal content) can be found in the long sequence which begins: "In den Tod nämlich ist jedwede Gleichzeitigkeit eingesenkt . . ." and ends with "oh, die Gefilde der Väter" (78). This sentence, which is "about" time's collapse, at death, into simultaneity, is itself a symphony movement in miniature, formed by a series of inward or downward spiralling verbal triads, each triad ending in a new word or idea which leads to the next triad, thus the triads lead to one another, like a musical circle of fifths.

Here is the entire sentence, with differing symbols enclosed in parentheses embedded in the text to indicate the several different triads:

> (I) *In den Tod* nämlich ist jedwede Gleichzeitigkeit eingesenkt, alle Gleichzeitigkeit des Lebens und der Dichtung ist in seiner Allesaufhebung für ewig aufbewahrt, er ist erfüllt von Tag und Nacht, und sie durchdringen einander zur zwiefarbenen Wolke der Dämmerung; (II) *oh, der Tod* ist erfüllt von all der Vielfalt, die aus der Einheit hervorgegangen war, um sich in ihm wieder zur Einheit zu schließen, er ist erfüllt von der Herdenweisheit des Beginns und von der Vereinzelungserkenntnis des Endes, sie beide zu einer einzigen Sekunde des Seins zusammenfassend, zu jener Sekunde, die bereits die des Nicht-Seins ist, denn in unaufhörlichem Wechselspiel mit dem Seinsablauf (III) *steht der Tod,* und anablässig wird der (A) *in ihn einmündende,* (B) *von ihm empfangene* und (C) *ursprungswärts rückgewandte Zeitenablauf* zur Einheit des —— (a) *Gedächtnisses* verwandelt, zum (b) *Gedächtnis der Welten und Aberwelten,* zum (c) *Gedächtnis des Gottes:* —— /// nur (1) *wer den Tod auf sich nimmt,* vermag

den Ring im Irdischen zu schließen, nur (2) *wer des Todes Auge
sucht,* dem bricht nicht das eigene, wenn es ins Nichts schauen
soll, nur (3) *wer zum Tod hinlauscht,* der braucht nicht zu flüch-
ten, der darf bleiben, —— denn (α) *seine Erinnerung wird* zur
Gleichzeitigkeitstiefe, und (β) *wer in die Erinnerung taucht,* dem
erklingt der Harfenton jenes Augenblickes, in dem das Irdische
sich zum unbekannt Unendlichen öffnen soll, (γ) *geöffnet zur
Wiedergeburt und Auferstehung unendlicher Erinnerung* ——,
(a') *Kindheitslandschaft,* (b') *Lebenslandschaft,* (c') *Todeslandschaft,* sie sind Eines in ihrer unwandelbaren Gleichzeitigkeit,
heraufahnend die (x) *Landschaft der Götter,* die (y) *Landschaft des
Ur-Anfanges* und des (z) *Ur-Endes,* unwandelbar geeint von dem
Reif des über sie hingespannten, siebenfarbig regenverhauchten
Bogens, oh, die Gefilde der Väter.

The first triad is marked with Roman numerals I–II–III, and
contains three longer ideas on death; each begins or ends with the
word "death" (*Tod*). The second triad is marked with A–B–C, and
is a triad of time flowing into death; this A–B–C triad is transitional, leading into the new idea of memory (*Gedächtnis*). When
the final third of a triad is reached, there arises the natural expectation of a new triad in the reader's mind, just as in a musical structure a leading tone gives the auditor certain expectations of what
will come next. The backward flow of time (*der rückgewandte Zei-
tenablauf*) back towards nonexistence in death transforms its
events into memory. With memory comes the start of a new triadic
structure (marked a–b–c), the memory (of man), of the cosmos,
and of God. With the end of the "memory" triad comes a break
indicated by the colon after *Gedächtnis des Gottes;* this caesura
marks a return to the original theme of death in the next triad
(marked 1–2–3); however, this "development" of the original
theme of death now includes the idea of individual man: *Wer den
Tod auf sich nimmt,* etc. The end of this triad signals the start of a
new triad, a return to the theme of memory, but with the substitution of *Erinnerung* (remembrance) for *Gedächtnis* (memory). This
triad of remembrance is marked by the sound of a harp, and this
sound marks the introduction of the infinite into the theme of
earthly life (*dem erklingt der Harfenton jenes Augenblickes in dem
das Irdische sich zu unbekannt Unendlichen öffnen soll . . .*). This
triad, marked α–β–γ, combines themes of infinity and remembrance, as the harp marks a chord of death, memory, and infinite

knowledge. The brief triad of *Landschaft* words (*Kindheits-, Lebens-, Todeslandschaft*) collapses the time of an individual life through memory, and this triad is amplified in the final triad of simultaneity, *Landschaft der Götter, des Ur-Anfanges, des Ur-Endes*, an increase in "volume" which acts as a final flourish to signal the end of this semantic symphonietta. Thus the semantic functions of Broch's words are arranged in musical patterns, in this sample typically triadic.

But beyond the semantic level, the structure of the sentence presents simultaneity in a characteristically musical fashion. Various elements of the sentence point forward or refer backward to repetitions or elaborations of the same theme. The triads (for example, those with *Tod*) reinforce the repetitive quality of music, but other techniques are also used. Opposition, inversion, chains of meaning which run first in one direction, then another, are common throughout. For example, *Vielfalt* (variety) proceeds out of *Einheit* (unity), and then returns back to unity. Often the text will reverse direction vertically, sometimes looping slowly and sinuously, sometimes suddenly and jaggedly. An example in the quoted passage is the cadence which begins: *denn seine Erinnerung wird zur Gleichzeitigkeitstiefe . . .*, where first there is (semantically) a downward impetus: *wer in die Erinnerung taucht*, then an upward motion: *geöffnet zur Wiedergeburt und Auferstehung unendlicher Erinnerung*. The harp explicitly marks a musical moment of cognition. Leitmotivs reach backwards and forwards through the sentences: as with *lauschen* and the recurrent references to "ring."

This passage epitomizes Broch's strategy of eliminating sequentiality; while Joyce, Mann and Proust attempt simultaneity indirectly, Broch directly attacks sequential and logical expectations. Proust and Mann try to collapse time, even while discussing time and its effects, with leitmotivs, epiphanic revelations, and so on. Joyce does not make time a theme as do Proust and Mann: but he presents a helter-skelter pattern of events and information which the reader must piece together: the final effect of simultaneity in Joyce is a hard-won one, requiring the reader essentially to reread the work.[42] But Broch, as shown in the above passage, "undoes" time more directly, in real time, so to speak, through lyric narration. The ultimate simultaneity of death is called "Twilight" (*Dämmerung*), and it refers to the extinction of individual knowledge and free will, combining the "herd knowledge" of the beginning of life with the individuated knowledge of the end of life into a single second of existence which becomes the eternal "now" of nonexistence. This passage exemplifies Broch's two approaches: simultaneity as an express theme, and simultaneity as a quasimusical technique.

Musical Inspiration: Broch and Barraqué

Jean Barraqué (1928–1973) was a French serialist (sometimes known as "row") composer; when the philosopher Michel Foucault introduced him to the French translation of *Vergil* in 1955, he was so impressed by it that he determined to devote his creative life to a gigantic musical work based on texts from the novel. Today Barraqué is somewhat obscure,[43] but during the 1960s and 1970s his music was played at avant-garde music festivals, and was much admired. He is sometimes compared to his contemporary and colleague Pierre Boulez.[44] His works are few and largely incomplete.[45] Barraqué's cycle *La Mort de Virgile* was to have had five parts: one for each of Broch's chapters, and a recapitulation.

Broch and Barraqué have certain similarities. Like Broch, Barraqué admired Beethoven and Debussy,[46] because they were innovators in a time of cultural hiatus. He also wanted, like Broch, a perfect fusion of aesthetic and technique. Although his technique was serialist, he could be considered a Romantic modernist in style,[47] because he preferred the emotional impact of pure sound over strictly formal considerations, and because he was "attracted to those writers who have succeeded in winning a transcendental, affirmative poetry out of their personal situation as outsiders, philosophers and prophets."[48]

Both Broch and Barraqué were involved in projects which have an open-endedness, an incompletability, which Barraqué explicitly called "ceaseless incompletion";[49] his project was impossible from the outset, like Broch's and Virgil's goal for art — to break through the barrier of the "earthly absolute."[50]

Barraqué was a serialist because he embraced Boulez's position "those who have not acknowledged or assimilated serial thought have condemned themselves to silence."[51] Young composers like

Barraqué espoused Webern's techniques: applying abstract compositional principles not just to pitches (like Schönberg), but also to rhythm, dynamics and timbre. One methodology would order all four parameters, so the resultant music would have unity. Thematicism, which creates fixed identities by unvarying association between constants in at least two parameters of music (usually pitch and rhythm,) was to be done away with. In the end, Barraqué felt that Webern's strict adherence to theoretical principles produced music that was ultimately tame or sterile.[52]

Still, Barraqué remained true to serialist principles: his major innovation was the technique of "proliferating series." This idea enormously increases the options available to the row[53] (one mathematical series generates another, and this in turn becomes another row), while making it formally much more complicated. While this form is rational, based on integers, its ultimate effect is irrational, for its content is so enormously variable that the listener cannot "follow" such music in the usual sense. Barraqué wanted to place the listener in this situation; he wanted music which would be "entirely inaccessible to analysis."[54] The rationale of its structure should not be apparent,[55] its "dialectic" should not distract the listener.[56] Unlike Broch, Barraqué did not write commentaries on his work, but it is known that, unlike most serial composers, he thought that music at heart is the expression of emotion or feeling, which cannot be analysed.[57] The creative motivation behind Barraqué's music is thus not formulaic orthodoxy but affective impact.

Barraqué's music also reflects the ideas of Broch's novel in its effect of simultaneity. Like the French critic Maurice Blanchot,[58] Barraqué admired the formal unities of Broch's art, and was obsessed with the predicament of the artist facing death (he died in his forties of acute alcoholism). The theoretical unity of Barraqué's music, based on rows of pitch, timbre, rhythm, or dynamic, is far too complex to be perceptible, but it negates time in quite another, and more immediately emotional way: since there is no theme to "follow," the listener feels caught in the present, in the "everlasting now" of Virgil's confrontation with the absolute.[59] This feeling is intensified by Barraqué's registrations: percussive effects, sudden and violent changes in dynamics and pitch, and incomprehensible fragments of text reduce the music to pure sound; without thematicism, there is no equivalent to Broch's idea of "one phrase, one idea." There is only "now." Much of the text of Broch's novel shows this to be the fearful state in which Virgil finds himself in his final hours, trapped in the present,[60] despite his heightened perceptions of past and future.

The music also has moments of "astonishment," Heideggerian astonishment (Staunen) at the fact of existence itself, an awareness precluding any further insight, such as knowing what exists or why. These moments are brought about by certain "privileged situations" (Barraqué's word) where rows converge or a pitch or pitches suddenly stand out, sometimes in conventional harmony. At these moments[61] the effect is like a sudden "clearing" (Heidegger's *Lichtung*),[62] analogous to Virgil's "*Überwachheit*" ("utter wakefulness"), but these moments are accompanied by a failure of comprehension, the subliminal feeling that there is here something to understand, but what? Virgil's situation is like that of the listener (the *Lauscher* of part 1) in these moments, in a near-epiphany that is not to be, for with Barraqué these moments occur only as part of his dialectic structure; they cannot be sustained, and lead only to an inevitable reversal, to moments of intense despair. Barraqué's dialectic structure is a musical analog of Virgil's wild swings from hope and insight to despair and darkness.

Barraqué is, moreoever, a skeptic of language. In a reflection of Virgil's despair over his *Aeneid*, and Broch's ultimate pessimism on the uses of poetry, Barraqué has torn Broch's text to bits, separating and distorting syllables into pure sound, incomprehensible as language. Long musical rests, extended silences, increase one's sense of despair of language. So in both ways, the very words which inspired the music in the first place are thus undermined.

Broch was dead before Barraqué's incomplete effort began, but he would no doubt have been impressed by such a sincere appreciation of his novel, though perhaps not by the music itself. Broch's theoretical appreciation of modern music and its cognitive and historical inevitability did not coincide with his actual musical tastes, but he was, as his essays show, positive about the future of music.[63]

Music, Time, and the "Everlasting Now"

The concept of "everlasting now" is one of the most prominent themes in *Vergil*. It first appears in the elegiac passages in part 2 (92–98): *das ewigwährende Jetzt,* and is associated with simultaneity and stasis all through the work — Barraqué's *Le temps restitué,* a (completed) portion of his cycle *La Morte de Virgile,* uses the phrase in the section called "Portail de la Terreur" (Pforte des Schreckens, or Portal of Fear.)[64] Barraqué's music, with its "impasses," points out the musical aspect to Virgil's situation, who feels himself caught in an everlasting now. This aspect involves time.

It is obvious that time and the idea of "now" are related, but how? In Aristotle's definition of time: "the *counting* of movement according to before and after,"[65] Aristotle says that time needs "now" to exist. Without "now" there would be no time, and no "now" without time, for time manifests itself as "before" and "after."[66] But "before" and "after" are never really present, only "now" is present. (Aristotle uses *arithmos:* number, for counting, which implies discontinuity — one counts discrete, nonspatial things (ideas, horses, dots). One cannot count continuous phenomena, which have extent and duration, and are measured, not counted. Aristotle thus did not consider time as a flow, but as a succession of discrete instants of "now." Time is not continuous, but discrete and discontinuous. It is not infinite (that is, without limit, or *apeiros*), but rather, unendingly recurrent. So time is really a counting of "nows."

Man's awareness of time is completely determined by the present — as is Virgil's, trapped between "not yet" and "never more." One cannot choose one's position in time, as one can in space. Thus, nothing geometric or spatial can be compared to time.

> Zeit strömte oben, Zeit strömte unten, die verborgene Zeit der Nacht, wiedereingeströmt in seine Adern, wiedereingeströmt in die Bahnen der Gestirne, raumlos Sekunde an Sekunde gefügt, die wiedergeschenkte, wiedererwachte Zeit, überschicksalshaft, zufallsaufhebend, ablaufsentbunden das unabänderliche Gesetz der Zeit, das ewigwährende Jetzt, in das er hinausgehalten wurde. (92)[67]

To Virgil, the stream of time is *not* a flow but a ceaseless series of nows, second by second — "now" is always the same, and yet, each respective present is not the same. Aristotle says we are first aware of time when the soul can distinguish between two nows, a prior and a later.

The musical ramifications of this view of time relate to music's undeniable relationship to numbers and counting. As for music in literature, one could say that music is counting, and literature is recounting, or narrating. This is the difference between *Zählen* and *Erzählen*, another way of stating the dichotomy of music and words. (In classical Greek, *logos* was used for both number and word.) This is the central idea of the work *Nennen und Erklingen*[68] (Naming and Sounding) by the Greek-born German musicologist Thrasybulos Georgiades, who explores the relationship between music and language.

In Georgiades' view, language is the activity of naming nature, and has absolute meaning (in any given language) while music is nonmimetic, non-naming and "means" nothing. (As he puts it, music turns away from nature and the world, music is "the singing of the angels to God.") A single syllable of language can be unambiguous, while a tone in isolation is meaningless. Relational intervals give music at once its form and its meaning, and these intervals, tones, are number-determined. Music's connection with numbers and counting excludes language.

Georgiades takes Aristotle's concept of time further: time is not a flow, and it is not *in* time. Time is *perceived* as recurrence[69] but time is, says Georgiades, an *es währt* (enduring). Time has no other quality.[70] The concept of *es währt* frees us from the notion that time is a flow. "Time remains and does not change; it does not run out,[71] it remains with us, as "lasting" (*das Währen*), as "everlasting (*das Immerwähren*). This is where Georgiades' analysis of time illuminates Broch's Virgil: Virgil is poised in the everlasting now of the question,[72] of knowledgeless knowing, and it is in this imperfect recognition of the *es währt* by the subject that consciousness of the tragic condition, the certainty of death, arises. The perceiving consciousness "knows" the "content" of life, but also knows indistinctly about Time — the *es währt*. It knows Time-enduring, but only fragmentarily through the self perceiving an endless series of successive Nows (Time-recurring), each the same and yet different, the constant being the "I" perceiving. It is the consciousness of time which gives the self its identity, and it is different from all other cognition: spatial cognition presents itself directly to the senses as phenomena, as sensation: we are passive. With time, however, cognition is mediated by the "now," by recurrence of that which is counted. The mind is active, is forced into activity, counting, to make sense of the recurrent nows. The tragic condition, the knowledge of death, in essence is: our inability to identify ourselves with the concept of Time=*Währen*, and yet our "fractured" knowledge of it.[73]

Virgil (man) is imprisoned in the eternally recurring present, "bound to the perfection of mere repetition without growth . . ."[74] He is imperfectly conscious (nichtwissenden Wissens) of the contrast of his own mortality with universal, incomprehensible, impartial *Währen*. Virgil's consciousness of the tragic condition can be compared to the ontological "position" of music — music's only certainties are now and number, counting. Music has (for the listener) an element of *doing* which other arts do not. The other arts deal in sensation, a spatial sense, the object being passive, but musical perception is neither spatial nor passive, for it is rooted in numbers and in counting. The cognition of time and music result in activities of the thinking part of man, the *nous* — counting, distinguishing. Thus music has an ethical moment unknown to other arts.[75]

While both Georgiades and Broch agree that ethical activity produces an aesthetic result, they do not agree on the effect of music. Broch's music "upends" time, turns time to space, and Georgiades' music eliminates the spatial moment — it has no place and no extension. But both maintain in different ways that time is a creation of human perception.[76]

But beyond or behind man's perception of time is something else: for Georgiades, it is *es währt*, for Broch it is fate, *Schicksal*. This mute, impartial and unmoving *es währt* (Greek ειναι)[77] might be called the "absolute," the facticity of which causes the previously mentioned sensation of astonishment (Staunen, Greek, θαυμαζειν) which Virgil experiences at the fever's crisis.[78] Virgil sees this "absolute" as an impartial, stony, staring eye, beyond all operation of time or time's annulment.[79] This force operates without reference to human cognition, is independent of it. Georgiades, following Aristotle, defines time as an operation of human cognition — "Die Zeit ist nicht ohne den Nous (νοειν)."[80] Thus, for both Broch and Georgiades, time and thus simultaneity are still figurations of consciousness, not absolutes, while "Währen" is beyond humanly perceived time, and does not presuppose human cognition.

Virgil's insight into time and the "absolute" can be illuminated by Georgiades' analogy of music to "lasting" (es währt): as true time (not just time as perceived) is an *es währt* without qualifiers (ohne Substrat), music (Tönen) is an *es währt* with qualifiers, with content, with recurrent sound, apprehended in the "now." Nonetheless, music is not *in* time, like a thing, or speech, or thought, but something whose mode of being is enduring, *währen*; in music we begin to apprehend real time. We perceive music differently from objects: a thing is "out there," but music only *is* by coming into being. Music is not a something which "sounds," but the sounding itself. It starts, stops, and changes; in a sense, it forms time and is fundamentally constituted by time, because like time music is based on "now" and on "number." Broch's view of music is in agreement with this; Broch explicitly acknowledges music's basis in time in the essays on value in *Die Schlafwandler*. But music's aim is simultaneity: to bridge this apparent contradiction in Broch's writing one must distinguish between the *figuration* of simultaneity which music provides, and the utopian, nonachievable simultaneity which accompanies total cognition. In this utopian state, which Virgil approaches as he enters the realm of death, the ring of time is closed (453), and beginning and end are one. Time is no more. Music, like all else earthly, no longer exists. In the realm of earth, music, like poetry or *Dichtung,* is paratactic; but the parataxis of poetry and art is spatial, of music, temporal. At Virgil's death, the ring of time is broken; music can exist only in this world.

But even in the realm of time, music can still give a figuration of time annulled, in the "ethical moment" described by Georgiades, by highlighting that "everlasting now" which is all that music has at its disposal. The listener can only be in the present, can only know now and number — for short intervals, music can thus seem to still time. And so even while it focuses on time,[81] Virgil's narration in the *ewigwährendes Jetzt* is in this sense profoundly ethical and musical.

Jenseits der Sprache: Music as Meta-Language

When music is presented negatively in *Der Tod des Vergil,* it is associated with the failed earthly mission of art in general. This can be
seen in Virgil's identification of the artist with Orpheus, for example (KW 4, 128–29). It is a commonplace of poetry that it refers to
itself as music, as singing, as does Virgil — *Arma virumque cano
. . .*[82] and Broch often uses musical terms in referring to
"Dichtung" or "Dichtertum." Of course, the word "music"
(originally) is ambiguous: μουσικη was a combination of the arts —
singing, dance and poetry; thus, there are often (negative) references to *Gesang, Lied, Sänger,* etc. in this extended sense. "Song"
(as a synecdoche for "art") is merely a temporary palliative, illu-
sory, amoral: ". . . even Orpheus had not achieved his aim, the help
lasts (währet) no longer than the song . . ."[83] and so on. But music
per se, or as a language beyond language, a meta-language, is always presented as a positive value. Virgil sees the triviality, immorality, even cruelty of the pursuit of beauty, "das schönheits-
durchtränkte, schönheitsdurchtränkende Spiel, das selber schön-
heitsverspielt . . . die Zeit vertreibend, doch nicht sie aufhebend."[84]
Virgil is prompted to this insight partly by the sounds of the
drunken trio — "crowing tenor," "sleepy bass," and "screeching"
woman — in the street below his window. His revulsion at the
violence and obscenity of the trio becomes a horror at his own
failed life, and his emotions are mirrored in their ghastly laughter — a language that is not a bridge between men, but its opposite, and the opposite of music. Like music, laughter is an
"unspoken language," a "language outside of language," but beneath the boundary of human limitations, as music is above it (KW
4, 110). The drunken trio's perversion of music, their horrific
laughter is gradually transformed into another language which aspires to the condition of music, ". . . both languages beyond that
of speech — had joined to form a new speech, joined to the in-
scrutable speech which is completely untranslatable. . . ."[85]

As described in this passage, music in *Virgil* is an art approaching a pure, "higher" language of ideas beyond words, a
meta-language. This conception is most pronounced in the fourth
and final chapter, "*Die Heimkehr,*" in which Virgil enters the realm
of death.

As this chapter begins, Virgil has already lost consciousness. In his febrile semiconscious state, he imagines he is now in a long, black barque gliding swiftly out of the harbor. At the bow of the barque is the boy Lysanias, a symbol of Virgil's childhood self,[86] and thus a symbol of recurrent time. (At the close of the third chapter, Virgil's last earthly conscious act was to bequeath to Lysanias Plotia's ring, a symbol of the cyclic nature of time.[87] Lysanias's function is first described as a musical one: he is to sing at the ship's bow (KW 4, 413), a singing Hermes Psychopompos. But his function is unfulfilled: he does not sing. One hears only murmuring voices, and a soft rush of wind. Virgil has already advanced too far into the realm of death. Even the "tones of life," the "singing of the mountains," their very echoes, are a disappearing and unheard flutelike tone remaining in the world of the living. As Virgil's boat glides ever more slowly, its mass grows proportionally, eventually extending to the size of the universe. Time is gradually, then ever more rapidly, undone. Sound is replaced by an exponentiated silence, a "stillness within stillness"(418). A world outside time cannot express itself through music. Paradoxically, the figure of a singer, before he strikes the lyre, is used to express the silence: "im stummen Ertönen ihrer Stille," "in the mute sounding of its silence,"

> und in solcher Stille, unangeschlagen die Leier, erwartungslos das Warten, war auch das Singende und das Hörende, waren auch der Sänger und der Hörer zu neuer Gemeinsamkeit gebracht worden, da des Sphärenliedes gewaltige Stummheit nun aufrauschte . . .[88]

This strange image of an Orphic singer, silent in anticipation of striking the lyre, is the prefiguration of a reversal to come. For in this final chapter, time is not just halted, it is reversed. Virgil will in the course of events regress through the six days of Creation in reverse.

For now, Virgil's last act as an individual human being is to take a sip of water from the cup Plotius presents him: the cup has been transformed from ivory (a symbol of falseness) to horn, a symbol of the true dream (Wahrtraum) that will follow. Presently he is no longer Virgil, but nameless; only Lysanias retains a name, the *leidenlösende* (Greek λυσανιας, "ending sorrow") silent-singing psychagog in the land of death. "The knowledgeless knowing of the second immensity" is a "soundless music" (Musik ohne Töne)

(422). Broch uses the astronomical metaphors *Sphärenmusik* and *Sphärenlied* through his entire work from *Die unbekannte Größe* on. In this chapter it is apt as a description of "stumme Musik."[89] But what is this "mute music?" And why is it mute? It is the symbol of Virgil's still incomplete knowledge, the cognition which he cannot have even in his transition to death: Audible, *irdische* (earthly) music is only the mere echo of this silent music: Virgil's apprehension of silent music is the analog of his "knowledgeless knowing," his incomplete cognition of that towards which he is moving, that is, total knowledge of the Platonic idea,[90] as Broch means it: "cognizance, the knowledge of night, not yet of day, merely the apprehension of a knowledge to come, and yet a fully valid knowledge."[91]

Virgil's backward journey through creation puts the poet back into the role of Orpheus: the animals of the world gather around him as they rush headlong back to earlier stages of creation. This sequence is Broch's ultimate figuration of simultaneity and totality. Even as the strictures of time are finally burst,[92] the remains of the Virgilian consciousness are in the stars, in the vegetable/animal imbroglio of earthly creation, while the constellation of the Lyre, the constellation of music, sparkles in a "twofold triad"[93] in his heart:

> seinem Herzen eingestaltet, in zweifachem Dreiklang funkelnd das Zeichen der Leier glänzte. . . . [er war], längst nicht mehr Herz, nein, nur noch Leier, zur Leier geworden, sie sollte in ihren Sternsaiten jetzt endlich das Verheißene aufklingen, noch nicht das Lied selber, doch schon seine Ankündigung, die Stunde des Liedes, die Stunde der Geburt and Wiedergeburt . . ., die Stunde des Gesangs am Zusammenschluß des Kreises, auftönend die Welteinheit in einem letzten Atmen des Alls.[94]

The silent song announces, in potentiality, the beginning of a new age. In the very same phrase ("Atmen des Alls") from the 1912 *Notizen,* the onset of a new phase of the dialectic of creation arrives in a last "breath of the universe." The "closing of the circle," symbolized by the ring of Lysanias and Plotia, and the serpent, coiled around the *nichts* of time (441) signifies the unity of all time and all things, possible now after the sundering of the bonds of time. But the narrative is not yet at this point — the lyre cannot sound yet; still to come is the prevegetative, lifeless, mineral stage of earth's evolution (KW 4, 448–49) and the final stage of cosmic unity in nothingness, "Einheit!" (450). An epiphanic vision of a crystalline unity, symbolized again by a single eye opens up the heavens. Here the universe is in a precreationary state, crystalline, potential, "a fore-echo of the still unsung song of the spheres."[95]

Then, a literal turning point occurs: Da durfte er sich umwenden, da kam ihm der Befehl zur Umwendung, da wendete es ihn um"[96] (452). Time is reinstated, "for the ring of time had closed and the end was the beginning" (453; JSU, 481), and as all the astronomical and meteorological aspects of temporality resume a "sounding" begins, a concatenation of all hearable and thinkable harmonies, not potential, but actual:

> mehr als Gesang, war mehr als Leierschlag, war mehr als jeder Ton, war mehr als jede Stimme, da es alles zusammen und zugleich war, hervorbrechend aus Nichts und All, hervorbrechend als Verständigung, höher als jedes Begreifen, hervorbrechend als das reine Wort, das es war . . . (452–53)[97]

This "word" (λογος) is the pure Idea of Platonism; the essence of this word cannot be expressed in language: music, too, can only be an earthly echo of this Idea, but yet more suited than any word: "er konnte es nicht festhalten, und er durfte es nicht festhalten: unerfaßlich unaussprechbar war es für ihn, denn es war jenseits der Sprache."[98]

Notes

[1] Hermann J. Weigand, "Broch's *Death of Vergil.* Program Notes," in *Publications of the Modern Language Association of America* 62/2 (1947), 525–26. One of the earliest critical essays on *Virgil,* it is still one of the best.

[2] Steven Paul Scher, *Verbal Music in German Literature* (New Haven: Yale UP, 1968). Scher analyzes short passages or works by five German writers; two of these are verbal renditions of specific musical works; the others are less specific but still attempt to convey in words an experience of music.

[3] In his introductory essay, "Lexis and Melos" Northrop Frye points out this problem: "By 'musical' I mean a quality in literature denoting a substantial analogy, and in many cases an actual influence from, the art of music. It is perhaps worth mentioning, at the risk of being obvious, that this is not what the word ordinarily means to the literary critic. To him it usually means

'sounding nice.'" Northrop Frye, "Lexis and Melos," in *Sound and Poetry. English Institute Essays*, ed. Northrop Frye (New York: Columbia, 1956), xi.

[4] KW 4, 473–77 (trans. JAH). This introduction was intended by Broch for inclusion with the first edition, but was rejected by the publisher. It finally appeared, in slightly altered form, in *Almanach der Buchhandlung Martin Flinker* (Paris: Flinker, 1954), 5–9; and also in: Hermann Broch, *Dichten und Erkennen* (Zürich: Rhein-Verlag, 1955), 265–68.

[5] A representative comment: "Nur ist. . . . zu bedauern, daß Brochs oft feinsinnige Bemerkungen zur Musik, die interessante Fährten versprechen, generell in Allgemeinheiten bzw. in einen Hymnus auf den Logos/Mythos münden." (But regrettably, Broch's often sensitive observations, promising in their implications, end up as generalities or as a hymn to Logos/Mythos.) Marianne Charriére-Jacquin, "Zum Verhältnis Musik-Literatur in Hermann Brochs *Der Tod des Vergil*," in *Hermann Broch: das dichterische Werk. Neue Interpretationen*, ed. Michael Kessler und Paul Michael Lützeler (Tübingen: Stauffenburg, 1987), 8.

[6] KW 9/1, 13–29.

[7] Broch's Vergil has many striking similarities to Mann's novella. For a discussion of these similarities see Doris Stephan, "Thomas Manns *Der Tod in Venedig* und Brochs *Der Tod des Vergil*," *Schweizer Monatshefte* 1 (April 1960), 76–83. Both protagonists are dying poets, each led by a young companion into death (Tadzio is a "Psychagog," Lysanias is a "Seelenführer"), Aschenbach's gondola becomes a coffin, Virgil's litter a "Todesnachen," and both works are studded with classical quotations in antique meters: in Mann, Homer's *Odyssey*, Plato's *Phaedrus* and *Xenophon*, in Broch, the *Aeneid*, and Broch's own hexameters.

[8] Further examples: "ein jubelndes und doch kein hastendes Allegro, das Orchester ist hell gestimmt, im Einklang wird das lichte, schlanke Motiv unisono gebracht"; "Und nun, dämonisch, Scherzo . . ."; "Das Tempo hetzt vorwärts"; "allegro furioso"; "Koda." KW 9/1, 25–26.

[9] "Notizen zu einer systematischen Aesthetik," KW 9/2, 11–35, passim.

[10] KW 9/2, 128 quoted from 1933 "Das Böse im Wertsystem der Kunst," this idea appears in earlier writings.

[11] KW 9/2, 17.

[12] In a letter of July 24, 1944, Broch makes the following suggestions for a foreword in English being written by Jean Starr Untermeyer:

> iii) The method to approach such a task is a lyrical one, emphasizing the musical content of lyric; therefore the whole structure of the book is musicale (sic), namely in the sense that every theme is in connection with every other one, and by force of this connection can be "developed" and "enlarged" (in a musical sense) . . . the style, the long sen-

tences, etc. is a fonction (sic) of this method . . . what are you writing about "leitmotiv"?¿? The leitmotiv is a literary and not a musicale tool of expression, adapted by Wagner for music. [It] . . . has nothing to do with my musicale structure. . . . YUL unpub., f. 394.

[13] Untermeyer felt that Broch's repetitive use of certain words and phrases would not work in English. He wrote her:

I am very afraid that with your passion for changing words, this violent desire not to use the same word, you will make vanish this whole technic of leitmotivs . . . And this would make also necessary that you would have knowledge of the whole book, because only then can you find out the meaning of all these leitmotivs.

YUL, unpub., June 17, 1942, f. 389. This issue remained a contentious one between the author and translator.

[14] Broch. "*Bemerkungen . . .*" KW 4, 475.

[15] Manfred Durzak sees two uses of the term in Broch's writing: one, the specific literary genre, the other, dissociated from poetry *per se,* and signifying a particular form of consciousness and cognition, "nämlich die Erkenntnis des Irrationalen." Manfred Durzak, "Hermann Brochs Auffassung des Lyrischen," in *Hermann Broch: Perspektiven der Forschung,* ed. Manfred Durzak (Munich: Wilhelm Fink Verlag, 1972), 293–313.

[16] "Die unmittelbare Transformation der Zeit in den Raum." KW 10/2, 242. "*Gedanken zum Problem der Erkenntnis in der Musik.*"

[17] KW 9/2, 128. From: "Das Böse im Wertsystem der Kunst" (trans. JAH).

[18] Johann Peter Eckermann, *Gespräche mit Goethe in den letzten Jahren seines Lebens,* ed. Fritz Bergemann (Baden-Baden: Insel Taschenbuch Verlag, 1981), entry for March 23, 1879. However, this comment was first made by Schelling.

[19] M. H. Abrams, *The Mirror and the Lamp: Romantic Theory and the Critical Tradition* (New York: Oxford UP, 1953), 88–94.

[20] Abrams 94: "'A fine instrumental symphony,' James Beattie [*Essays on Poetry and Music,* 150] said, '. . . is like an oration delivered with propriety, but in an unknown tongue . . .' But when words are sung to the same air, 'all uncertainty vanishes, the fancy is filled with determinate ideas, and determinate emotions take possession of the heart.' In Germany, writers such as Tieck, Wackenroder, and E. T. A. Hoffmann (following the lead of Herder) praised symphonic music as the art of arts, just because it is indefinite, innocent of reference to the external world, and richly, because imprecisely suggestive."

[21] Manfred Durzak, *Hermann Broch, der Dichter und seine Zeit* (Stuttgart: Kohlhammer, 1968), 11–34. Durzak sees Weininger's influence in the early notebooks of Broch, in his *Ethik* essay, and in the concept of value as related

to time. Cf. Weininger's *Geschlecht und Charakter* (Vienna and Leipzig: Braumüller, 1904), 168–69. Durzak 18.

[22] Durzak 22.

[23] But Schopenhauer does say that in attaining cognition of the Platonic idea, art does arrest time: "so ist dagegen die Kunst überall am Ziel. Denn sie reißt das Objekt ihrer Kontemplation heraus aus dem Strome des Weltlaufs und hat es isoliert vor sich: . . . sie bleibt daher bei diesem Einzelnen stehen: das Rad der Zeit hält sie an . . ." *Die Welt als Wille und Vorstellung*, vol. 1, book 3, section 36, "Die Platonische Idee: das Objekt der Kunst" (Zurich: Diogenes, 1977), 239.

[24] "Die Musik ist nämlich eine so unmittelbare Objektivation und Abbild des ganzen Willens, wie die Welt selbst es ist . . . etc.," *Die Welt als Wille und Vorstellung*, vol. 1, book 3, 324.

[25] There are resonances also in Wagner: as Parsifal first enters the Gralsburg:

Parsifal: "Ich schreite kaum, doch wähn' ich mich schon weit."

Gurnemanz: "Du siehst, mein Sohn, zum Raum wird hier die Zeit."

[26] Other commonalities: Broch and Schopenhauer share a view of music as a language of feeling, of emotion, of the irrational, yet bound by rules of the Logos. Schopenhauer: "Daher auch hat es immer geheißen, die Musik sei die Sprache des Gefühls und der Leidenschaft, so wie Worte die Sprache der Vernunft . . . der Komponist offenbart das innerste Wesen der Welt und spricht die tiefste Weisheit aus, in einer Sprache, die seine Vernunft nicht versteht: wie eine magnetische Somnambule Aufschlüsse giebt über Dinge, von denen sie wachend keinen Begriff hat." *Die Welt als Wille und Vorstellung*, vol. 1 book 3, section 52, 326–27. Broch, KW 9/2, 136: "*Das Böse im Wertsystem der Kunst*": "Musik, obwohl am tiefsten dem Gefühl verhaftet, dennoch die rationalste Kunst, hat mit dem Kanon der Kontrapunktik ihre Syntax zum reinsten Ausdruck gebracht. Und nirgends ist es so deutlich wie eben in dieser rationalen und sichtbaren Syntax der Musik, daß diese trotz aller Strenge Ausfluß des schöpferischen Subjektes bleibt . . . das so irrational ist wie der Mensch selber." Also in the essay on music, in the translation essay, and other places Broch constantly emphasizes the rational/irrational polarity of music, if somewhat vaguely. Its rationality seems to stem from its syntactic rigor (*formaler Inhalt*), its irrationality from its inexpressible "content," its nonlinguistic "language."

[27] Notably in *Technische Bemerkungen zum Stil des TdV* and *Stilprobleme im TdV*, KW 4, 478–87. [Technical Remarks on *The Death of Virgil* and Problems of Style in *The Death of Virgil*.]

[28] He would later develop these ideas in the more detailed essay *Über syntakische und kognitive Einheiten* [On Syntactic and Cognitive Units]. KW 10/2, 246–301.

[29] "die Eidos-Einheit [εἶδος = form, shape, here idea] ist auf einen bestimmten äußern oder innern Weltausschnitt bezogen, der an einer bestimmten Stelle des Raumes und der Zeit lokalisiert ist und für die Dauer seines Bestehens als Ganzes erfaßt wird." KW 10/2, 249.

[30] "And though this striving for simultaneity (which is also indicated by the compression of events into a single day) cannot avoid the necessity of expressing the contiguous and the interwoven by means of the successive, or the unique by means of repetition, the demand for simultaneity remains nevertheless the real objective of all that is epical, in fact of all that is poetic." In "*James Joyce und die Gegenwart*," KW 9/1, 73, trans. Eugene Jolas, "A James Joyce Yearbook" (Paris: Transition, 1949).

[31] "Ein richtig konstruierter Satz bringt alle seine Teile in eine Simultan-Beziehung zueinander, und in der Simultaneität ist auch das Augenblickshafte und Statische enthalten." KW 4, 483.

[32] In German, *Satz* (sentence) and *Absatz* (paragraph) do have musical connotations: *Satz* is "movement," *Absatz*, "section."

[33] "Den Syntax-Einheiten dürfen und müssen daher Ideale der 'meinenden' Erkenntnis zugeordnet werden." KW 4, 481.

[34] "Jede Handlung trägt ihr Ende bereits in ihrem Anfang, und jedes Problem enthält bereits seine Lösung. Ebenso muß auch der Absatz oder das Kapitel am Ende stets zu seinem Anfang zurückkehren, wenn auch auf einer logisch höheren Stufe. In diesem Sinne hat jeder Absatz und jedes Kapitel zyklische Struktur," KW 4, 487 (trans. JAH).

[35] Charriére-Jacquin, 11.

[36] Which later became a very musical town, home to Monteverdi, Amati, Guernari, Stradivari.

[37] "Holy three, omnipresent, in the mystic Gothic it arises as the most visible symbol by far; near to God the double towers of the cathedral arise, embracing the stillness of their center, striving toward the infinite, protecting it from dissipating into the immeasurable, unity in trinity, triadic, world symbol, of the ego: this is what three says" (*Notizen zu einer systematischen Ästhetik*; KW 9/2, 18; trans. JAH).

[38] ". . . unendlich hingebreitete Seele, unendlich vom Zeitenring umschlossen, unendlich in ihrem Ruhen . . ." KW 4, 75.

[39] ". . . janusartig stets beiden angehörig, denen des Sternschwebens wie denen der Steinschwere, denen des Äthers wie denen der Unterweltfeuer, janushaft die doppelgerichtete Unendlichkeit, janushaft die unendlich hinerstreckte, dämmerhaft ruhende Seele . . ." KW 4, 75.

[40] "... wohl aber als ständige Wiederkehr empfindet, als die ständige Wiederkehr innerhalb ihres eignen Seins, als die Wiederkehr des allumfassenden saturnischen Ablaufes ..." KW 4, 75–76.

[41] "That the converse does not occur, that music can hardly be translated into words, is a sign that the multiplicity of syntactical units, such as those brought into being by music, is numerically necessarily greater than the richness of content-forms ..." KW 9/2, 66. (*Einige Bemerkungen zur Philosophie und Technik des Übersetzens*). (trans. JAH).

[42] See Joseph Frank, *The Widening Gyre. Crisis and Mastery in Modern Literature* (New Brunswick, NJ: Rutgers UP, 1963), 19.

[43] In 1989 a comprehensive performance and evaluation of Barraqué's work was mounted at the Almeida Festival in England. For a review of this festival see article by "JW" (John Warnaby) in *Musical Opinion* (London, Sept. 1989 (No. 1341, v. 112), 314–15. Recordings: *Le temps restitué,* Harmonia mundi, CD # 905199, *Concerto* (Harmonia mundi), *Chant àpres chant* (Astrée Records, AS75), *Séquence* (Astrée and MHS), ... *au délà du hasard* (Astrée AS50), Piano Sonata.

[44] In a review, Donal Henahan hints that Boulez may have sensed in Barraqué a rival, and tried to suppress Barraqué's music in performance. *N.Y. Times,* July 31, 1978.

[45] Barraqué's works are listed in "L'Inachévement sans cesse. Essai de chronobiographie de Jean Barraqué." Rose-Marie Janzen, *Entretemps* 5 (Paris, 1987), 119–30.

[46] G. W. Hopkins, *Musical Times* 107 (November 4, 1966), 952.

[47] He said the Romantic period was his favorite, and came to admire Wagner toward the end of his life. For a discussion of Barraqué written while he was still living, and the incompleted work he had planned, see article by "JA" (Jack Adrian) in "Counterpoint" section of *Music and Musicians* (London: Hansom Books) 21, no 244 (Dec. 1972), 6–7.

[48] G. W. Hopkins, "Biography of Jean Barraqué," in *Musical Times* 107 (November 4, 1966), 952.

[49] Jean Barraqué, "Propos impromptu," in *Le courrier musical de France* 26 (1969), 75–80. "Tout depositaire de la création doit l'accepter [i.e., la mort], comme il accepte sa propre mort, il doit s'achèver dans l'"inachèvement sans cesse."

[50] A review of the recording of *Le Temps restitué* makes this same point. Harald Pfaffenzeller, *Neue Zeitschrift für Musik,* July/Aug 1991, 89: "Broch's key thoughts demonstrate immediately the position of Barraqué's serial esthetic: between a rigidly and morally perceived creative urgency, and an insight into the inevitable incompletability of any creative act in the face of

death, or put another way, in the force field between construction and destruction" (trans. JAH).

[51] *Cahiers de la Compagnie Madeleine Renaud Jean-Louis Barrault,* iii. (1954), 32–45. Cited by Hopkins in "Barraqué and the Serial Idea," *Proceedings of the Royal Musical Academy* 105 (London, 1978/79), 13–24.

[52] "Barraqué and the Serial Idea," 17. He saw Beethoven as a composer who "could never have been satisfied with serial language as it was conceived by Webern . . . Beethoven possessed vast intuition, but it was so sure-footed that he never made mistakes, as we can prove by analysis." Hopkins cites Barraque's analysis of Beethoven's Fifth Symphony. MS and various notes (undated) in the possession of Mme Germaine Barraqué.

[53] Broch's music essay describes music's freedom: "Music has all of mathematics' formal freedom; like mathematics, musical thought is always in search of new formal elements (which in fact are constantly becoming available to it),. . ." KW 10/2, 242 (trans. JAH).

[54] Cited in G. W. Hopkins's biographical article in *Musical Times* 107 (November 4, 1966), 952, "une musique parfaitement incompréhensible."

[55] Barraqué echoes Mann's Leverkühn, who in turn uses Schönberg's thoughts (via Adorno); he states that the twelve-tone compositional technique works best when one doesn't "hear" it. Thomas Mann, *Doktor Faustus* (Frankfurt: S. Fischer Verlag, 1967), 193, and Theodor W. Adorno, *Theorie der neuen Musik* (Frankfurt: Suhrkamp, 1976), 63 and elsewhere.

[56] Ozzard-Low 52.

[57] Radio interview with Florence Mothe, cited by Hopkins. Here Mothe compares Barraqué to Schumann in emphasizing feeling in music.

[58] Blanchot, in his 1955 review of Broch's *La Morte de Vergile* wrote that it was "the answer . . . Not that his book tells us what unity is — rather, it is the picture of unity itself." James Miller, *The Passion of Michel Foucault* (New York: Simon and Schuster, 1993), 84.

[59] For example, "denn er ist hinausgehalten in das ewigwährende Jetzt der Frage, in das ewigwährende Jetzt nicht-wissenden Wissens . . ." (KW 4, 94) [. . . for he is held into the everlasting now of the question, into the everlasting now of man's knowledgeless-knowing . . .] (JSU, 99; and also KW 4, 112 and 146 and elsewhere).

[60] Cf. KW 4, 83–84.

[61] Ozzard-Low 54, cites G. W. Hopkins, "Barraqué and the Serial Idea."

[62] Ozzard-Low 47. Although Broch's letters reveal an antipathy toward Heidegger, there is nonetheless something in Broch's language evocative of Heidegger's vocabulary, with its use of terms such as "Verborgenheit,"

"Lichtung," even the use of "wesen" as a verb (for example, 154: "das nackte Ich weset).

[63] In a letter of December 12, 1947, Broch alludes to the "romantic" quality of Schönberg's music for his generation: "One must consider how quickly the unusual becomes commonplace; a Schönberg, who was still 'too difficult': for the last generation, today makes an almost 'romantic' impression," KW 13/3, 201 (trans. JAH).

[64] "car il est engagé dans l'instant perpétuel de la mise en question, dans l'instant perpétuel et du savoir fait d'ignorance . . ." (denn er ist hinausgehalten in das ewigwährende Jetzt . . .), KW 4, 94.

[65] Aristotle *Physics* 4. 11. 219b1.f, τουτο γαρ εστιν ο χρονος, αριθμος κινησηως κατα το προτερον και υστερον. "For time is just this: The number of a motion with respect to the prior and the posterior." *Aristotle's Physics,* trans. Hippocrates G. Apostle (Bloomington, IN: Indiana UP, 1969), 81.

[66] This is not obvious, as Georgiades points out that Kant never mentions "now" in his discussion of time.

[67] "Time flowed above, time flowed below, the hidden time of night flowing back into his arteries, flowing back into the pathway of the stars, second bound spacelessly to second, the regiven, re-awakened time beyond the bonds of fate, abolishing chance, the unalterable law of time absolved from lapsing, the everlasting now into which he was being held" (JSU, 97).

[68] Thrasybulos G. Georgiades. *Nennen und Erklingen. Die Zeit als Logos.* (Göttingen: Vandenboeck & Ruprecht, 1985). (All trans. JAH).

[69] The word for year and time is same: χρονος, implying recurrent time.

[70] Georgiades 53.

[71] Georgiades cites Kant: *Kritik der reinen Vernunft,* note 31, A143, B183.

[72] KW 4, 94, 112, 146, and elsewhere.

[73] Georgiades 51.

[74] KW 4, 116 (JSU, 122). Remarkably similar words are used in Mann's *Magic Mountain* chapter "Eternal Soup" to describe Castorp's sense of the present: "It is always the same day — it just keeps repeating itself. Although since it is always the same day, it is surely not correct to speak of 'repetition.' One should speak of monotony, of an abiding now, of eternalness." *Zauberberg,* 254; Woods 181.

[75] Georgiades 89. "Because all music knows as certain is 'now,' anything else it is can only occur as activity. But this activity, the essence of music, is time. Time urges me along the tightrope upon which I proceed, on which I am balanced like a circus acrobat. And thus I am in the sphere of the practical, of decision, ethics, responsibility: you should: you should <u>dare</u> it. I continually

opt for the next 'now,' and I create it . . . It is the sphere of action which makes the man. This is the reason the Greeks spoke of the ethical constructive power of music, of μουσικη παιδεια."

[76] KW 4, 331.

[77] Cf. Georgiades' citation of Parmenides in the foreword — το γαρ αυτο νοειν εστιν τε και ειναι, 48: "For certainty and 'it is' are the same thing" ("die Gewissheit und das 'ES IST' sind dasselbe"). For Georgiades, νοειν is not "thinking" but "certainty," related to the idea of noticing, stumbling upon something. The ideas of recurrence, counting, and consciousness are all present here in the concept of νοειν, to notice, come upon.

[78] KW 4, 151: ". . . it was the eye of stony emptiness, the torn-open eye of a fate, which no longer participated in any occurrence, neither in the passing nor in the annulling of time, neither in space nor in spacelessness, neither in life nor in death, neither in creation nor in discreation, an unparticipating eye in whose glance there was no beginning, no ending and no concurrence . . ." JSU, 158.

[79] This vision reappears at the climax of Virgil's experience (450).

[80] Georgiades 48: "Time does not exist without thought."

[81] For example, 281, 311, 314–15, 318–19, 322, 328–29, 331, 332, et al.

[82] Virgil's final direction to his literary executors: "Die Gesänge dürfen nicht zerrissen werden . . ." KW 4, 411.

[83] KW 4, 129; JSU, 135.

[84] KW 4, 117: "the beauty-saturated, beauty-saturating game in which beauty was at play with itself, passing the time but not annulling it . . ." JSU, 123.

[85] KW 4, 110–11; JSU, 116. For the most part, throughout the *Vergil,* Broch remains consistent with the thoughts expressed in the Schönberg essay, with respect to music's supralinguistic quality, its untranslatability into language.

[86] For convincing interpretation of the mythic figures of the novel as Jungian archetypes, see: Koichi Yamaguchi, "Das Seelenproblem und der Mythos in Hermann Brochs *Der Tod des Vergil*" (Kessler/Lützeler), 201–7.

[87] For example "er erkannte Ur-Enkel und Ur-Ahn im Zusammenschluß des Ringes," 437.

[88] KW 4, 419 ("and in this stillness, the lyre unstruck, the waiting without expectation, fuses the singing and hearing, the singer and the hearer, into a single harmony; for the silent power of the spheric song was now stirred to sound."), JSU, 445.

[89] KW 4, for example, 419, 428, 432, 433, 438, 440, 451, 452.

[90] In Ernestine Schlant's words: "Die Platonische Idee bedeutet ihm die Idee einer allumfassenden Totalität, wie sie sich zum Beispiel in einem einheitli-

chen Weltbild ausdrückt," *Die Philosophie Hermann Brochs* (Bern: Francke Verlag, 1971), 11.

[91] JSU, 452; KW 4, 426: "Wissen war es, Nachtwissen, noch nicht das des Tages, nur Wissen um künftiges Wissen, und eben damit doch schon wieder vollgültiges Wissen."

[92] "es zerbarst die Schlange der Zeit," 443.

[93] The double triad describing Lyra's stars hearkens back to the importance of the musical triad in Broch's early writings. Cf. chapter 1.

[94] KW 4, 446: "transferred to his heart, sparkling in a twofold triad, shone the sign of the lyre, . . . his heart that long since had ceased being a heart, only a lyre, ah yes, now a lyre, as if at last the promise were to ring out among its starry strings, not the song itself but the annunciation of it, the hour of song, the hour of birth and rebirth, . . . the singing hour at the closing point of the circle, crying out the unity of the world on the last breath of the universe . . ." JSU, 473.

[95] This final sequence contains many echoes of the Johannine *Offenbarung* (Revelations), not least the emphasis on music.

[96] *Offenbarung* (Revelations), I, 12: "Und ich wandte mich um, zu sehen nach der Stimme, die mit mir redete."

[97] KW 4, 452–53: "and that which sounded was more than song, more than the striking of the lyre, more than any tone, more than any voice, since it was all of these together and at once, bursting out of the nothing as well as out of the universe, breaking forth as a communication beyond every understanding, breaking forth as a significance above every comprehension, breaking forth as the pure word which it was . . ." JSU, 481.

[98] KW 4, 454: "he could not hold fast to it and he might not hold fast to it; incomprehensible and unutterable for him: it was the word beyond speech." JSU, 482.

6: Thomas Mann's *The Magic Mountain* and *Doctor Faustus*

THOMAS MANN'S APPRECIATION OF MUSIC was by his own admission that of an informed and enthusiastic amateur; his exposure to late German romantic music was typical for his time. Along with the large doses of Schopenhauer and Nietzsche which he ingested in his youth, he contracted a serious case of Wagnerism from which he never completely recovered, and his musical taste remained, like that of most concertgoers today, firmly rooted in the late nineteenth century. But for Mann, the central role which music played, that most German of the arts, can hardly be overstated.

The two works which exhibit most clearly Mann's interest in music are *The Magic Mountain,* written at the height of his creative middle period, immediately after struggling to come to terms with his own views on Germany and being German in the *Betrachtungen eines Unpolitischen* (1918, translated as *Observations of a Non-Political Man*), and *Doktor Faustus* (1947), written during Mann's American exile just before the final decade of his life. The earlier work is a sardonic, yet comic look at a fragmented and decadent Europe descending into the divide of Great War. The later work is a profoundly tragic life story of a composer, presented as an allegory of the fate of Germany in the twentieth century. Each of the works is "musical," but in radically opposed ways. While *The Magic Mountain* is placed in this century, the music it is concerned with is primarily that of the nineteenth. It uses literary leitmotivs to a greater degree than any other work of Mann's, and its chief concern is the subject of time; music, though an important theme, is not central. *Doktor Faustus,* on the other hand, has as its subject the life of a composer and the music he creates.

These novels stand in contrast not only to one another, but also to the works of Broch and Kafka discussed in this study. Kafka's approach to music is negative, a denial of music both in technique and in its epistemological potential; Broch's, as we have seen, is radical, thoroughgoing, and in *Vergil,* all-encompassing in the narrative flow. With Mann, musical techniques and subjects are blended in with a more conventional narrative technique.

What follows is a musical survey of the entire novel *The Magic Mountain:* an attempt to catalogue the various works and themes having to do with music in the novel, and to relate them to the fate of its hero. Following this is an essay which sees in Mann's deliberate choice of the Schönberg twelve-tone system of composition a creative misreading of Adorno's analysis of modern music, the result of this misreading being a musical allegorization of German fascism.

The Magic Mountain:
Thomas Mann's *Danse Macabre*
to the Music of Time

In his introduction to *The Magic Mountain,* a talk given in English (but written in German) for an audience of Princeton literature students in 1939, Mann describes his novel as a *"Zeitroman,"* and gives two reasons: "First, in a historical sense, . . . it seeks to present the inner significance of an epoch, the prewar period of European history. And secondly, because time is one of its themes: time, dealt with not only as part of the hero's experience, but also in and through itself."[1]

Mann describes his hero's experience as "hermetic enchantment" within the timeless, and the book as seeking to "abrogate time itself" (Zeitaufhebung) by giving "complete presentness at any given moment to the entire world of ideas that it comprises."[2] This anticipates Hermann Broch's explanation of the goal he had in writing *The Death of Virgil,* namely the abrogation of time. Broch attached ethical value to this goal, but in Mann the intent is aesthetic, not moral: the goal is pleasure. He urges the reader, on completing the work, to read it again. Mann says that a work of art is "meant to give pleasure, to entertain, and enliven." Though he certainly believed with Horace that art should both entertain and uplift, here he is emphasizing the pleasure his work should bring, comparing it to that afforded by music. Like Broch in discussing his *Vergil* a few years later, Mann says, "To me the novel was always like a symphony." He uses the verb "compose" to describe his writing, saying "music has always had a strong formative influence upon my style of writing."[3]

In his introduction, Mann highlights one important compositional aspect of his novel, the leitmotiv (that "most unmusical" of musical aids, as Hermann Broch remarked). While it is a perhaps over-used term, it describes repeated key phrases and ideas (literary or musical) meant to recall or anticipate other ideas or events. In a five-hour Wagner opera, there are typically only two or three dozen separate leitmotivs, but in a novel such as *The Magic Mountain* the writer can employ many more. Some of them are recurrent *ostinato*-like repetitive phrases or words,[4] others are infrequent, subtle, perhaps accidental. Verbal leitmotivs recur in ever more varied contexts as one moves through the work, and perfectly serve Mann's express goal of abrogating time, of giving "complete presentness at any given moment to the entire world of ideas that it comprises," as Mann said in his Princeton remarks. The reader can accomplish this "magical" effect himself, this "nunc stans" as Mann says, by reading the symbolic and allusive formulas both forward and backward.

This technique (simpler than Broch's more systematically worked out ideas and perhaps clearer on the phenomenon of *Zeitaufhebung*) appears to have a magic formula in it, perhaps appropriately for a book that is about a Magic Mountain and a hermetic enchantment. Mann was known within his family as "Der Zauberer" (sorcerer) and was fascinated by formulas (cf. *Doktor Faustus*), and by the occult (cf. the chapter "Highly Questionable" in *The Magic Mountain*). In the former work, the demonic powers connected to the creation of music according to a twelve-tone formula are probed deeply to tragic effect.

The Magic Mountain, though, is not a tragic work, though by no means is it the brief comical "satyr-play" that Mann originally planned as a counterpart to *Death in Venice*. Goethe's description of his *Faust* as "very serious jests"[5] applies to this work, too, Mann says; he finds this a good definition for art in general. Though its "jesting" quality is remote from Broch's *Vergil*,[6] the works bear striking similarities in the musicality of their construction, their musical effect, and in their concern with time, both historically (the epoch in which they take place), and with the effect of simultaneity, that is, the abrogation of time. Further commonalities are the investigation of the nature of time itself, and its connection in the human imagination to death.

The present chapter investigates Mann's novel on three levels: (1) the musical construction of the novel and its discussion of music and specific musical compositions; (2) leitmotivs and their relationship to (1); and (3) time as a theme itself, and its abrogation by the techniques of (1) and (2). These three strands investigated here are not separate; they are all functionally and formally intertwined in the composition of the novel itself.

Mann's novel is a *Zeitroman* (novel of time) in several different senses. First, it takes place in a specific period, 1907 to 1914; this "serious jest" took twelve years (1912 to 1924) to write, a period of momentous change in Europe and in Mann's own life, as witnessed in his *Observations of a Non-Political Man*. But the novel is also about time itself, and how it is perceived differently under different circumstances: Mann's reading of Henri Bergson's *Time and Freedom* is palpable in the novel. The word "time" and its variants in German: (*Zeit, zeitlos, zeitigen, zeitlich*, and so on) is one of the most frequently occurring words in the Magic Mountain: it appears over 450 times. Indeed, the only nouns occurring more frequently are the protagonists' names, and the words *Augen* (eyes) and *Frau* (woman).[7] The novel begins with the author's statement of purpose, the *Vorsatz*, a somewhat ambiguous word which usually means "intention," but here can be read as Introductory piece, or "prelude" (*Satz* is the word used for musical movement). The very first words, though, it seems quite clear, are among the last that Mann wrote — the outcome of the novel and its length are hinted at in the conclusion of the *Vorsatz*, and Mann did not know when he began the work how it would end. In any event, the *Vorsatz* discusses time, the first of many such instances. Ironically apologetic, Mann states the obvious: stories must be about the past, as the very word implies (history = *Geschichte* = that which has happened (*geschehen*)), and the narrator is the "murmuring conjurer of the imperfect tense." (German calls the narrative past tense the Imperfect, as though the past were not really over — the first of many confusions about time in the novel.) Although Mann says the events of the novel are "long ago,"[8] the reader will know differently: at the novel's conclusion he will be able to date the novel's action to the seven years commencing August 1907 — "long ago" means simply the bygone age of Europe before the Great War. As a culture, the nineteenth century continued right up until the War's outbreak. Time is here a mysterious element whose measure remains elusive, but this measure has something to do with the momentous turn of events which carved a deep chasm between "now" and "then." Time is change, and time without change is meaningless.

Mann concludes this prelude with the ironic hint: we will not be finished with this young man in seven days or seven months, but "for God's sake surely it cannot be as long as seven years!" (W, xii). With this false prediction the book's obsession with the magic number seven is announced.

Now that we "have begun," as Mann instructs us, let us examine the chapter divisions. There are seven chapters, of ever-increasing length, and each successive chapter takes up not just more space, but more time as well, an acceleration reflecting the hero's changing perception of time. When he first arrives time passes slowly; still the denizen of the low lands, Castorp greedily holds on to passing time. But as he stays on the mountain, time speeds up, loses its former significance, its value, and the chapters speed up. The first three chapters comprise only two days; after five chapters we are only through six months; after six, only two of the seven years have passed. The final chapter must run out the remaining five years.

In the first chapter (called *Ankunft*, arrival, as in Broch's *Vergil*) we are immediately confronted with the issue of time — Castorp arrives for his three weeks' visit slightly earlier than planned: his cousin picks him up at an earlier point in the trip, and after two days' travel Castorp feels the power of change in location as well as time. Space can assume powers we normally ascribe to time, says the narrator. Although three weeks seem a long stretch to Castorp, to his cousin Ziemssen they are a mere "day." For his part, Castorp is shocked that his cousin will need to spend six months here till cured (although Ziemssen never really accepts the sanatorium's prodigality with time; this eventually prompts his fateful decision to leave prematurely). For now Castorp is resisting this prodigality, but he will change.

The novel has scattered little digressions on the nature of time throughout, in conspicuous places, not unlike the essays in Broch's

Schlafwandler. In chapter 1 there is none, just Ziemssen's comment (W, 14) says that quick or slow, time really doesn't pass at all; this is no life for him.

Chapter 2 begins with a narrative descent into the past and the mysteries of time: here time is symbolized by the silver baptismal bowl of the Castorp clan. Consecrated water, flowing through the generations and yet caught in the silver ewer, symbolized both the flow and stasis of time. Time is sometimes an "everlasting now" and sometimes an endless flow; this is the "presentness" of the image of the bowl.[9] The magic number seven is also hidden here: the Castorp family generations number seven, and the boy is seven at the time his grandfather shows him the bowl again. But time as perceived here is not objective clock time, but Bergsonian perceived time; the grandfather has outlived his era; further, an even more remote past — the Renaissance, or even the Middle Ages — seems to live on in him.[10] His conservatism and *Vormärz* (pre-1848) sensibilities are preserved and handed down to his grandson.[11] This generational link is mirrored in the depiction of Settembrini's inheritance of the liberal tradition from his grandfather.

Castorp from early on has had a somewhat casual attitude towards time; he was held back in school several times: not the brightest or hardest working of students, he developed early on a tendency to take his time, if not exactly to waste it. This wantonness with the stuff of life itself will stand him in good stead at the Berghof sanatorium.

And though he finally went to live with his guardian to begin work, he was ambivalent towards work: he reveres the concept, but does not love the fact. Time, unhampered by labor, free time, is what he most loves.

In chapter 3, Castorp begins to suspect the different nature of time on the mountain when he discovers the "Half-Lung Club," the curious band of pneumothorax patients who have no sense of time, who lark about the compound playing tricks with their "whistling" lungs, and just as suddenly and unceremoniously die, or when Settembrini (*sette*: seven) seems surprised at his intention to stay only three weeks. The narration makes palpable Castorp's slow sense of time: we sit through all five meals with him, bit by bit gaining clearer impressions of the other patients at his table.[12] Castorp has his second dream at the end of this chapter, in which he sees the nature of Time: it is a thermometer with no scale, no measurements, the so-called "Silent Sister." As Thieberger notes,[13] it is the special privilege of dreams to allow "felt time" (Bergson's *temps hétérogène*) to supplant objective or measurable time (*temps homogène.*) The immeasurability of felt time is symbolized by using the "silent sister" (which takes seven "long" minutes!).

In chapter four, Castorp's time confusion mounts as a big snowstorm blows up on his third day; he wants to know if summer is now over? It's only early August, after all. His cousin hastens to reassure him, summer is not over, but that seasons as he knows them don't really exist here; winter days can occur in midsummer, and spring days in midwinter, so seasons have meaning but often just for the length of a day. "Das ist ja eine schöne Konfusion," says Castorp, reasonably enough.[14]

As if in response to this confusion, the narration now digresses briefly on the nature of time itself. The next four chapters each have a similar excursus, in which the narrator pauses to look at the shifting perceptions of time from both the hero's viewpoint, and in common experience. This sequence explores the paradox of short-term versus long-term "ennui" and "amusement." Time passes quickly when one is amused, yet in retrospect, a life of amusement seems longer than a monotonous one (*langweilig* vs. *kurzweilig*); all this introduces Castorp's own feelings of Bergsonian time: he feels he has been there an eternity, regardless of the calendar (W, 103).

The paradox of ennui is that when one day is like all days, then all seem like one. From this point, the three-day mark, the next narrative break comes when Castorp's status changes from from visitor to patient: he is ordered to three weeks of bed rest when a spot is found on his lung. This break is chapter five's "Eternal Soup," which presents time as the eternal "now": the nurse bringing in the broth today is indistinguishable from the same moment yesterday and tomorrow — to the invalid each day is the same day. Mann uses the phrase *stehendes Jetzt* (or *nunc stans*). Castorp in his fever is the comic equivalent of the mortally ill Virgil in his fevered dream of "Fire: The Descent."

The next digression on time occurs in the "Changes" section of chapter 6, six weeks after Castorp's erotic encounter with Clavdia Chauchat at the Mardi Gras party, at the end of his seventh month. Time: what is it? the narrator asks. "A secret, insubstantial and omnipotent" (W, 339).[15] As in Aristotle, time is an accounting for the changes which motion brings about between "earlier" and "later." Time is an active process, not just observed change. It "brings forth," it "zeitigt" ("betides") change. The motion by which time is measured is circular (clocks, planetary rotation), but sitting in his "Liegestuhl" Castorp experiences time as a quiet *flow*, "the web of silently flowing earthly days" (W, 341). Such are Castorp's constantly altering perceptions of time, demonstrated in these three digressions. The last digression comes immediately after Ziemssen's untimely death: the seventh and final chapter starts by discussing time and music, comparing the need for time in both music and narrative. Time is to music and narrative as space is to bodies. It is not possible for a narrative to be "present" like a work of visual art; it requires "Nacheinander" (things in sequence), and referring to the novel at hand, "and even if it would try to be totally here in each moment, would still need time for its presentation." But this total "being here" ("*ganz da zu sein*") is exactly Mann's goal, through leitmotiv: to give "complete presentness at any given moment to the entire world of ideas that it comprises."[16] Here Mann wrestles with the same paradox Broch meets in his plan for *Vergil*: it is not possible to present a narrative in such a way as truly to abrogate time: one can only attempt to simulate this with other means. Mann uses leitmotiv, Broch uses lyric in verbal constructions of enormous length. This digression refers back to a remark of Ziemssen's concerning these matters; now the narrator grants the reader may be confused: *when* did Ziemssen speak about music and time? This may be unimportant to the reader, but Ziemssen's untimely passing in "A Good Soldier" has prompted this entire discussion. In fact, Ziemssen's "alchemistically enhanced" observations on music and time, though not part of his "upright" nature[17] are not only a way of bringing the reader's attention back to an earlier part of the work: they lead us to one of the most interesting interpretative points of the novel: what is the significance of music to the characters themselves, and what possibilities does this significance have for the interpretation of the novel as a whole?

Unlike *Doktor Faustus*, the characters of *The Magic Mountain* are clearly unsophisticated about music. Castorp himself seems to be the only character of the novel who has a real love of music, not unlike his creator Thomas Mann. Hermann Weigand notes Castorp's "Germanness" is epitomized by this attraction to the medium of music rather than the word;[18] the Italian Settembrini evokes the verbal, the classical, the liberal Western European;[19] Castorp is representative of German *Todesromantik,* musical, inarticulate, Northern. At first Castorp is bewildered by the Italian's verbal fluency, although he later appropriates some of Settembrini's ideas and phrases for himself. But still, music "is the medium towards which he instinctively turns, as a flower does to sunlight."[20] Mann made his Faustus a composer for the same reason: the nature of the German's relationship with the world is "abstract, mystical, that is, musical."[21]

At first Castorp seems not particularly discriminating about music — Hans Castorp loved music "with all his heart" (W, 36). The music that prompts this statement from the narrator is "morning music" from the hotel down the hill, a small pickup orchestra or band. After a choral interlude the band plays a march, to which the bereaved (yet comic) Mexican mother unwittingly trudges along. The patients often enjoy this kind of music: superficial and kitschy. At the end of his second day, Castorp again changes for bed and hears hackneyed, "symmetrical" operetta tunes being played by the same band as on the previous night.

A conspicuous example of the narrator's ambivalent attitude towards the music of the Magic Mountain occurs on Castorp's fifth day, at the biweekly Sunday band concert on the terrace. Most of the patients attend, with the younger ones lounging here and there on the steps and walks. The group is described as the picture of self-indulgent vapidity and decadence. Their physical pleasures (meals, sexual adventuring, wine) are described in such detail that music seems just another indulgence for them. Indeed, Settembrini wittily suggests (quoting Nietzsche) that Castorp's three "drugs" constitute Germanness:

> "Beer, tobacco and music," he went on. "Behold the Fatherland! I rejoice to see you in your element, Engineer — you have a feeling for national atmosphere, it seems." (W, 110)

But the uncomplicated music provokes a complicated reaction from Settembrini: he is no fan, he says, of music without words, that is, absolute music: "there is something only semi-articulate about it, something dubious, irresponsible, indifferent."[22] There are other ironically meant musical references associated with the Italian humanist: he quotes Papageno's aria, "Der Vogelfänger bin ich ja" from *Die Zauberflöte,* referring to Behrens's penchant for snaring patients into long stays;[23] Castorp dreams of him in this role that night;[24] Settembrini's Freemasonry (a central theme of the opera) is presented in opposition to music and musical sensibility: the cousins' experiences on the Magic Mountain can be seen as a kind of masonic initiation, a comic echo of Tamino's and Pamina's ordeal. Settembrini is against the Germanness, the death-romanticism of music.

Castorp remains sensitive to music throughout, indeed, his appreciation of masterpieces from the operatic and symphonic Romantic repertoire has come quite a way by the chapter "Fullness of Harmony." As a leitmotiv this sensitivity is linked, by his very facial expression while hearing music, to the themes of death and disease, the primal aspects of his experience on the Magic Mountain.[25]

Although music in the abstract is strongly associated by leitmotiv with Castorp's German nature, many of the works of music named specifically in the text are often neither of German origin, nor necessarily of best quality: the music heard by the patients is often described disparagingly as "light," "tasteless," "hackneyed," or similarly. As in Broch's *Die Schlafwandler,* the superficial quality of the music emphasizes the cultural exhaustion of the epoch and the decadence of the societies allegorically presented in the novels. Representative instances of this use of music lie readily at hand, for example: (a) Castorp's repeated references to Settembrini as a "Drehorgelmann," an organ grinder; (b) Castorp's insomnia caused by the insipid music of the hotel concert — and his whistling it (the height of musical Philistinism) to drown out his neighbors' amorous noises; (c) march music in inappropriate circumstances: the grieving Mexican mother and Hofrat Behrens in Castorp's dream; (d) hackneyed march music in various hotel concerts; (e) the Mendelssohn wedding march repeatedly played by a neurotic guest, and so on.

But where music is more closely associated with Castorp, it takes on a more serious function in revealing to the reader, and to Castorp himself, his own inner nature. Castorp is sensitive to music, we are told: he is both "musikalisch" and "sensitiv" (Z, 193).

Although musical amusements are sometimes classified as a narcotic, like Castorp's cigars or his daily dose of porter, in the rarefied mountain air these latter two pleasures have begun to pall: the cigars are tasteless,[26] and the alcohol too strong; but the narcotic effect of music gets stronger as his stay lengthens. Castorp even sings a bit from time to time: In "Table Talk" he hums a little ditty he heard years before, and which he now judges too sentimental: "One word from thy sweet lips / Can strangely thrill me. / Within my heart it slips / And raptures fill me."[27] Castorp impatiently rejects this kind of sentiment, almost embarrassed at his own thoughts. This seemingly trivial incident shows Castorp in the beginning stages of self-knowledge, and music accompanies this process at certain critical points. Earlier, in a reverie about his boyhood infatuation with his schoolchum Hippe, he sings a bit as well: music seems to allow him a certain freedom of expression. Significantly, during the lecture that Settembrini gives about "politically suspect" music, Castorp makes almost no argument;[28] but he is not persuaded, and almost in rejoinder to this lecture, on his walk later that day he sings his boyhood songs with "operatic" abandon.[29] Ziemssen has a more pragmatic attitude towards music — he finds it useful in gauging the otherwise elusive passing of time: He says an "unpretentious" concert number lasts perhaps seven minutes, and that these minutes "amount to something." They have "a beginning and an end," and don't "get swallowed up" in the humdrum of life (W, 112). But he is actually referring to the time one must give to "Merkurius," the omnipresent thermometer, and here the magic number is a curious link between music and illness.

Settembrini's decidedly non-German attitude towards music also is at odds with the concept that music should annul time; "it lends an awareness, both intellectual and precious, to the flow of time. Music's moral value is that it "awakens time . . .," (W, 112), it brings time to life. Mann is not as clear about the ethical component in music; rather, in *The Magic Mountain,* there is an opposition between states of wakefulness, of rational cognition, promoted by the Italian humanist Settembrini, and states of dream and sleep, of irrational cognition, which are associated with Castorp, with "German-ness" and with music. Settembrini also rejects music's "natural" appeal and "clarity" as meaningless (W, 111) whereas Castorp's love of nature and music are closely associated:

he "loved the purl of water as much as he loved music — perhaps even more" (W, 117).

Castorp's love of music becomes more evident and more serious as the novel progresses. As he is lying in his horizontal cure position in "The Thermometer," his fever slowly rising, he hears snatches of *Carmen, Il trovatore,* and *Der Freischütz. Carmen* is a kind of leitmotiv in itself,[30] as it comes up several times in the later course of events, and Weber's *Freischütz* does as well. Perhaps coincidentally, Castorp is first diagnosed with genuine illness at the point at which he rejects Settembrini's critique of music — this point marks the beginning of an association of music and death which will also continue through the entire work. He hears the second band concert of his stay from his bed, wearing that reverent/dreamy expression associated with his musically receptive state. Music is a kind of barometer of Castorp's growing independence from the opinions of Settembrini; he borrows his epithet "politically suspect," using it sarcastically. But his fever reaches a new height when he suggests to Ziemssen that they hear the spa orchestra play *Carmen* (Z, 325).

The chapter called *Totentanz* (Danse Macabre) is named for a musical (as well as dramatic and iconographic) form used by Liszt and Saint-Saëns, among others.[31] This chapter points to many events to come, including several deaths, and comes just before the "Walpurgisnacht" episode in which Castorp openly declares his love for Clavdia. In a sense it has a musical form as well: exposition, theme and variations, and finale. The opening statement announcing the death of the Austrian gentleman rider is the thematic exposition; this is to be a round dance of death, in which Castorp will be the partner of seven consecutive "moribundi." The dance starts with a *Liederabend* in which the tubercular soprano sings a Strauss song which is an oblique reference to illness: "Ich trage meine Minne."[32] Settembrini leaves in disapproval. Music's narcotic association with tobacco and alcohol is still an undercurrent here: Castorp notes with pleasure that people make music all over the world, under even the most peculiar conditions, perhaps even on polar expeditions. This is the same formulation he used earlier to express his surprise that Joachim does not use tobacco (Z, 69). Castorp views the corpse of the Austrian, his head cocked and his face bearing the familiar expression he adopts when listening to music (Z, 401). Now Castorp begins his "experiment," though not in the sense meant by Settembrini's *placet experiri*; he pays visits and sends flowers to seven terminal patients, each one a macabre variation of the fatal illness infecting them all.[33] The flowers which all receive from Castorp are linked with the theme of "earth," humus ("erdig," "feucht," etc.), and with the words of the Latin burial prayer, *requiescat in pace, sit tibi terra levis*. The Latin language itself is a leitmotiv throughout, with a dual significance: it is both the language of humanism and the language of death.

Frau Stöhr commits one of her many "howlers" in this chapter: she has confused an aria from *Freischütz* with *Tannhäuser*, a minor detail, but the first of many references to the Wagner opera to follow. In the "Walpurgnisnacht" chapter, the *Zauberberg* is transformed first into Mephistopheles' Blocksberg for Carnival and then into Tannhäuser's Venusberg, with Clavdia and Castorp its lovestruck inmates.

The finale of *Totentanz*, the cousins' outings with Karen Karstedt, exposes them to more music. The cousins escort Karen on a stroll through Davos where first they watch a skating competition: the competitors, some of them patients, cavort on the ice to band music. Both patients and audience, tanned and sleek, look deceptively healthy, though of course they are not. Next, the three walk to the bobsled run, which is used both for racing and for expeditiously fetching corpses down from the Schatzalp, a fact which figured into Castorp's dream of his cousin's death. The sled run also has a band: and both these athletic sites grotesquely share musical accompaniment to distract onlookers from the Dance of Death. On another occasion the three attend a silent movie, and this movie interweaves themes of music, time and timelessness, and the opposition of *Kultur* à la Settembrini to barbarism. The customary small orchestra plays, its "present rhythms" matching "vanishing phantoms from the past which despite limited means ran the gamut of solemnity, pomposity, passion, savagery, and cooing sensuality."[34] The violent and erotically explicit film is described as catering to its audience's, and thus their civilization's, secret wishes. The movie's focus on "love and murder . . . naked bodies, despotic lust . . . cruelty, prurience and fatal desire . . ." parodies the escapades and desires of the patients of the Berghof. The film's barbarous obscenities are the creation of technological innovation, an illusion made by actors who have now scattered, but the projector can "give them back to the element of time," just as earlier Settembrini had said that "music awakens time"; here the figures are transplanted to a new time, "tricked out with music." Music's role in this justifies Settembrini's mistrust of it — indeed, the film's effect on the viewers is very like that of music, in Settembrini's view: reducing them to inaction and "nerveless silence," which amounts to (Settembrini's term) "Orientalism," that is, passivity and irresponsibility. The film gives the illusion of annulling both time and space,[35] the "there" and "then" is transformed into the "here" and "now" by hurtling pictures and music.

The fourth and next-to-last movement of this finale to the *danse macabre* is literally a macabre dance: the impossible Frau Stöhr leads the three into a café with many enthusiastic, if ill, clients dancing the night away. As the evening progresses and the music gets more lively, it is reported that many a dancer from one of the local sanatoriums has "danced his way to eternity here" (W, 312) "first tossing back the beaker of life and then hemorrhaging one last time *in dulci jubilo*." Frau Stöhr's mangled quote (she says "in dolce Jubeljau") again exhibits the double use of Latin — which here combines a ghastly *placet experiri* on the part of the patients, with Castorp's morbid interests. Church Latin and its rites of burial is the "official language" of death (W, 288). The scene has an infernal feel, with its heat, "fiery" movements, red-jacketed players, with its irresponsible pleasure-seekers in their final hour, a *Totentanz* indeed. The chapter ends in the little Davos-Dorf graveyard, appropriately;[36] the watchword here is silence, not music: but this "Schweigen" speaks volumes, the little *putti* figure with its finger to its lips is the emblem of silence demanded in the presence of death, the *genius loci* of the Magic Mountain in general (Z, 440; W, 315). The single file "march" (German: *Gänsemarsch*) of the three to the graveyard recalls earlier misplaced marches, and Castorp at the scene's close has the same dreamy "musical" expression he so often wears when in the presence of death or listening to music.

Of course, the music actually heard on the Magic Mountain up to this point has not been "great" music; mostly banal entertainment music, it is just background, unworthy of the scorn of a Settembrini, but nonetheless supporting his "suspect" view. Later, when Castorp discovers the supply of recordings and the gramophone in "Fullness of Harmony," there is more at stake musically, since the operatic and orchestral selections are from the "great" European tradition.

Following the *Totentanz*, a new musical movement begins with "Walpurgisnacht," the Witches' Sabbath traditionally thought to be celebrated in the Harz Mountains on May Day night.[37] In Goethe's *Faust*, the Walpurgisnacht scene, and the dream following it, are a grotesque operatic parody, with choruses and antiphonal songs. Mann's chapter has many direct and indirect citations from Goethe's Walpurgisnacht for parodic effect, and to musical accompaniments; it is a virtuosic weaving together of the novel's main strands: love, death, disease, and time.

The section begins with the calendar: a magic seven months have now elapsed since Castorp's arrival, twelve since Ziemssen's. Since Shrovetide is at hand, Castorp wants to know how the sanatorium celebrates Carnival; Settembrini says, "Magnifik!" and goes on to quote Mephistopheles: it will be as much fun as in the Prater.[38] Castorp likes the idea[39] of Carnival in such an odd setting, echoing Joachim's words about the utility of music in marking out the divisions of time,[40] but Settembrini compares it to the parties insane asylums give for their inmates.[41] After dinner a violinist starts the musical entertainment — she is described as having a face like a tapir's, a Faustian touch. The numerous *Faust* citations underscore the real purpose of both scenes: sexual initiation of the hero (rejuvenated Faust, virginal Castorp), with musical accompaniment. The bowdlerized obscenities of old witch Baubo and Mephistopheles are parodied by Settembrini, who compares Frau Stöhr and her broom to Baubo's entrance riding a pig,[42] and the play's phallic jokes reappear as the pencil Clavdia lends Castorp. As another young patient plays the piano, Castorp pulls up a chair and begins his long conversation with Clavdia in French, a language *"sans responsabilité"* for him. When he rambles on about timelessness and eternity, the piano stops briefly as the dancers who had been whirling around them gradually depart, leaving the two alone; now the conversation takes a decidedly erotic turn, as Castorp invokes the trinity of body, love, and death, anticipating his later fascination with Tannhäuser's Venus-aria,[43] as we shall see.

But for all his Germanness, Castorp stumbles drunkenly onto the meaning of his passion for Clavdia only in French; the switch of languages accentuates Castorp's lack of sophistication, for all the Faustian allusions of this Witches' Sabbath are lost on him: much later in the novel he will gain insights from a *Faust* but it will be the German translation of Gounod's Francophone Faust. The music of Carnival, which begins with noisemakers at breakfast, and reminds us of Mephistopheles' complaint about instrumental music:

> Ich höre was von Instrumenten tönen!
>
> Verflucht Geschnarr![44] Man muß sich dran gewöhnen.

In truth, it never rises above the level of amateurish *Hausmusik,* an appropriate music for Carnival and for Castorp's clownish profundities in a strange language.

Time's rhythms continue in "Changes," with the narrator literally ringing the changes of time and its indefinable fascination for the narrator and the narration. Six weeks have passed since the Carnival night, the night he had been with Clavdia "for one wicked, riotously sweet hour, an hour quite inconsistent with some delicate little song from the flatlands . . ." (Z, 344), this being the clichéd song quoted above: "Wie berührt mich wundersam oft ein Wort von dir . . ." (Z, 194). Such a song will not do for this "Kätzchen," that is, for Chauchat, and *in nuce* shows again Castorp's growth.

For the next few months, music slips into oblivion. Easter comes, and Pentecost six weeks later: the contrapuntal role of Naphtha[45] is introduced, and before long, we have reached the one-year mark in Castorp's stay of "three weeks"; now it is Joachim who leaves the Magic Mountain, not Castorp. It is Castorp who now becomes "lost to the world" (der Welt abhandengekommen),[46] who must stay (or rather, chooses to stay) in the "underworld" to which those mortals are condemned who have eaten, like Persephone, of the food of the shades.[47]

If there is a chapter in the Magic Mountain comparable to a *stretto,* where all the various thematic strands are virtuosically interwoven, it is "Snow." The major themes of death, disease, love, time, and music all appear in the sequence of visions which attend Castorp's foolhardy excursion on skis into a blizzard. Death, or the threat of death, here has an immediacy which was hitherto absent in the narrative. Suddenly the narrative, with its horrific hallucinations, casts off the macabre humor and disinterested pose it had assumed for the last twelve months.

The chapter begins with a prologue which is a series of variations on several themes contained in remarkable, Stifteresque landscape description; the theme of snow is the most important: snow as the manifestation of sublimity in the quotidian of Berghof life, and is in all its various forms the predominant leitmotiv.[48] "This major theme is interspersed with leitmotivs we have seen all through: the deceptively healthy artificial tan of certain patients, the physical infirmity of seemingly healthy military officers, sexual highjinks, liberties given and taken, the abrogation of time as recompense for the "lifeless life" all had signed up for, the aether-like thinness of the air, the "horizontal" way of life are all repeated here. Lying down, lying, reclining, all the forms which this word can take emblematic of the passivity of the patients, and Castorp.[49] The "horizontal" aspect of life is an important theme, looks both backward and forward: Castorp in his *Liegestuhl*:

> Snow was falling silently. Everything grew more and more blurred. Gazing into cottony nothing, eyes easily closed and drifted into slumber, and at just that moment a shiver passed over the body. And yet there could be no purer sleep than here in this icy cold, a dreamless sleep untouched by any conscious sense of organic life's burdens; breathing this empty, vaporless air was no more difficult for the body than non-breathing was for the dead (W, 463).

This passage evokes all the prior "horizontal" experiences while anticipating Castorp's temptation to succumb to the deadly embrace of the storm. Castorp's dilettantish dabbling in the occult is anticipated: "This soft, ghostly pantomime was extremely entertaining" (W, 463; Z, 643). Castorp's revelations are swathed in veils ("Schleier"), are unveilings (Z, 643, 656, 669). He "loved life in the snow"; it reminds him of those other primal experiences of his holidays at the ocean; his impulse to wade too far into the crashing waves will be repeated in his near-fatal excursion into the snow. Both elements have the appeal to Castorp of release from constraints of time and responsibility, not unlike the effect of music, or of conversation in French. Castorp realizes that a part of him wanted to get lost on his hike into the blizzard (Z, 656), that

forces of irrationality and perversity are combining to make him ignore his "upright" fear of the elements. These elements have their
own weapons: the wind cuts into "flesh like a knife," the "wind
swung its scythe at him" — this a faint echo of his friend Hippe
(archaic form of *Sense*, "scythe"), and of the subtle connection of
love and death in the elements to which Castorp has so willingly
exposed himself. Thus, this passage makes "musical" use of variations on the theme of snow, and uses leitmotiv conspicuously.
There is a third musical technique, as well; that of evoking music
itself, and of silence.

   "Es war das Urschweigen, das Hans Castorp belauschte. . . ."[50]
As he begins his perilous adventure, we see our hero listening to:
nothing. *Musikalisch und sensitiv*, his head tilted in the "musical"
position, his senses alert also to the silence which is music's close
relation, Castorp resembles Virgil: both fevered dreamers for
whom music and silence are languages beyond speech. Like Castorp, Virgil "lay and listened"; Virgil is recumbent, too, but not in
his *Liegekur*, not in an effort to get well, but just as aware of death;
with Virgil, man lies in three ways, sleep, love, and death, and a
thematic of the body in recline is common to both works: Aware
that he is overstepping a boundary, Castorp knows "this world
with its fathomless silence does not receive a visitor hospitably"
(W, 467), feels "rather impudent standing there on his deluxe skis,
listening to the primal silence), to the deadly hush of the winter
wilderness" (W, 467). Virgil, too, in his musical genius, can listen
to that which makes no sound, "a hearkening of the landscape and
the soul" (JSU, 80). And finally Virgil, after a lifetime of listening,
hearkens to death: "er lauschte dem Sterben": he was listening to
dying. And so it is with Castorp in his vision in the snow: in his
unconsidered, lowlander's way, he deliberately and flippantly exposes himself to the primal, sublime, unknowable infinity of the
snow, to silence, to the abrogation of time, and he sees the inter-
connectedness of all life and its primal urges with death, through
eros. Virgil readies himself to die, and in a way Castorp is doing
the same: his death is remote (though not so far off as he thinks)
but his life-affirming experience in the snow is also a brush with
death. Like Virgil, Castorp's fever-ridden dream insights arise from
a Jungian[51] overlay of mythical and fantastical figures; Castorp
dreams of southern landscapes, Goethe's and Hölderlin's German

dream of classical Greece; he has (like these poets) never been there, but he is part of the "great soul" which dreams it through him. And like Virgil's final hours, his dream is synaesthetic — a rainbow appears in the mist "like music," like "the sound of harps, joined by flutes and violins. The surging of blue and violet was especially marvellous" (W, 481). Castorp confuses hearing and seeing, as the vision intensifies, he compares it to the childhood memory: a superb tenor aria, which starts high but with each successive note, removes veils one by one from a passionate harmony, till reaching a final note of tear-shimmering splendor. Thus, the veils of rainclouds part in Castorp's dream to reveal the deep blue Mediterranean: this echoes Aschenbach's classical dream of Apollonian beauty as well as Goethe's Faust.[52] In Aschenbach's and Castorp's dream the Apollonian calm suddenly gives way to a horrifying vision of Dionysian bloodlust. But Castorp comes to terms with his double vision more successfully than does Aschenbach, in whom the forces of disorder finally prevail. Castorp's insight is that man must not allow the fact of his inevitable extinction to dominate his thought, that man's dignity is that he is master of his contradictions, and they exist only through him. Though death's power is great — it is "freedom and kicking over the traces (Durchgängerei), chaos and lust" — and reason is helpless before it, yet love is stronger. Form and civilization (Gesittung), community and society, all come from love. Castorp's final reckoning of the meaning of his vision, just before he awakens, is in itself a contradiction:

> I will keep faith with death in my heart, but I will clearly remember that if faithfulness to death and to what is past rules our thoughts and deeds, that leads only to wickedness, dark lust, and hatred of humankind. *For the sake of goodness and love, man shall grant death no dominion over his thoughts.*[53] (W, 487)

It is no wonder Castorp cannot really retain this difficult lesson. Like Thomas Buddenbrook and his reading of Schopenhauer, Castorp cannot consciously retain all these contradictory ideas, yet in some way he is changed, for he is now ready for life as it comes, and for death, which at the novel's end is very near. His fleeting insight, which vanishes with his dream, is like musical cognition, like trying to remember a forgotten melody, but musical cognition for both writers nonetheless has the power to affect human consciousness through extrarational means.

Castorp's most significant musical experience comes near the end of the novel, in "Fülle des Wohllauts" (Fullness of Harmony).[54] The administration has provided a gramophone for the patient's diversion, and after an introductory demonstration, Castorp returns to the parlor on several occasions alone to listen to the recordings available. Here it is apparent that the specific pieces of music chosen by the narrator are consciously woven into the text of the novel as a whole. Unlike Broch's *Schlafwandler*, where the selection of music is arbitrary, merely a plausible background, here it has a definite rationale, as Symington notes. For instance, the first selection is "an overture of Offenbach" which turns out to be "Orpheus in the Underworld," a sly reference to Behrens as the Rhadamanthus of the Underworld, to Castorp's loss of Clavdia/Eurydice in the aria "Ach, ich habe sie verloren" ("Alas I have lost her"), and to Behrens's having "kept" his Eurydice for a time; even the gramophone is a physical reminder of the Underworld and of Clavdia: several times it is compared to a coffin, its lid is *verjüngt* (tapered, though Woods translates: "beveled"), and its arm is described in words which remind us of Clavdia's arm.[55] Moreover, Behrens's statement about the instrument, "the German soul, up to date" is a signal that music and its importance to Castorp in this chapter will be paramount.

The following pieces of music are discussed in "Fullness of Harmony" with the salient points of Symington's analysis summarized:

1. The *Largo al factotum* from Rossini's "Barber of Seville" is a critique of Settembrini's linguistic virtuosity and Italianate repetitiveness (welscher *da capo* Geschmack), and of his revolutionary progressive political ideas (via Beaumarchais's text).

2. The horns of the theme and variations recall not just a hoary symbol of German romanticism, but the warning horns of the lifeguard of Castorp's childhood beach, of Settembrini's shouts to him in "Snow," and the various horns of *Carmen*, textual passages past and still to come.

3. The aria from "La Traviata," "*sempre libera,*" is a reference both to the tubercular state of the *Dame aux camélias* and of the

Berghof resident most interested in liberty and pleasure, Clavdia Chauchat.

4. The Rubinstein violin piece, played as if "behind a veil" is a continuation of the *Schleier* thematic associated with music, with Clavdia, with landscape depiction, and with the homoerotic attraction of Hippe.

5. Several popular dance numbers come next in the series of records. One of them, the tango (danced earlier by certain patients) is "destined to turn the waltz into a dance for grandpas" (W, 629). (This ambivalence toward foreign dances is also a feature of *Huguenau;* here, the reader cannot know whether it is Castorp or the narrator's opinion.)

6. The "Barcarolle" duet from "Tales of Hoffmann"[56] is an obvious allusion to the Walpurgis-night events experienced by Castorp.

7. Wolfram's aria from *Tannhäuser:* "Blick ich umher in diesem edlen Kreise" an indirect allusion to Castorp's Tannhäuseresque hymn to his Venus at the Carnival party, as well as to the circle ("Kreis") of revenants in the upcoming "Most Dubious" sequence, when the specter of Ziemssen is conjured up in a séance.

8. "Da mi il braccio" is from *La Bohème,* another work with a consumptive heroine; the reference to Mimi's arms is a leitmotiv seen often in connection with Clavdia.

The next selections, which the narrator dubs Castorp's "favorites," do not evoke from Castorp dozy, open-mouthed reveries (which music had tended to do) but rather an involved, earnest attempt at understanding, interpreting, and relating the situation described in the music to his own.

9. The first is a series of records containing the final scenes from *Aida,* where Radames is brought before the tribunal of priests, found guilty of treason, and sentenced to be entombed alive. The opera subtly undercuts Settembrini's influence. Though Verdi's name is not mentioned — he is merely Settembrini's "compatriot" — the opera's commission for the opening of the Suez Canal is mentioned, "a work of technology that would bring nations closer together" (of which Settembrini's would presumably approve), even though it was inspired by an "Oriental despot" (of which he would not approve). As he hears the final scenes, Castorp notices how the heavenly harmonies cover, "or triumph" over the

ghastly physical realities of the final gruesome death and inevitable physical decay of the two lovers; this particular music combines his sympathy "for death" with his interest in the transfiguring power of music — Mann had once referred to the ending of *Aida* as an "Italian *Liebestod*."

10. Debussy's *Prelude to the Afternoon of a Faun* is the only wordless music in Castorp's catalogue of favorites; Castorp loves its unabashedly programmatic nature, and it is described in Mann's lush "verbal music," in a way quite different from *Aida*. The tragic release of the opera's finale is succeeded by an indulgent dream of pagan pleasure: like the faun, Castorp (called "goat-footed Hans") is lying back on a little mound of grass — the erotic figure of the satyr merges with Castorp, the lover of Clavdia Chauchat: both figures are free from any sense of responsibility or honor ("There was no 'defend yourself' here," as in the judges' admonition to Radames for his illicit love of Aida); here Castorp sees himself as hedonist, and the musical eroticism of this piece as life-oriented as the prior was death-devoted. Mann describes this music with adjectives from Wagner and Schopenhauer,[57] a narcotic of oblivion and time-annulment ("Hier herrschte das Vergessen selbst, der selige Stillstand, die Unschuld der Zeitlosigkeit.").[58]

11. The third of Castorp's "favorites" is Bizet's "Carmen," where the heroine's themes of "freedom" and "pleasure" are meant to remind us of Clavdia. Carmen is a figure of consummate vitality, but her character is musically and emotionally interwoven with fate-and-death thematics (Schicksalsmotiv); this facet of Carmen makes her an object of fascination for Castorp — Mann's early comment to a friend that he wanted to create in the *Magic Mountain* a novel which was "lebensträchtig, aber weiß vom Tode," that is, a novel which was "teeming with life but informed by death," is an apt description of Bizet's opera. This is, moreover, not the first time the subject of *Carmen* has come up; the narrator tells us that *Carmen* is a work "he had heard and seen repeatedly in the theater and to whose plot he had even alluded once in conversation — in a very crucial conversation." This "crucial conversation" is the one between Peeperkorn and Castorp, in which Castorp tactfully conveys to Peeperkorn that he had indeed loved Clavdia on that long-past Carnival eve (which he refers to as the "twenty-ninth of February"). During this conversation, Castorp

summarizes the plot of *Carmen,* and in doing so clearly compares the "fate" of Don José with his own, stating indirectly that just as Don José threw away his life for a woman, so, in effect, has he:

> For the sake of her love . . . I subordinated myself to the principle of irrationality, to the principle behind the genius of illness, . . . to which I have remained true up here . . . I have forgotten everything, broken off with everything, with my relatives and my profession in the flatlands, with all my prospects. And when Clavdia departed, I waited for her, just went on waiting up here, so that the flatlands is entirely lost to me now, and in its eyes I am as good as dead.[59]

And this does eventually prove to be true. The *Carmen* texts (in German translation) which are cited seem to have a peculiar relevance to Castorp's retreat from life, just as Don Jose has become a deserter from the army: "O folg uns in felsige Klüfte, wilder, doch rein wehen dort die Lüfte" (O follow to the mountains fair, the hills and crags and purest air) (Z, 889; W, 639).

12. In Gounod's "Faust" Castorp finds a musical work with a peculiarly German theme; as if to emphasize the direct line of communication, Castorp (like most Germans till recent years) hears this French opera in German translation (and *Carmen* as well). The aria is the final prayer of Valentin, Marguerite's soldier brother slain by Faust. The *Faust* allusions of earlier chapters continue here. Goethe's text has Valentin's last words: "Ich gehe durch den Todesschlaf/ Zu Gott ein als Soldat und brav." *Als Soldat, und brav* is the heading of the subchapter where Ziemssen dies, and when the aria speaks of Valentin looking down from heaven on his sister, Castorp is moved "to the depths of his soul" thinking of Joachim looking down at him. This association of Ziemssen with Valentin becomes even stronger in "Most Dubious": Castorp has inadvertently left the *Faust* recording lying about and the recording is played during the séance when the specter of Ziemssen is conjured up.

13. The most important musical selection here, and of the whole novel, is Castorp's last "favorite": Schubert's "Der Lindenbaum." It is the only one of the five where Mann both gives the title and cites the the first line: Mann wants no ambiguity here (Z, 891). It is also the only German work among the recordings, besides *Tannhäuser,* which gets rather short shrift here, after being

parodied anonymously in "Vingt-et-un" (Z, 759–60). Castorp's catalogue of works is mostly *welsch,* that is from more Settembrini-like cultures: here is an exception, notable and last in the lineup. Schubert's song is a work of high art nourished from German roots in folk culture. So the records he listens to reflect both his deference to Settembrini and his own romantically German nature. The works also encode cryptic reminders of the current situation: Debussy's faun and Wagner's Tannhäuser are voluptuaries of the erotic, ironic contrasts to Castorp's enforced celibacy; Don José and Radames are soldiers who go against their sense of duty, ironic comments on Ziemssen. (Castorp as Don José has been noted above.) Gounod combines these two aspects with the figures of Faust and Valentin.

Placing this German work last hints at its significance for the narrator, who assumes the reader knows it both as a folk song and as the sublime masterpiece Schubert made of it.[60] Mann concedes that what he is trying to say with this song is "tricky," its proper "intonation" will need the "greatest care." The narrator now indulges himself in semiotics: any object created by the human spirit, thus a signifying object, points beyond itself, is the expression of a more general spirit and intellect, a "whole world"[61] of emotion and thought which has found its "more or less" perfect symbol in this particular object. Furthermore, it is not just the song that is significant, but also the perceiver: Castorp has grown enough spiritually not merely to love and understand this song; no, Castorp consciously loves the "world" which stands behind it; moreover, he can subject this love to certain "scruples" (Gewissenszweifel); for he is aware that the world behind this song is — Death. His aesthetic and romantic predilection for death, his fascination with its manifestations in illness and sexuality are encrypted somehow in his love for a German Romantic song. What is happening here? Commentators have wondered why Mann did not end the novel with the insights of "Snow," when Castorp, on his own *Winterreise,* so to speak, appeared to have learned the lesson of balancing the power of death in his thoughts with the strength of life and love in his heart. Is he any further along here?

At first appearance, it would seem that Castorp's *Sympathie mit dem Tode* is as strong as ever, and his love of the Schubert song is more evidence that the insights of "Snow" are transitory; the narrator tells us, shaking his head in wonderment, that though the song was born of the *Volk*, though it comes from "the profoundest, most sacred depths of a whole nation's emotions — its most precious possession, the archetype of genuine feeling, the very soul of human kindness" (W, 642), it is indeed suffused with the idea of Death. This is a defining characteristic of German Romanticism, which from Herder on found wellsprings of inspiration in folk poetry, as our narrator is well aware. When the narrator feigns the protest: "But that is sheer madness! A beautiful, marvelous song like that? . . . What hateful slander!" he is, for pedagogical reasons, arguing against what he knows to be true. In the folksong as well as in Schubert's cycle the linden tree is meant to be a symbol both of the beauty of the singer's youth and the peaceful repose awaiting him in death.

Castorp recalls his mentor Settembrini's word "Rückneigung," backsliding; is he backsliding here to his old sympathies? In a sense, he is: but with a difference; he has learned in his years on the Magic Mountain that Settembrini's life views are also only partial, and that the Italian humanist's indefatigable optimism also needs to be tempered by some of his own German insights: that death is both the parent and the child of life, that such is the nature of life, and this song is the epitome of this tragic condition:

> But what's this? Hans Castorp's sweet, lovely, fair song of nostalgia, the emotional world to which it belonged, his love for that world — they were supposed to be "sick"? Not at all. There was nothing more healthy, more genial on earth. Except that this was a fruit . . . a fruit of life, sired by death and pregnant with death. (W, 643)

Surely it has not been the Schubert song which has taught Castorp any lessons; no, Castorp's receptivity to the song only illustrates the changes which have already taken place in his heart; through it Castorp appreciates directly and unconsciously what life is, as expressed by the song — life, bounded by death. Mann's term *Selbstüberwindung*, overcoming the self, expresses the progress Castorp has made, like the *Bildungsroman* hero he is, in integrating seemingly irreconcilable viewpoints within himself, and at the same time subjecting these ideas to healthy doubt. This doubt even includes his love of the song: he understands that the "soul-enchantment" proceeding from such music may indeed have a certain "suspicious," yes, even "politically suspicious" aspect to it, as Settembrini had said.

One need not be a genius, all one needed was a great deal more talent than the author of this little song about a linden tree to become an enchanter of souls (Seelenzauberkünstler), who would then give the song such vast dimensions that it would subjugate the world. One might even found whole empires on it, earthly, all-too-earthly empires, very coarse, very progressive, and not in the least nostalgic . . . (W, 643).

Symington sees the specter of Wagner in the word "*Seelenzauberkünstler,*" soul-enchanter; perhaps this passage alludes to the uses and misuses of Wagner's music in the coming decades, as *Doktor Faustus* in its turn would confirm. The narrator gives at some length an analysis of the song from his wonted "informed amateur" viewpoint: as Symington has noted, the narrator finds certain phrases "overpowering" (bezwingend) where the melody's third verse rises slightly, then falls: "so manches liebe Wort," "als riefen sie mir zu," and "entfernt von jedem Ort." It is the peculiar ability of music to afford insights that the narrator does not want to (indeed, cannot) get "too close" to with words, using these passages as examples. These lines return at the novel's end in a subtly leitmotiv form.

The narrator refers to Castorp's "fate" as partially a result of his susceptibility to the emotional sphere which this song epitomizes[62] (W, 642); he grants that this comment is made somewhat "darkly"; and purposefully obscure it certainly is — our narrator does not spell out what this emotional sphere contains, but we can assume the complex of eros/illness/death with which so much of the work has been concerned. The term "fate" (Schicksal), however, also looks ahead to the last pages of the book and Castorp's possible death in the Great War, and Castorp's fate is hinted at obscurely in the last paragraphs of "Fullness of Harmony," as Castorp indistinctly but surely arrives at inner harmony through "intuitive half-thoughts" which "soared higher than his understanding." Alone with his thoughts in the night, he sits by the foreshortened "coffin" that is the gramophone, that is his cousin's, his grandfather's, and others' coffins before it. The young man who was the "song's best son may yet have been the young man who consumed his life in triumphing over himself and died, a *new* word on his lips, the word of love, which he did not yet know how to speak" (W, 643). The reference is to Castorp, of course, and to the end of the novel. The song, it turns out, is indeed a "magic song" worth dying for (es war so wert, dafür zu sterben, das Zauberlied!). "But he who died for it was no longer really dying for this song and was a hero only because ultimately he died for something new — for the new word of love and for the future in his heart" (W, 643). Castorp will not die for a song, but for the insights it affords him — the overcoming of his old self and its "German" obsessiveness with darkness and death, through integrating that self into a newly awakened emotion of love for life, for love itself, and for a world which will come after him.

This statement, borne out by novel's end, predicts the end of an age through the coming war. Castorp's seven-year dream on the Magic Mountain is finally broken; war's thunderclap awakens the *Siebenschläfer*[63] hero and disperses the "anthill" of Berghof inmates to their various homelands. Castorp packs his bags, is ironically described as a kneeling penitent, and this posture recalls his abjection in the hymn of love he sang to Clavdia Chauchat on that long-ago Carnival night, as well as the *Tannhäuser* of the grammophone sessions.[64] The Zauberberg is a Venusberg no longer, however. Inverting Goethe's *Faust II,* whose hero sleeps off his crimes and awakens in a mountain meadow to sublime visions, Castorp wakes on the mountaintop from his dreams and his visions, and must descend into the war-mad world of men. Broch ends his *Vergil* also with the end of a world age as well as of an individual, and, similarly, with the idea of the new word beyond language. As in Broch, a "ring of time" is closed, so here an era; as Virgil's consciousness is finally extinguished he hears "the word beyond speech"; Castorp will die, "a new word on his lips, which he did not yet know how to speak."

Unlike Broch, Mann ends his novel with a concrete work of music with well-known words, placed at the very end of the novel. As Castorp is running through the mud of the darkened battlefield, a hellish landscape of fire and thunder and explosions, we hear him, improbably, singing snatches from "Der Lindenbaum." And the lines he unwittingly sings are the very ones the narrator earlier termed "magical," which he did not wish to "abuse with words";[65] although it was the musical change which caused him to select these words, there is another reason for their appearance in this final moment of the novel. The song as a whole can be read as a retelling of the hero's progress to the present point. Like the narrator of *Winterreise*, he has indeed been dreaming sweet dreams among the "shades" of the Berghof these seven years. The linden tree he lay under was within the gates, near the fountain (that clear water Castorp loves as much as music), was thus a haven, which he has now abandoned, as he has abandoned the "horizontal"[66] mode of life. He has joined battle, has marched seven hours, exhausted, into mortal danger, and our narrator does not give Castorp much chance of surviving. Nonetheless, we hear him sing of "loving words" which he has carved on the linden tree bark, while all around him blasted tree trunks jut into the darkness, reminders of how the darker side of the forces at work in Castorp's soul have been playing out in the the "flat" world. These phrases he sings were indeed "*bezwingend*,"[67] to use the narrator's adjective, and they show Castorp still struggling to balance the sides of his nature, the fascination, indeed "compelling" attraction which death still has for him. The leaves on the branches rustle as if calling out to him with the words of love which he once carved.[68] If this music takes us back to the "Harmony" episode, other allusions refer us back to Castorp's "Snow" insights, a comparison of the soldier's dire reality now against the classical vision which raced through Castorp's imagination then.[69] These references to Castorp's past insights point out how very tentative is his ability to integrate himself, to overcome his contradictions. The final stanza of the song, with its "cold winds," also refers back to "Snow": and as those winds did not deter him then, neither will the winds of battle deter him now. The narrator's divided loyalties reflect Castorp's own unresolved conflicts directly:

> Instead, there they all lie, noses in the fiery filth. That they do it with joy, and also with boundless fear and an unutterable longing for home, is both shameful and sublime, but surely no reason to bring them here to this. (W, 705)

With no pat answers or judgments on Castorp and his progress, the narrator bids him farewell, but reserves a faint glimmer of hope, not for Castorp, but for the forces of life and love which will outlive him: he recalls intimations of Castorp's "dream of love," and asks, after releasing his hero into a battlefield *Götterdämmerung*, if from this "worldwide festival of death" this love might not again arise? With this final question, Mann imposes a heavy burden on the little song of the lime tree: can the spiritual divide which Castorp learned about from this song be bridged through the cognition which it also affords? In this work, the narrator is hopeful that it can.

Doktor Faustus:
"Strict Style" as an Allegory of Fascism

> Die Unmenschlichkeit der Kunst muß die der Welt überbieten um des Menschlichen willen. Die Kunstwerke versuchen sich an den Rätseln, welche die Welt aufgibt, um die Menschen zu verschlingen. Die Welt ist die Sphinx, der Künstler ihr verblendeter Oedipus und die Kunstwerke von der Art seiner weisen Antwort, welche die Sphinx in den Abgrund stürzt.[70]

In his essay "Deutschland und die Deutschen," written at the same time as *Doktor Faustus,* Mann discusses the Faust legend's relevance to the German spirit, and especially to music: he finds it a "great error" that neither the legend nor the poem connected Faust with music, for music is a "demonic realm," and if he is to be representative of the German soul, Faust should be musical, since (as noted in the above section on *The Magic Mountain*) the relationship of Germans to the world is "abstract and mystical, that is, musical."[71] So in his Faust novel, Mann's ultimate confrontation with the questions of the artist and society, it is hardly surprising that Mann makes his hero a composer.

But it may seem at first glance surprising, given Mann's musical predilections, that he draws his hero as an exponent of the "twelve-tone" or "serial" music of Arnold Schönberg and the Second Vienna School; this innovation comes out of Mann's connection with Theodor Adorno, whose influence on *Doktor Faustus* has been well documented by Mann and his commentators. Adorno, both a composer and a philosopher, lived near the Manns in Los Angeles during the war years, and Mann appropriated much of Adorno's *Philosophie der neuen Musik* (Philosophy of Modern Music) throughout his novel. Adorno's ideas lend authenticity and power to the musically technical passages which Mann could not have written without help. Beyond this, however, these borrowed ideas enrich the political and philosophical aspects of the work. It will be shown that Mann's "humanist" reading of Adorno's *Philosophy of Modern Music* intentionally presents an esthetic evocative of fascism. Since the political content of the novel is the fate of twentieth-century Germany and its descent into fascism, the introduction of a musical "mirror" of fascism lends unity and strength to a long and diffuse work.

Mann was already at work on the novel in 1943 when he first wrote to Adorno, asking for help with the description of the *Arietta*-theme of the Beethoven Sonata op. 111.[72] Given his musical tastes and expertise, he might have drawn his Faust-figure as a Stravinsky, a Debussy, or even as a Cesar Franck.[73] Sometime in 1943 Mann received the typescript of Adorno's *Philosophie der neuen Musik,* which Adorno was in the process of editing at that time. (The original typescript with Mann's annotations and underlinings is in the library of the Thomas-Mann-Archiv, Zürich.) Adorno was to make many changes to this version, which as "Schönberg und der Fortschritt" now comprises one part of the *Philosophie der neuen Musik.* While there is virtually no available correspondence between the two men covering this period, it is clear that after reading the typescript Thomas Mann decided to make Adrian Leverkühn a serial composer.

In order to see the effect of the Adorno-montage on the novel, one can set up the analogy: Leverkühn: Germany; art: politics; serial Music: National Socialism. If Leverkühn is symbolic of Germany, then art can symbolize politics, and serial music, a type of art, can be seen as analogous to a particular kind of politics, Nazism.

It is irrelevant whether Thomas Mann correctly understood Adorno's meaning, or whether he accurately understood twelve-tone theories of composition. Mann knew of and accepted differences between "his" version of serial technique and Schönberg's actual methods; he even maintains that his book, with its pact, its black magic, lends twelve-tone composition a character that in reality it does not possess.[74] Accordingly, in his appropriation of Adorno, even when quoting verbatim, Mann freely adapts the meaning to his own purposes.[75]

In chapter twenty-two, where Leverkühn explains to Zeitblom his concept of the "strict style" (*strenger Satz*, Mann's phrase for serial composition), he precedes his explanation with a description of the historical situation in which music presently finds itself. Since Adorno was a Marxist, it is not surprising that many of Leverkühn's words resonate with political overtones,

> einen Systemherrn brauchten wir, einen Schulmeister des Objektiven und der Organisation, genial genug, das Wiederherstellende, ja das Archaische mit dem Revolutionären zu verbinden,[76]

to which Zeitblom replies that this "archaic revolutionary" schoolmaster sounds "very German." Here Adrian refers to an earlier discussion of the music theories of Johann Conrad Beissel, whose "Herr- und Dienertöne" (master and servant tones) are recalled in the word "Systemherrn." With Zeitblom emphasizing the "very German" quality of Leverkühn's concept, a reader cannot fail to hear in this statement key concepts of German National Socialism: strong leader, organization, and a restoration of archaic concepts of the past combined with pseudorevolutionary ideologies. Sinister echoes of the Nazi concept of the "master race" (*"Herrenvolk"*) are contained in Beissel's terminology. These concepts are in part repeated and strengthened in the later political discussions of the Kridwiss circle.

In their analyses of the historical crisis of music, both Adorno and Leverkühn discuss freedom. Both see the adoption of twelve-tone technique as a necessary, indeed inevitable alternative to the sterility of twentieth-century art. Paradoxically, by making music less free, less spontaneous, more determined, serial technique frees music from its bonds of sterility and impotence. Adrian says that in a time of dissolution of all objective allegiances, freedom is beginning to "mildew" talent, to become "sterile" (DF, 190). In Adrian's mind, this time of dissolution was the early twentieth century, but in the narrative frame it is a pointed allusion to the Weimar republic as well. Later Zeitblom completes the allusion on the political account in the "Kridwiss" chapter; freedom, fallen "into their laps" as a result of the defeat in World War One, was never to be taken "seriously" as a frame for the future; it was rather "ephemeral," "meaningless," and "a bad joke" (DF, 365).

The philosophic paradox of freedom is reflected both in music and in politics: freedom in fact is a dialectic, and tends towards its own negation, a constant theme in *Doktor Faustus*. Adorno:

> Musik, welche der historischen Dialektik verfiel, hat daran teil. Die Zwölftontechnik ist wahrhaft ihr Schicksal. Sie fesselt die Musik, indem sie sie befreit. Das Subjekt gebietet über die Musik durchs rationale System, um selber dem rationalen System zu erliegen.[77]

Since Adorno sees the transformation of music by the twelve-tone system as a dialectical extreme, from which he hopes for a "recovery," his admiration for Schönberg does not necessarily extend to the system itself (a term for which Schönberg preferred to substitute "method"): "Durch Organization möchte die befreite Musik das verlorene Ganze, die verlorene Macht und Verbindlichkeit Beethovens wiederherstellen. Das gelingt ihr bloß um den Preis ihrer Freiheit, und damit mißlingt es."[78]

Leverkühn is not so cautious in his embrace of the new aesthetics. Though aware of its dangers, he is eager for the new system, for within it music will find in "objectivity," "protection and security" from a freedom which has become too "subjective." While aware that freedom tends to its dialectic reversal, Leverkühn maintains freedom does not "cease being freedom" because of "laws, rules, compulsion, system" (DF, 190).

Zeitblom, the humanist, immediately mistrusts Leverkühn's reversal of the meaning of freedom — put politically, this would no more be freedom than that of a dictatorship born out of a revolution. (Though he is suspicious, Zeitblom too is swept along with the general conformism of the time, undercutting his humanistic-sounding statements; Lukács calls him a "Raabean" character who cannot hide his own considerable accommodation to fascism.)[79] In the "Kridwiss" political circle, the dialectical nature of political freedom is a paraphrase both of Adorno's and Leverkühn's utterances but with a decidedly undialectical-sounding nihilism. The members of the circle no longer believe in "free institutions," for freedom necessarily is self-negating; freedom for one is only at the cost of reducing the freedom of others; thus, its fate is "self-abolition" (DF, 365). Leverkühn's willing belief in the subjugation of music to a system that denies freedom (in order to find it anew)[80] thus finds a close parallel in the cynical utterances of the protofascist Kridwiss circle.

Another theme of both the political and musical aspects of *Doktor Faustus* is that of form and organization. Fascism as a political system places organization over freedom, and form over meaning. These antinomies take many forms in the text, most notably in Leverkühn's exposition of the "strict style," and in the conversation with the devil, in chapter twenty-five. The citation from Adorno above on organization gives the basic idea of this antinomy. In an earlier passage Adorno identifies another paradox of twelve-tone music: its seeming rationality is in fact contrived, arbitrary and a closed system ultimately with no sense beyond a belief in its own "correctness," a superstition: its "legitimacy" is "imposed" on the material (A, 67; MB, 66).

With this as a theoretical backdrop, it is appropriate to examine Leverkühn's explanations and Zeitblom's reception of the "strict style" with respect to questions of organization.

Organization in music, as presented in *Doktor Faustus,* can be charted on two axes: harmony-homophony, and atonality-polyphony. Harmony and homophony are thus associated variously with subjectivism, personal expression, and liberal humanism, while atonality and polyphony are associated with objectivity, impersonalness, barbarism and authoritarianism. (DF, 355, 280–81), with Zeitblom affiliated with the former and Leverkühn with the latter. Subjectivism is associated with the personal, with individual liberty, and with expressiveness. Objectivism is in turn associated with intellect and order. Therefore, although harmony and polyphony are both methods of organization, polyphony tends to privilege organization before content or expressive value: and harmony vice-versa.

The novel holds consistently to this ethical categorization of musical modes of organization. (However, Beethoven is specifically exempted from this categorization: he is at once the master of harmony, polyphony and the strict style of the fugue.) Nor is this categorization necessarily self-evident: one could argue for instance the independence of each note of the dodecaphonic row, or the independence of the voices in polyphony as a paradigm of democratic pluralism, and the hierarchical configuration of the conventional harmonic system as a model of authoritarianism and elitism.

But Mann aligns himself with more traditional musical aesthetics in this sense.

On the question of organization within music, Adrian and Zeitblom first show their differing affinities when discussing the curious phenomenon of Beissel. Quoting Terence, they both agree that he uses "reason" in "acting foolishly" ("mit Vernunft albern zu handeln,") to which Adrian adds, that he had a sense of order at least, and foolish order is better than none at all. (DF, 71). The cliché of the German love of order is an influence on young Adrian's aesthetic development, too. Even if the mature Adrian would have despised Beissel's worn-out harmonic based on the triad, he would still have admired his "cooling down" the "cow-warmth" of the music by the vigorous imposition of a system of order. In the closing lines of the chapter Adrian stresses that music's need for order is an atonement for its innate sensuality. This dualistic view of music, rejected by Zeitblom with the exhortation to "love" it, not subject it to antinomies (DF, 72), is characteristic of Mann.

In his later definition of the strict style, Leverkühn says it gives primacy to the organization over all other musical elements: "Ich meine damit die vollständige Integrierung aller musikalischen Dimensionen, ihre Indifferenz gegeneinander kraft vollkommener Organisation" (DF, 191).[81] This is an appropriation of Adorno's phrase "Indifferenz der Materialdimensionen gegeneinander" (A, 57). "Die vollständige Integrierung" and "vollkommene Organisation" are in themselves reminiscent of Nazi terms like "Gleichschaltung." "Die Indifferenz" finds echoes in "die Indifferenz von Harmonik und Melodik" (Adorno's meaning as seen by Mann (A, 64 and DF, 193), and later in the sinister discussion of the Kridwiss-circle: "Diese Achtlosigkeit, diese Indifferenz gegen das Schicksal des Einzelwesens" ("indifference toward the fate of the individual") (DF, 365). Even the conspicuously named student Deutschlin, in the student group "Winfried," refers to the primacy of the organization over the individual, the hallmark of the totalitarian state — the state's sovereignty consists in its coming *before* any individual, despite the "*Flausen*" (fancy ideas) of the *contrat social* (DF, 122). The effect of this method of organization on "freedom" is quite specific: "Jeder Ton der gesamten Komposition, melodisch und harmonisch, müßte sich über seine Beziehung zu dieser vorbestimmten Grundreihe auszuweisen haben . . . Es gäbe keine freie Note mehr" (DF, 192).[82] There would be no more "free notes." Thus Adorno's peculiar use of language gives Mann in his appropriation of Schönberg's musical theories certain phrases with marked political and sociological resonances. The organizational tendencies of serial music and totalitarianism are brought together through free use of the Adorno material.

The self-conscious and arbitrary nature of the creation of the row is a source of concern to Zeitblom. Moreover, serial music's intellectual and theoretical nature make it a problematic allegory for Nazism, which despite its propaganda of racist doctrine and historical necessity was anti-intellectual and anti-theoretical. It preached a doctrine of naturalness and immediacy. Kretschmar sees the first criterion of a culture in a certain naïveté, unconsciousness and naturalness (DF, 62); Adorno states that the twelve-tone compositional technique works best when one doesn't hear it. Similarly, Zeitblom asks Leverkühn if the system will be heard in the music, the latter says no, but its presence provides "unknown" aesthetic pleasure by virtue of its "cosmic order" and legitimacy (DF, 193). This puzzling statement is in effect a paraphrase of Adorno's view that the "rationality" of twelve-tone music is "opaque to itself" (MB, 66). The image is retained on the political level: as Adrian speaks of music as "gebunden durch sich selbst bereiteten Ordnungszwang, also frei" (DF, 193),[83] so, too, in the "coming" world of violence, the spirit "gar nicht auf den Gedanken kam, nicht frei zu sein. Sie war es subjektiv durchaus — innerhalb einer objektiven Gebundenheit, so eingefleischt und naturhaft, daß sie in keiner Weise als Fessel empfunden wurde" (DF, 369).[84]

The arbitariness and unnaturalness of the "system" is concealed; its reason for being transformed from "Willkür" (arbitrariness) to magic. The novel develops effectively the theme of music as a demonic art, an essentially Faustian pursuit. Mann was influenced by his reading of Adorno to emphasize the irrational, "magical" elements of music. Adorno said that the rules of musical composition spring from a rationalist urge to regulate and dominate ("ordnend erfassen") nature (A, 66; and similarly, DF, 194). But he saw the means to this regulating and dominating as irrational, paradoxically: this means was numerology, astrology, and it was not at all odd that many of the adepts of new music were susceptible to astrology (A, 67; and similarly, DF, 194).[85] To be sure,

Adorno also gives rational explanations for the "Vorkomponieren" (precomposing) of a row (acoustic and psychological) (A, 67), but, interestingly, Mann did not adopt these: he wanted to emphasize the irrational.

The thematic of compulsion links serial music indirectly to Fascism. As mentioned above, there is an implicit coercion in twelve-tone music which comes from its precomposed (*vorkomponiert*) quality — nothing "unthematic" can arise in it (A, 59; also DF, 487). Again, "there are no more free notes" (A, 64). Within the row there is another kind of compulsion: with every new tone in the row, the choice of remaining tones is diminished, and with the last tone, there is no choice at all. The compulsion is undeniable (A, 73). Truly, the new music can be seen as the artistic equivalent of an all-encompassing necessity; though even Nietzsche saw the essence of great art "that in all its moments it could be different," Schönberg said, "Art is not a product of Can but of Must"[86] (A, 45–46).

The coercive quality of twelve-tone music is itself the result of historical necessity, not arbitrarily conceived; as much as the music must conform to the rules, the rules themselves are an adaptation to the historical necessity within the material (A, 65). For Leverkühn, music is compelled to yield to the dialectic of history in his conversation with the Devil: tonality gave the chord its "specific gravity." But the chord has lost it through an irreversible historic process. (DF, 240)

The motive of coercion is carried into the act of composing. Since the row, the "self-imposed rule," is preformed, the material controls the content. The artist is called upon to answer the questions imposed by the material, and to come up with the "uniquely correct answer" for each moment (DF, 240). The artist is not free, but under the constraint of the self-imposed row. Zeitblom makes several references (DF, 175; DF, 480 for example) to the German people having put themselves into an analogous situation, choosing, by their headlong rush into the "torture chamber" of fascism, the final determined condition of the police state.

Closely allied to this theme is an undercurrent of violence. The affinity of twelve-tone music for violence comes not from its peculiar choice of subject matter (though violent plots in Leverkühn's *Apocalipsis cum figuris, Dr. Fausti Weheklag,* and actual works like Schönberg's *Erwartung,* Berg's *Wozzeck* and Adorno's favorite,

Lulu, are not atypical) — but comes, rather, from its indifference to tonal harmonics, and the effect of this on the listener. It routinely deals in minor seconds and ninths as governed by the chance of the row. These frictions as well as hollow fifths and fourths, have no compositional purpose in themselves. They are the sacrifice which music must make to the row (A, 84). In Mann's descriptions, this quality makes Adrian's music capable of describing the pain and despair of the world. Indeed, this is the sole purpose of art: to be the "unmediated and untransfigured expression of suffering in its actual moment" (DF, 241)." The harshness and severity of both form and effect reflect the world around it (A, 47–48).

Because twelve-tone music is of necessity limited thematically, Adorno sees "acts of force" replacing melodic and harmonic nuances.[87] This allusion to historical changes finds an echo in the Kridwiss discussions: "Force" give them a firm footing.[88] When the individual values of truth, freedom and reason are suspended (political analogs of the bourgeois harmony, melody, and their traditional use), Zeitblom sees the domination of "force, authoritarianism, and dictatorship of belief" (DF, 368).

Mann strengthens the connection of strict style to fascism even more: both are atavistic, and barbaric. New music and old music are both polyphonic; and music tends to atavism, to regress to its elements, according to Kretschmar's lectures on Beissel (DF, 66). Of course, Beissel's music did regress to its elemental units, for he found the traditional chorale too complex. But unlike Beissel's music, the atavism of the new music was not simplification or purification. It was a purposeful return to older, more ascetic ways of music-making. Kretschmar suspects that harmonic music has a "guilty conscience" relative to polyphonic music, and this sometimes results in a reflex return to older solutions in societies when crisis approaches. It is that "rider of paradoxes," Chaim Breisacher, who first attributes barbarism to polyphony (DF, 282), and also who first exhibits that "preservationist radicalism" ("Radikalismus der Bewahrung") which is characteristic of fascism. The Nazis' infamous pledge to rebarbarize Germany is first spoken from Leverkühn's mouth.[89]

True "Kultur," then, is "barbarisch"; civilization, *Gesittung,* is admirable, but only to insulate society from the barbarism which accompanies true culture. Here Adrian makes the connection between polyphony and (barbaric) *Kultur*. In Zeitblom's detailed description of the *Apocalipsis cum figuris*, which immediately follows the Kridwiss discussions, the work is shown as consciously using primitive musical means — the gong, the glissando, the cry, and so on. Although Zeitblom is at pains to reject the epithet "barbaric," he appears to protest too much. Atavistic Adrian's music certainly seems, as Zeitblom describes its *Massen-Modernität*. It reverts to an older rhythm pattern more closely related to speech, just as the new music's *Sprechstimme* style does (DF, 372). Zeitblom himself doubts Adrian's asseveration that the opposite of bourgeois culture is not barbarism, but the community (DF, 373). This because he has the humanist's suspicion of aestheticism being allied with barbarism.

The curious link of aestheticism and barbarism, Zeitblom feels, is hard to comprehend. Certainly aestheticism is a difficult label to pin onto serial composers as described in the Adorno text, unless one sees in their fierce, lonely and unappreciated struggle to regenerate their art a form of aestheticism. Indeed, for Adorno the whole point of the attempted reform of music is to increase its relevance to society. It should also be a bulwark against the rising barbarity of mass-produced, consumer-good music (A, 112). But for Thomas Mann, aestheticism, as represented by the George-like figure of Daniel zur Höhe and his disciples, was suspect because it is cold, elitist, and *weltfremd*. Adrian's personality is repeatedly described this way, and in this context Adrian is seen as an aestheticist.[90]

In the "Teufelsgespräch," the devil (in his Adorno-persona) promises Adrian that he will have the courage to attempt the barbaric — the doubly barbaric, because he follows an epoch of bourgeois refinement (DF, 244). This barbarism should result in the reunion of culture with the cultic, and move music and *Kultur* generally back to its original mythic, prereligious function. This refusion, or confusion, of the elements of *Kultur* with the *kultisch* is, of course, equivalent to the Nazi assignment of culture to the mystic level of the *völkisch*. After the Kretschmar lecture Adrian becomes fascinated with Beethoven's struggle to write and validate the *Missa solemnis* in an age of secularized art (DF, 62). He feels that music will move from the status of the personal, the culturally self-oriented, to a "lower" function serving a "higher" authority, and that the current (ca. 1900) condition of culture is "transitory."

The inevitability of Germany's decline to catastrophe is brought out in many passages of Zeitblom's narrative, especially in the recounting of the Kridwiss group discussions. Zeitblom's helplessness in the face of the rising tide of Fascism is partly due to his self-identification as German. As shown by his comments in praise of German valor, submarines, and technical know-how, Zeitblom cannot stop being a German, and his attitude towards the coming events is conflicted. He is horrified by what he hears at the Kridwiss house, but too timid to put forth a real objection. His powerlessness is the metaphor of Europe's inability to escape its historical dialectic. What has happened to music, happens to Germany. One reason *Doktor Faustus* is at base such a tragic and troublesome work is the clear implication of the inevitability of the German fate.

This quality of powerlessness against history is exactly the Devil/Adorno's message to Adrian: The Devil/Adorno explains the sweep of historic inevitability: the old is not enough, one must reach for the new, even if the new is negative and nihilist. The new is at the same time older than the old. The old-new, the "archaisch-revolutionär," symbolized here in atonal polyphony and fascism, are concepts of dialectic philosophy. The image of the wheel which moves both forward and backward as it moves along, as mentioned in the Kridwiss section, is a dialectic image. With two self-contradictory movements, motion nonetheless occurs. For Adorno, music as represented by twelve-tone music is at a dialectic crisis: the moment of synthesis is at hand. Its future is uncertain; music wants to flee toward "order," but cannot; it is overpowered by historical necessity creating change in all things, and it has become a metaphor of the world it is rebelling against; music's future, like that of all culture, is gloomily uncertain.

> Die bestimmte Freiheit, in welche sie ihren anarchischen Zustand umzudenken unternahm, hat sich ihr unter den Händen ins Gleichnis der Welt verkehrt, gegen die sie sich auflehnt. Sie flieht nach Vorwärts in die Ordnung. Die aber will ihr nicht geraten. Indem sie der geschichtlichen Tendenz ihres eigenen Materials blind und widerspruchslos Folge leistet und sich gewissermaßen dem Weltgeist verschreibt, der nicht die Weltvernunft ist, beschleunigt ihre Unschuld die Katastrophe, welche die Geschichte

aller Kunst zu bereiten sich anschickt. Sie gibt der Geschichte recht, und darum möchte diese sie kassieren.[91] (A, 108)

Paradoxically, this redeems music; moribund music, ravaged by the disease of time and change, still has the paradoxical chance to survive. "Das jedoch setzt die Todgeweihte nochmals ins Recht, und verleiht ihr die paradoxe Chance, fortzubestehen."[92]

Similarly, Zeitblom sees Germany at its end, canceled by history, as Beethoven's Ninth Symphony is canceled by Adrian's *Weheklag* (DF, 481): In the real world, Zeitblom dares not see any hope for Germany. But the antinomies within Adrian's composition stir him to express, however faintly, on the level of art, the "hope beyond hopelessness" (DF, 490). Zeitblom sees the *Weheklag*, a monument to the *ur*-expression of music as Lament (DF, 485), as most exemplifying the peculiar freedom of expression which only the unfree "strenger Satz" can accomplish. A dialectic process will again reverse the changes wrought in music, and perhaps in history.

> Nur daß der dialektische Prozeß, durch welchen . . . der Umschlag von strengster Gebundenheit zur freien Sprache des Affekts, die Geburt der Freiheit aus der Gebundenheit sich vollzieht . . .[93]

The total hegemony of form over material brings about its release from bondage:

> [die Komposition] kann sich nun völlig ungebunden ergehen, das heißt: sich dem Ausdruck überlassen, als welcher jenseits des Konstruktiven, oder innerhalb ihrer vollkommenen Strenge, wieder gewonnen ist. (DF, 487)[94]

It is important to distinguish between Adorno and Mann. Adorno saw the nihilistic and negative vector of art as a response to the events of the twentieth century. Mann's application of his reading — whatever it may have been — is aimed at a different target. Leverkühn's esthetic values at once anticipate and (through the double time frame) parallel the crisis of fascism. For this reason Mann uses only the expository passages of the *Philosophie der neuen Musik,* none of the passages detailing Adorno's criticisms of serial music. Adorno's hope for the future of music rests on principles not far from Mann's humanism — hope for "wintering over," that is, music's recovery, depends on its emancipating itself from twelve-

tone music: but not by returning to the "irrationality" which pre-
ceded it, but to the "free composing" and reception of the "critical
ear."[95]

It is not difficult to see the political parallel to this statement.
But Zeitblom is not so hopeful, does not see a way out — not out
of the artistic cul-de-sac of Adrian's music, nor out of Germany's
abyss. But, like Adorno, Zeitblom dares hope for a dialectical *Um-
schlag* (reversal) in the work of art, if not in history. He likens the
"totale Konstruktion" of Adrian's final work to the "tiefste Heillosigkeit" (profoundest hopelessness) of the theological discussion.
He allegorizes the paradox of Adrian's music to the theological
doctrine of saving the unsaveable, that the nihilism of Adrian's music — so bleak and hopeless that it truly is the cancellation of Beethoven's — will reverse itself to hope.

It is useful to examine the endings of *Doktor Faustus* and *Der
Zauberberg* with respect to the hope, or lack of hope, which each
narrator offers, which results from the different attitudes the author
had towards the contemporary events in each case. Each of these
major musical works finds its end in the *Heillosigkeit* of war and of
Germany's part in it. The "irrationality" which music had found its
way into, but not yet out of, as Adorno saw it, allegorizes the political irrationality into which Germany had fallen. There is something of this irrationality in Castorp's fascination with death and
illness, portrayed negatively, but it is also inextricably linked to his
understanding of life and art, particularly music, as symbolized in
Schubert's "Lindenbaum." Both Broch and Mann know the importance of irrational perception for art and for civilization, and
both show artists in their inability to break through the barriers
which the irrational represents, which is ultimately death. Castorp's
response to music comes from his unconscious perception of this
barrier. For Virgil and Leverkühn this barrier is the inspiration for
art, but art which ultimately must miss its goal, for their perception
is limited to the earthly absolute. Virgil finally learns and accepts
this limitation, and his death is his release from it. Leverkühn does
not accept limits, and in consciously joining forces with the demonic irrational forces in music, he is destroyed by them. The
profound negativity of *Faustus's* ending shows Castorp's fascination with the irrational transferred to the conscious level, no longer
held in check. In the earlier work, the responsibility for war is in-

ternational, not German. Castorp's "mystical, abstract" musical nature, his German-ness, in short, is not (yet) connected to political events. In the later work, the connection is made: Mann's pessimism is directed at Germany and the German-ness in the soul of his musician hero, for whom he can only hope for a miracle beyond faith, for whom he can only wish God's mercy. This tiny hope, applicable only implicitly to history, is all *Doktor Faustus* will allow. The use of serial music as an allegory of fascism brings this hope beyond the level of art, to the historical.

Notes

[1] "The Making of *The Magic Mountain*" in *The Magic Mountain*, trans. H. T. Lowe-Porter (New York: Alfred A. Knopf, 1964), 725.

[2] "The Making of *The Magic Mountain*," 724.

[3] Thomas Mann, *Der Zauberberg* (Stockholm: Bermann Fischer Verlag, 1946), xix. (The German has an untranslated extra sentence here: "Was mich betrifft, muß ich mich zu den Musikern unter den Dichtern rechnen": "As for me, I must count myself among the poetical musicians."

[4] Purely as examples, some very common ones: "Wir hier oben," "Merkurius," "Kirghisenaugen," "horizontal," "liegen," "Liegekur," and variations, "Sorgenkind des Lebens," "feuchte Stelle," "Flachland," "leichtes Fieber," and variations," etc.

[5] "Diese sehr ernsten Scherze": letter of March 17, 1832 to Wilhelm v. Humboldt.

[6] Forms of *lachen* (laugh) and *lächeln* (smile) occur well over one hundred times each.

[7] *Wortindex zu Thomas Mann: Der Zauberberg*, Francis Bulhof (Austin: Xerox University Microfilms, 1976).

[8] Thomas Mann, *The Magic Mountain*, trans. John Woods, (New York: Alfred A. Knopf, 1995), 7. (Further references to Woods's translation indicated with W, and page number.)

[9] "The boy looked up at his grandfather's narrow gray head which was bent over the bowl again, just as it had been in that long-vanished hour he was talking about, and a familiar feeling stole over him — a strange, half-dreamy, half-scary sense of standing there and yet being tugged away at the same time, a kind of fluctuating permanence, that meant both a return to something and a dizzying, everlasting sameness, a feeling that . . . he had been waiting for, hoping it would touch him again," (W, 22).

[10] See the description of Senator Castorp's portrait, W, 24: "It showed Hans Lorenz Castorp in his official dress as a town councillor — the sober, even godly attire of citizens from a vanished century . . ."

[11] The term *zergliederungsfeindlich* (resistive of analysis) used here to describe the boy's reverence for his grandfather is a forward-referring leitmotiv: Castorp undergoes *Seelenzergliederung* (psychoanalysis, comically put).

[12] Hermann J. Weigand, *Thomas Mann's Novel "Der Zauberberg"* (New York: D. Appleton-Century Co., 1933), 18.

[13] Richard Thieberger, *Der Begriff der Zeit bei Thomas Mann* (Baden-Baden: Verlag für Kunst und Wissenschaft, 1952), 25–65.

[14] Thomas Mann, *Der Zauberberg* (Frankfurt: S. Fischer Verlag, 1952), 131. (Edition follows original edition of 1924.) Further citations from German marked "Z" with page reference.

[15] W, 339.

[16] In context: ". . . das Gesetz der Zeit und des Nacheinander aufzuheben, indem sie in jeder Hervorbringung ganz da zu sein versuchen, aber doch nur so, wie der Roman 'Der Zauberberg' selbst und auf eigene Hand sich an der Aufhebung der Zeit versucht, nämlich durch das Leitmotiv, die vor- und zurückdeutende magische Formel, die das Mittel ist, seiner inneren Gesamtheit in jedem Augenblick Präsenz zu verleihen." Stockholmer Ausgabe, xi. (This forward is not contained in the S. Fischer Frankfurt edition.)

[17] W, 532. "Upright" for *brav,* an inspired rendering when one contrasts the word "horizontal" to this attitude.

[18] Weigand, in the chapter, "What is German?" 107: Germany is called "das unliterarische Land." But while "lacking the power of articulate speech, (it) has its own vehicle of expression, and that is 'music' . . . music stands for the language of the emotions, for poetry in the broadest sense."

[19] His very name invokes the *Risorgimento* writer Luigi Settembrini.

[20] Weigand 113.

[21] Thomas Mann, *Rede über Deutschland und die Deutschen* (Berlin: Suhrkamp Verlag [formerly S. Fischer Verlag] Sonderdruck, 1945), 11.

[22] W, 111. Weigand notes how paradoxically similar this utterance is to propaganda Wagner himself made for his music dramas. Cf. *Das Kunstwerk der Zukunft, Wagners Gesammelte Schriften,* vol. 10 (Leipzig: Hesse und Becker, 1914), 100.

[23] Naphtha at one point warns Castorp that Settembrini is a *Seelenfänger* (soul catcher), a variation of the Papageno character.

[24] Behrens whistles to two female patients (in bird form), Z, 126–27.

[25] For example, when he sees his hand under X-rays, and when he stands by the bed of the dead equestrian gentleman.

[26] Marie Mancini, Castorp's Italian cigar brand, is in fact the name of Louis XIV's first mistress; she too lost her appeal at high political "altitude."

[27] "Wie berührt mich wundersame oft ein Wort von dir / Das von deiner Lippe kam und zum Herzen mir," Z, 193; W, 137.

[28] The physical appearance of the assembly of patients underscores Settembrini's point.

[29] "mit opernhaften Armbewegungen" (Z, 163). Translated as "theatrical" by Woods.

[30] Nietzsche's favorite opera after his rejection of Wagner also features prominently in *Doktor Faustus*.

[31] The Middle Ages saw the proliferation of this form of public dance in graveyards. Later in Germany it became a danced drama in which the figure of Death was shown seizing people in the midst of life without distinction of class or profession. Holbein made a series of woodcuts on the theme of the *Totentanz*.

[32] "I bear my song of love within my heart" (W, 285). The original: "Ich trage meine Minne vor Wonne stumm, im Herzen und im Sinne mit mir herum."

[33] The "speaking names" of the patients provide sardonic humor: Leila Gerngroß, who presumably would "gern groß werden," that is, "grow up," will definitely not (described tellingly as "die Kleine," as she is); while she seemingly cannot get enough liquids, Fritz Rotbein's problem is getting enough food (his name an unpleasant reminder of his need for a rib resection). The third, Frau Zimmermann has too much air in the lungs, and a constant alarming giggle; the three form a *danse macabre* themselves.

[34] W, 311. Woods's translation says "trivial music": but here "kleine Musik" means a band. The longer passage: "die ihre gegenwärtige Zeiterzgliederung auf die Erscheinungsflucht der Vergangenheit anwandte . . .": "Zeiterzgliederung" or "time-dissecting" can mean rhythm or the marking of time by filling it with discrete units of sound, as Ziemssen says in "Politically suspect"; it also echoes the term: "Seelenerzgliederung," or Krokowski's "suspect" analyses.

[35] "Space was negated, time turned back" (W, 312) [Der Raum war vernichtet, die Zeit zurückgestellt; Z, 436].

[36] In the Romantic musical realizations of the Totentanz the dance ends with the dead returning to the graveyard to resume their "horizontal" positions by sunrise.

[37] Of course, it is not May: the date of Shrove Tuesday of "Walpurgisnacht" can be exactly deduced; it is March 3, 1908, a leap year: and as strange things will occur in this chapter, things out of the ordinary calendar of events for our hero, and which will not be repeated, it is understandable that one commentator places the events (metaphorically, at least) on the twenty-ninth of February, as Castorp does too in his conversation much later with Peeperkorn. Eckhard Heftrich, *Zauberbergmusik: Über Thomas Mann* (Frankfurt: Klostermann, 1975), 115, 120.

[38] "Das ist so lustig wie im Prater," and musically, "Dann sind wir gleich in Reihen hier die glänzenden Galanten," quotes from Goethe's "Walpurgisnacht."

[39] As he similarly commends the ubiquity of music and tobacco in even the strangest places.

[40] "we should mark the passing of the year in the usual way, its turning points, I mean, so that the monotony gets divided up." W, 317; Z, 442.

[41] "Even in the *maison de santé* they throw balls now and then for the fools and cretins, or so I've read — why not here? The program includes various *danses macabres*." W, 316.

[42] The animal all try to draw blindfolded is a pig, which Heftrich sees as a cryptic allusion both to Baubo's mount and Circe's enchantment (Heftrich 113).

[43] Heftrich 28.

[44] ". . . gab es im Speisesaal allerlei Töne aus scherzhaften Blasinstrumenten, schnarrend und tutend . . ." Z, 444; the first music we hear of Carnival is that of noisemakers. Heftrich notes Mephistopheles' dislike of music as of divine origin; Mann's reference parodies this.

[45] Although "vollständig unmusikalisch," that is, completely unmusical (Z, 609).

[46] From the Rückert poem "Ich bin der Welt abhanden gekommen" in Mahler's setting doubtless familiar to Mann.

[47] Settembrini's caustic remark: (Z, 486) "Nun, Ingenieur, wie hat der Granatapfel gemundet?" (or, "How did you like the pomegranate?"), a reference to this myth.

[48] "Colossal masses of snow, more snow than Hans Castorp had ever seen in his life" (W, 461). Forms of *Schnee* are everywhere, "monströs und maßlos," "es schneite Tag für Tag und die Nächte hindurch," "übermannshohen Schneewänden zu beiden Seiten," "auf die liegenden Massen schneite es weiter, tagaus, tagein," "Schneequalm und Nebeldunst," "bleiche beschienene Schneeflächen," "Massen von Neuschnee," "ungeheuren Schneeflächen," "Gebirge völlige im Schneenebel verschwunden," "Schneestürme, die . . . das

stöbernde Weiß massenweise hereintrieb," "ausgefüllt von Flockengewimmel," "Gestöber," "wirbelten," "quirlten," "das war kein Schneefall mehr, es war ein Chaos von weißer Finsternis," to give a few examples.

[49] As Virgil also reflects on all his memories of lying, reclining as he lies dying.

[50] Z, 649. "It was primal silence to which Hans Castorp listened as he stood there, leaning on one pole, his head tilted to the side, his mouth open . . ." (W, 467).

[51] "We don't form our dreams out of just our own souls. We dream anonymously and communally, though each in his own way. The great soul, of which we are just a little piece, dreams through us so to speak . . ." thus Castorp's self-commentary on his own dream (W, 485).

[52] 4721–24:

"Allein wie herrlich, diesem Sturm ersprießend,
Wölbt sich des bunten Bogens Wechseldauer,
Bald rein gezeichnet, bald in Luft zerfließend
Umher verbreitend duftig kühle Schauer . . ."

[53] "Ich will dem Tode Treue halten in meinem Herzen, doch mich hell erinnern, daß Treue zum Tode und Gewesenen nur Bosheit und finstere Wollust und Menschenfeindschaft ist, bestimmt sie unser Denken und Regieren."

[54] This episode has been analyzed in detail by Rodney Symington in his article, "Music on Mann's *Magic Mountain*: 'Fülle des Wohllauts' and Hans Castorp's 'Selbstüberwindung,'" from: *Echoes and Influences of German Romanticism: Essays in honor of Hans Eichner* (New York: Peter Lang, 1987), 155–82.

[55] "in weichen Gelenken beweglichen Hohlarm," though this does not come through in the Woods translation.

[56] "Belle nuit, ô nuit d'amour, souris à nos ivresses, Nuit plus douce que le jour, o belle nuit d'amour!

[57] The word "wonnevoll" (Z, 866) and the phrase "Verneinung des abendländischen Aktivitätskommandos" respectively.

[58] Strangely, this sentence is omitted in the Woods translation. In Lowe-Porter's translation: "Forgetfulness held sway, a blessed hush, the innocence of those places where time was not" (Lowe-Porter 646). We are reminded again by the word "Stillstand" of Settembrini's mistrust of music as an opiate, with a propensity towards "knechtischen Stillstand" (Z, 158) [slavish inertia] (W, 112).

[59] W, 601–2: the German more clearly links the "Schicksal" of Castorp and Don Jose with death: And though Castorp says the story is really "rather pointless" he still must ask, "why did it occur to me?" And Peeperkorn knows better than he — he offers to repay him for the "injury" he has done him in-

advertently. Moreover, Castorp's lament about his "fate" recalls the Mahler song mentioned earlier ("Ich bin der Welt abhanden gekommen" [I have become lost to the world]) "so daß ich nun dem Flachland völlig abhanden gekommen und in seinen Augen so gut wie tot bin." The Mahler-Rückert text: "Sie (die Welt) mag wohl glauben, ich sei gestorben . . . und wirklich bin ich gestorben der Welt."

[60] "We all know that there is a great difference between . . . this splendid song . . . as an art song and as a tune in the mouths of children and everyday folks" (W, 640).

[61] This "whole world" is what Broch is driving at in his shorthand formulation, the "impatience of cognition" (Ungeduld der Erkenntnis): art is the way in which this impatience is satisfied: the goal of art is to somehow encompass the whole world in its adequate object, without the plodding, progressive route of experiment and discovery taken by science.

[62] Wir wissen, was wir sagen, wenn wir — vielleicht etwas dunklerweise — hinzufügen, daß sein Schicksal sich anders gestaltet hätte, wenn sein Gemüt den Reizen der Gefühlssphäre, der allgemein geistigen Haltung, die das Lied auf so innig-geheimnisvolle Weise zusammenfaßte, nicht im höchsten Grade zugänglich gewesen wäre (Z, 893).

[63] "Seven-sleeper": a hibernating rodent, as well as a folk-tale Rip Van Winkle figure.

[64] "And so he sank back down on his knees, his face and hands raised toward a heaven darkened by sulfurous fumes, but no longer the ceiling of the grotto of sinful delight" (W, 703).

[65] "Diese zauberhafte Wendung, der wir mit Worten nicht zu nahe treten mögen . . ." (W, 641; Z, 891).

[66] Though Castorp's life is preserved, for the moment, by one last *Liegekur:* he throws himself down, avoiding a direct hit from an enemy shell, just before getting up to sing again.

[67] "overpowering" (W, 641). The root of *bezwingend* is *Zwang,* compulsion, coercion.

[68] Whether or not Castorp remembers the context of his words, Proust's (Marcel's) linden-leaf tea comes to the reader's mind as another way of remembering the past.

[69] The original German is strongly similar to the phrases in the "Snow" episode.

[70] Theodore W. Adorno, *Philosophie der neuen Musik, Gesammelte Schriften,* vol. 1 (Frankfurt: Suhrkamp Verlag, 1975), 125. Mann marked this passage with underlining in his copy of Adorno's typescript. Because Adorno's German is so idiosyncratic, and appears in Mann's text in only slightly altered

form so often, the quotations in the main body of text are left in German. Translations are given in notes. "The inhumanity of art must triumph over the inhumanity of the world for the sake of the humane. Works of art attempt to solve the riddles designed by the world to devour man. The world is a sphinx, the artist is blinded Oedipus, and it is works of art of the type resembling his wise answer which plunged the sphinx into the abyss." *Philosophy of Modern Music,* trans. Anne G. Mitchell and Wesley V. Blomster (New York: Seabury Press, 1973), 132. Further citations marked MB, with page number.

[71] Thomas Mann, *Rede über Deutschland und die Deutschen* (Berlin: Suhrkamp Verlag [formerly S. Fischer Verlag] Sonderdruck, 1945), 11.

[72] Letter of October 5, 1943, to Adorno, in Hans Wysling, ed., *Dichter über ihre Dichtungen*, vol. 14/III (Munich: E. Heimeran, 1975), 15.

[73] Hansjörg Dörr, "Thomas Mann und Adorno. Ein Eintrag zur Entstehung des 'Doktor Faustus,'" in *Literaturwissenschaftliches Jahrbuch* 11, Neue Folge (1970), 295.

[74] *Die Entstehung des Doktor Faustus,* in Thomas Mann, *Schriften und Reden zur Literatur, Kunst und Philosophie,* vol.3, Moderne Klassiker, Fischer Bücherei, ed. Hans Bürgin (Frankfurt: S. Fischer Verlag, 1968), 105.

[75] This idea is also explored in Hans Wisskirchen's essay, "Die ästhetische Bewältigung des Faschismus im Doktor Faustus," from the volume *Zeitgeschichte im Roman: zu Thomas Manns Zauberberg und Doktor Faustus* (Bern: Francke Verlag, 1986), 160–95.

[76] Thomas Mann. *Doktor Faustus* (Frankfurt: Fischer Taschenbuch Verlag, 1967), 190. Further quotes will be indicated by DF and page number.

[77] Adorno 68. Further citations will be indicated in the text by "A" preceding the page number. "Music, in its surrender to historic dialectics, has played its role in this process. Twelve-tone technique is truly the fate of music. It enchains music by liberating it. The subject dominates music through the rationality of the system, only in order to succumb to the rational system itself" (MB, 66–67).

[78] A, 69. "By means of organisation, liberated music seeks to reconstitute the lost totality — the lost power and the responsibly binding force of Beethoven. Music succeeds in so doing only at the price of its freedom, and thereby it fails," (MB, 69).

[79] Georg Lukács, *Essays on Thomas Mann* (London: Merlin Press, 1964), 84–85.

[80] Adorno states that no rule is more repressive than the self imposed one (A, 69).

[81] "I mean the total integration of all musical dimensions, the neutrality of each over against the other by means of complete organization" (W, 204).

[82] "Each tone in the entire composition, melodic and harmonic, would have to demonstrate its relation to this predetermined basic row . . . Free notes would no longer exist" (W, 205).

[83] "Bound by the self-imposed constraint of order, which means free" (W, 207).

[84] ". . . the force, the authority of the community — premises so axiomatic that it never entered science's head that it might not be free. They were thoroughly subjective — within an objective restraint so natural and ingrained that it was in no way felt to be a shackle" (W, 388).

[85] Schönberg, who was so superstitious about the number thirteen, that he numbered his musical measures 12, 12a, and 14, in fact died on Friday the thirteenth. Gunilla Bergston, *Thomas Manns Doktor Faustus. Untersuchungen zu den Quellen und zur Struktur des Romans* (Tübingen: Niemeyer, 1974), 224.

[86] "Noch Nietzsche hat das Wesen des großen Kunstwerks damit bestimmt, daß es in allen seinen Momenten auch anders sein könnte. Schönbergs Stücke sind die ersten, in welchen in der Tat nichts anders sein kann: sie sind Protokoll und Konstruktion in einem. . . . [Schönberg:] Kunst kommt nicht vom Können, sondern vom Müssen."

[87] "Die Nuance endet in der Gewalttat — symptomatisch vielleicht für die historischen Veränderungen, die zwangsmäßig mit allen Kategorien der Individuation heute sich zutragen" (A, 79).

[88] "O, ja, die Gewalt schuf einen festen Boden unter den Füßen. Sie war anti-abstrakt, und sehr gut tat ich, mir in Zusammenarbeit mit Kridwissens Freunden vorzustellen, wie das Alt-Neue auf dem und jenem Gebiet das Leben methodisch verändern werde" (DF, 369). "Oh yes, force gave one firm footing, it was anti-abstract, and in concert with Kridwiss's friends I found it easy to imagine how these old-new ideas would systematically change life in one arena or another" (W, 388).

[89] ". . . daß wir sehr viel barbarischer werden müßten um der Kultur wieder fähig zu sein . . . Willst du mich hindern, in der homophonen-melodischen Verfassung unserer Musik einen Zustand musikalischer Gesittung zu sehen — im Gegensatz zur alten kontra-punktisch-polyphonen Kultur?" (DF, 62).

[90] The link of barbarism and estheticism can be considered in light of Broch's dichotomy between ethics and esthetics in art: ethical art has an esthetic result, but art which aims for esthetic effect only produces kitsch, or evil in the value system of art. The end effect of Leverkühn's estheticism in reducing music to its elements, "barbarizing" it, in effect, is regressive, kitsch, and therefore unethical, evil, in terms of Broch's esthetic theories.

[91] (A, 108): "That certain freedom, into which it undertook to transform its anarchistic condition, was converted in the very hands of this music into a

metaphor of the world against which it raises its protest. It flees forward into order. However, success is denied it. It is obedient to the historical tendency of its own material — blindly and without contradiction. To a certain degree it places itself at the disposal of the world-spirit which is, after all, not world-logic. In so doing its innocence accelerates the catastrophe, in the preparation of which the history of all art is engaged. Music affirms the historical process and therefore history would like to reap the benefits thereof" (MB, 112–13).

[92] "Music is doomed, but this historical processs in turn restores it to a position of justice and paradoxically grants it a chance to continue its existence" (MB, 113).

[93] ". . . the dialectic process by which strictest constraint is reversed into the free language of emotion, by which freedom is born out of constraint . . ." (W, 510).

[94] ". . . the work . . . thus can now unfold outside all restraints — that is to say, abandon itself to expression, which, being beyond the constructive form, or inside its perfect strictness, has now been reclaimed" (W, 512).

[95] "Mit anderen Worten, aufs Ueberwintern ist nur zu hoffen, wenn die Musik auch von der Zwölftontechnik noch sich emanzipiert. Das aber nicht durch Rückfall in die Irrationalität, die ihr vorausging und die in jedem Augenblick heute von den Postulaten des strengen Satzes durchkreuzt werden müßte, welche die Zwölftontechnik ausgebildet hat, sondern dadurch, daß die Zwölftontechnik vom freien Komponieren, ihre Regeln von der Spontaneität des kritischen Ohrs absorbiert werden" (A, 110).

7: Kafka and Silence: An Alternate View of Music

WITH RESPECT TO MUSIC, a greater contrast than Kafka to the works already discussed can hardly be imagined, for in all of Kafka's narratives there is scarcely a mention of music. Unlike Thomas Mann's characters, many of whom discuss music, attend performances, compose, or perform themselves, Kafka's characters are in near-complete ignorance of this art. Broch, who so admired Kafka, would also find nothing in his style to compare with the musicality of his own prose. Kafka's spare Prague German is in a way the very antithesis of a musical style.

Kafka himself was unmusical, of this there is no doubt. Though enthusiastic about the theater, Kafka in his diaries reveals little interest in concerts, operas, or the public musical life of Prague. He writes to Milena Jesenska, "Do you realize that I'm completely unmusical, of a completeness which in my experience simply doesn't exist elsewhere?"[1] In a letter of 25 August 1920 he allows that being unmusical isn't necessarily a misfortune, and that "to understand musical people you need to be almost unmusical," a typically enigmatic statement which reveals his antipathy for things musical in general. He seems to have been fascinated by Grillparzer's story *Der arme Spielmann* (The Poor Musician, 1848); though he at first denies this interest, and in sending Milena a copy of the story warns her that he finds the work curiously repellent and pathetic. In his conversations with Gustav Janouch, Kafka does discuss music and his mistrust of it in a way which is oddly reminiscent of Settembrini in *The Magic Mountain:*

> Music creates new, subtle, more complicated, and therefore more dangerous pleasures . . . but poetry (*Dichtung*) aims at clarifying the confusion of pleasures, at raising them to consciousness, purifying them and therefore humanizing them. Music is the multiplication of sensuous life; poetry . . . disciplines and elevates it.[2]

However, the very absence of musicality and music as a theme in his prose does not prevent the reader from noticing that Kafka does indeed present, however tentatively, the potential power of music, not so much as a form of art, but as a metaphor for a latent metaphysical force at work behind the foreground of human existence. The current chapter will present a few of the very infrequent instances of examples of music in Kafka's prose in an attempt to show the extensive reach of music and musicality in German prose of the modernist era, even in as unmusical a writer as Kafka. The works are chosen chiefly as contrast to the other two writers in this study; however, certain similarities are also noted. The works are *Amerika* (1927), "Die Verwandlung" (The Metamorphosis, 1916), "Untersuchungen eines Hundes" (Investigations of a Dog, 1922), and "Josefine die Sängerin oder das Volk der Mäuse" ("Josephine the Singer or the Mouse-Folk," 1924).

In *Amerika*, the text touches on music in several passages. Shortly after Karl Rossmann's arrival in New York, he is ensconced in the futuristic steel apartment building belonging to his uncle; after detailed descriptions of such modern American innovations as the building, the imposing mechanical desk in Karl's room, and the general conurbation visible from his sixth-floor balcony, Karl hints to his uncle that he would like to have a piano. A week later a piano arrives and is whisked up to Karl's room on a freight elevator. As in Broch's *Die Schlafwandler*, the piano does not signify great music; it just reflects the status and wealth of Karl's uncle. Karl is not very accomplished, and plays only briefly before jumping out of the chair, filled with "foolish joy."[3] Strangely, Karl places great hopes on his musical abilities, even imagining as he falls asleep that his playing may have a "direct influence upon his life in America."[4] Karl plays folk ballads which remind him of his homeland, songs which soldiers sang to one another in their barracks. Karl is hoping somehow to use music to convert his strange new American surroundings into the familiar European ones of his youth. Of course, this does not work: ". . . but the street, if he looked down it afterwards, remained unchanged, only one small section of a great wheel which afforded no hand-hold unless one knew all the forces controlling its full orbit."[5] The uncle puts music for American marches and the national anthem at his disposal; the narrator deflates any further expectations of music by slyly hinting that Karl may not be much good at playing his piano: his uncle asks him, "quite seriously," if he might not rather learn the violin or French horn.

Later, at the dinner at Pollunder's, for a brief moment it looks as if Karl's musical talents will be useful for impressing Pollunder's daughter Clara, but nothing much comes of this; eventually Karl does manage to play some sort of "air" for her on her instrument, and even plays his wistful ballad again for her. With tears in his eyes, Karl confesses, "I'm no good,"[6] and, of course, he is not. Despite the fact that he had given his uncle to understand that he loved music, here he performs, perversely, as a "hack"; the German uses the word "hudeln," to do slipshod work; he plays the piece too fast for the hearer to comprehend it; moreover, he allows that he doesn't need music, he can't read music very well, he says. The reaction to Karl's playing is ambivalent; Clara finds it "quite good," and Mack, who has been listening from outside, gives a lengthier commentary: "you play very well . . . it's certainly amateurish enough, and even in these two airs, which have been set very simply and which you have practised a good deal, you made one or two mistakes; but all the same it pleased me greatly, quite apart from the fact that I never despise players of any kind . . ."[7] (This equivocating about both music and its performance is also featured in *Josefine*.) All of this performance comes immediately before the Cinderella hour of midnight, when Karl's disenchantment takes place; he receives the letter from Uncle Jacob notifying him of his disinheritance. He has botched the performance of music, which Clara had so desired,[8] and so the imminent downward turn in Karl's fortunes is prefigured or perhaps even caused by this seeming indifference to the art to which he had once been so expressly partial. Karl's musical carelessness reflects his false consciousness, the burden of guilt which he carries with him from the Old World to the New, and this carelessness is punished.

The figure of Brunelda who appears in the episode "The Refuge" (*Asyl*) is another of Kafka's peculiar strong women with fierce tempers: she is a singer who can be seen as a distant precursor of Josephine the mouse-singer. This ferocious woman has been forbidden by the neighbors to sing, but still makes her voice heard in frequent attacks of rage against her servants and male companion. A negative image of singing, and of music in general, is the message in this chapter; the neighbors all listen to their gramophones at loud volume, but this mechanized music does not really interest them; as in Broch, this is "dead" music. Nor does the reader ever hear the famous singer Brunelda actually sing; a political demonstration beneath their balcony windows occupies the neighbors as well as Karl Rossmann, but even the name of the candidate is inaudible. Only a loud brass band with drums manages to communicate its message, to encourage the residents to support the candidate; opponents shout their opposition, and soon a general cacophony results, with brass instruments, campaign slogans and gramophones all contributing to the chaos.

Adding to the general negativity associated with music is Brunelda herself, with her operatic name, profession, and the conspicuous opera glasses with which she peers at everything around her. The earlier chapter, "The Road to Rameses," has already introduced this negative view of opera: Karl is at first quite taken with his tormentors Delamarche and Robinson, and is impressed partly by Robinson's English rendition of an operetta tune from Karl's homeland; he even likes it better in English than in the original, a statement which might call into question the depth of Karl's musicality. The narrator notes the indifference of America to music again, as before when Karl plays his piano in his uncle's house: "the city at their feet . . . remained apparently indifferent" to the little open-air concert which the three give on the road. Again, Karl is not seeing things as they are: music, as before, causes him to misread his situation.

The final fragment of the novel, "The Nature Theater of Oklahoma," is a parody of Judgment Day; it can also be read as a parody of American advertising and personnel recruitment agencies. The racetrack in Clayton, the site of this recruitment for the Nature Theater of Oklahoma, is a Chautauqua, a revival meeting, and a Promised Land all at once. When Karl climbs out of the subway from New York and finds himself in Clayton, his ears are assaulted by the blaring of hundreds of out of tune trumpets. These are blown by angels, of course, American ones, stationed on hundreds of pedestals of various sizes. Like Karl, these musicians play none too carefully: "It was a confused blaring; the trumpets were not in harmony but were blown regardless of each other."[9] But these angels seem rather to be blocking the entrance than encouraging applicants. Karl, undaunted, climbs over the podium to get to the other side, and as he does so, the angels he passes by cease their playing and gaze after him, in apparent wonderment at his initiative. And Karl, it seems, can play the trumpet as well as the piano. Remarking that they play poorly, he takes an instrument from one of the angels, whom he by chance knows, and plays a song from his past, from some bar he used to frequent. The trumpets are real ones, not just noisemakers, he notes. But even if the instruments are real, the Nature Theater is bogus, as his friend Fanny suspects. She has a job here, in the recruitment area, but she has never seen the Theater, and to all appearances, neither has anyone else present. The blaring horns are supplemented by a troupe of men dressed as devils, also playing trumpets and drums, adding further to the Judgment Day atmosphere, but the whole exercise seems to be a Ponzi scheme, where the only thing real is the "pitch": all are welcome, but to what? Recruiting others? This feeling of insubstantiality, of deception, is emphasized by the angels' manner of leaving. Without further ado, they (and the male devils) have decamped for another rally. As the orchestra disappears, Karl expects that now more people will be encouraged to apply, but this proves wrong.[10]

It must be remembered that this, like Kafka's other two novels, remains unfinished; but Max Brod's rosy view that Kafka intended the novel to end on a positive note is not supported by anything in the novel's depiction of Karl Rossmann's downward-spiralling career.[11] In this first novel of Kafka, then, music is negative, false, and where it has an allegorical purpose, it points to failure, disconnect, and isolation. But as a detail the music contributes to the novel's overall effectiveness.

Kafka's shorter prose pieces deal more directly with music *per se*. In "Die Verwandlung," Gregor's sister Grete is a talented violinist whom he had hoped, before his transformation, to send to a conservatory to continue her musical studies. Now helpless, he can barely remember what her playing was like. One evening he hears the sound of her violin coming from the kitchen, and is drawn out of his room to listen. "Was he a beast, if music could move him so?"[12] It is the music which makes the degraded protagonist-insect remember his human emotions, forget his degraded current state. Music shows him the way to a kind of spiritual food ("Nahrung":

sustenance) he has longed for,[13] but it also ushers in the story's de-
nouement as well as dramatically reinforcing the contrast of Gregor's horrific physical situation to his intact emotional self hidden
within.

In "Investigations of a Dog,"[14] music becomes a metaphor for
supraverbal perception. A dog looks back at his long life, and remembers a crucial formative incident from his youth: while walking
through the woods, he comes suddenly upon a "troupe" of seven
dogs, who act like no other dogs he has ever seen. Most striking of
all, they refuse to greet him, a major transgression of a universal
dog law. Instead of acknowledging his presence, they proceed to
perform a kind of circus act: they line up in formations, walk
around on their hind legs, and do gymnastic stunts. The whole is
accompanied by music, a music which the narrator simply cannot
comprehend, even while acknowledging its great power over him.
He mistakenly thinks that the dogs themselves are making the music, instead of merely performing in time to music. It is some kind
of band music and it exerts a powerful force on him:[15] just as he is
on the point of asking them to explain what is happening, the music takes hold of him, spinning him around, and throwing him this
way and that in a frenzied tarantella, finally releasing him from its
power and depositing him in the middle of a confused jumble of
wooden stakes. From this refuge he observes the performing dogs
closely, and sees that they perform not willingly, but under some
compulsion: "it was not so much coolness as the most extreme tension that characterized their performance; . . . why were they
afraid? Who forced them to do what they were doing?"[16] Once
again, he asks them to clarify, and he is ignored. The dogs continue to perform their unnatural acts, transgressing without shame
or guilt against canine moral codes, finally disappearing with their
music into the darkness from which they had come. Music, the
blaring of brass, signals a missed epiphanic moment for the dog.
Who forced them? He cannot say. In the story's opening lines, he
senses something incomplete, not right, with his perception of the
world about him.[17] When he comes closest to breaking through, to
seeing through the *Bruchstelle* (fracture), music, perversely, throws
him off the track. Emrich uses the word "musikalisches Gesetz"[18]
to express the noncommunicability of the message which the dog
is so near to, yet so far from. The narrator cannot decide finally

whether this is music or noise; music in the sense that it contains some truth he wants to know but cannot, and noise in the sense that it is the summation of many truths, each interfering with and canceling out the other. This seems clear in the text: "a clear, piercing, continuous note which came without variation literally from the remotest distance — perhaps the real melody in the midst of the music."[19] This "beguiling music" may well contain the answer the dog is looking for, but he cannot filter out the truth from the music ("konnte die Antwort von der Musik nicht sondern"). Emrich compares this musical message to the telephone's humming in *The Castle*: the conversations of all the Officials represent the sum of all knowable truths, and thus are incomprehensible.[20]

This crucial experience of his youth sets the future course of the young dog's life: he cannot leave off from his efforts to explain it. This need to understand what happened, he says, robbed him of his childhood and started him on the course of scientific investigations which eventually become his life. These investigations concern the dog's system of procuring food. Thus, this is another example of the theme of *Nahrung* in Kafka (cf. *The Metamorphosis* and *A Hunger Artist*). Here, the investigation concerns the central matter of dog-life, that is, the source of food.

Ritchie Robertson[21] takes an allegorical view of this enigmatic story which yields useful insights. In this allegory, dogs are below the level of cognition which would enable them to see the existence of human beings in the world. The first dogs are a circus act. The narrator dog has wandered into the tent of a travelling circus; thus the overly bright day (spotlights), and the haze (smoke) within the tent. The thicket of sticks into which the dog is driven would be the chair legs of the gallery. Alongside this allegory, music is used as a signal of confusion and blindness; music appears to overwhelm the narrator three times:[22] In his confusion, he thinks the animals make the music, rather than just dancing to it. The human masters who are forcing the trained dogs to do their routines are invisible to the narrator. This cognitive blindness is evident when the narrator dog, a pariah who seems to live apart from men, says: "For what is there actually except our own species? To whom but it can one appeal in the wide and empty world?"[23]

The dogs know that their sustenance comes partly from the earth, and partly from above; in terms of this allegory, then, from that which has been left there for them (or perhaps carrion), and partly from the hand of man. The hand of man is also behind the confusion attending the "soaring dogs," *Lufthunde,* an allusion to German *Luftmensch,* a person who can live on seemingly nothing. For these *Lufthunde* are pets, lapdogs, who are mostly carried around in the arms of their owners. The narrator regards them with envy and contempt; contempt for their idleness, and envy of their leisurely, luxurious existences, which they can devote to "artistic" endeavors.

During his musings on his life, the narrator dog describes the original dogs, his distant ancestors, as somehow having more "authentic" language ("The true Word could still have intervened . . . and that Word was there, was very near at least, on the tip of everybody's tongue, anyone might have hit upon it."[24]) But now that truth, that word is gone, even if one could look inside oneself it would not be there. What is it, this truth that dogs will not consciously know or impart to one another? Is it knowledge of the compact dogs have with man? This would explain the lost authenticity of the race, the greater submissive (*hündisch*) quality of dogs today. The narrator tries to explain the difference between his generation and his ancestors': back then, dogs had not yet become as *hündisch* (this means "beastly" as well as "submissive"). All dogs pathetically assume that *Nahrung* (nourishment) comes from the earth or the sky at least partly as a result of their efforts at watering the earth (the chief dog law: "Make everything wet, as much as you can"). The narrator even sees in the dogs' "water" the chief source of food found on earth. However, he is mistaken, not only about the role their peculiar *Bodenbearbeitung* (soil preparation) plays in the food chain, but also about the importance of sayings, dance and song in procuring food. He says, in his investigations, "The people in all their ceremonies gaze upwards."[25] In terms of the allegory, the rituals which the dogs perform with words, dance and song can be seen as tricks, begging routines performed by animals to procure food from the humans, but for whom cognitively there is no category; phrases like "in die Höhe," and "von oben herab" are evasions, repressing the cognition that dogs are not alone.

In the final section of the story, the narrator dog tells of his attempt to understand the nature of nourishment by starving himself, a dog equivalent of mortification of the flesh. Alone, forsaken by all other dogs, he is half dead with hunger and exhaustion; he is seeking the insight of the hermit in ecstasy, to escape "this world of lies," to escape even himself, "a citizen of falsehood."[26] He is awakened by a large hunting dog. This dog tries to make the narrator leave; he must leave, for this dog must hunt. Neither understands the reason for this compulsion (as before with the circus dogs), but it is clear that this dog is accompanied by hunters, human beings, and as they are discussing this compulsion, music again enters the narrative. As before, the narrator dog thinks he hears the hunting dog start to sing: the hunter denies this, but admits that he will be singing soon. The narrator resists the insight that the music might come from another, noncanine source, just as before with the circus dogs. This melody which he hears hovers in the air "according to its own law."[27] This music has an extracanine origin which the narrator dog can only perceive in his ecstatic, starved state, his "Außer-sich-sein" (the word ecstasy, ek-stasis, means "being outside of oneself") — it can only be the music of the hunting horns, deafening and sublime.[28] The melody strains the capacity of the dog's perception; he wants to relate what he has heard and seen, but "later it seemed to me that such things could not be told."[29] At the same time that it delivers the unheard message, music obliterates the insight that they are not alone in the world.

The central function of music as the bearer of an unheard and unhearable message is consistent with the general tenor of this enigmatic story, and with other interpretations of the existential situation of the narrator and the dogs. The narrator's presentiments of another world, of a higher order, take him only to ecstasy, not insight. He still imagines music to emanate from other dogs, and he expands his scientific investigations to include this "music of the dogs." Just as he imagines that food production really is the result of dogs' pawing the ground, marking their territory, and producing food from "above" via ritual and song, he likewise thinks that music is the product of dog culture. In one respect, his observations are correct: he says it is possible to investigate music production more "dispassionately" than food production, since the results don't particularly matter to dogs. For them, the practical consequences of food procurement are highly important; they remain, indeed, too "doggish" to be objective in carrying out food-deprivation experiments;[30] they just gobble it down when their hunger is too much. There is an even more negative association here: the dogs are unknowing, and afraid of knowing more than they do. The conspiracy of silence which the dogs mutely agree to allows them to keep their illusions intact, that they are the only creatures who matter.[31] It is the not knowing which allows them to maintain their "freedom" — the dog admits, he does not want to trade half knowledge for complete knowledge; why not? "Easy to answer: Because I am a dog."[32] And, true to his dog nature, when he expands his researches to dog music, nothing much comes of it; "It is regarded as very esoteric and politely excludes the crowd."[33] Also true to his nature, the "border area" of study — which examines that music which does in fact successfully conjure up food — is the area of music which interests him the most. But even here he has no success at musical research. He suspects a more deep-seated reason for his scientific incompetence: an "instinct," and "by no means a bad one." This instinct turns out to be the wish to preserve freedom: this instinct, for the sake of knowledge (*Wissenschaft*), not the *Wissenschaft* that he has been discussing, but one of a higher order, has caused him to value freedom. He senses that the freedom that he now possesses is a miserable thing, but still it is freedom. This sarcastic final line[34] points clearly to the dog's need to preserve his state of innocent ignorance of the real state of things in the world. To investigate too closely the musical phenomenon *per se* would bring him too dangerously close to the knowledge which he fears. The whole can be interpreted narrowly as *Wissenschaftskritik* (critique of science) or more broadly as a satire on the biased nature of humankind's epistemological explorations, in whatever area.

Music is in a sense the reverse of silence, as it is the opposite physically and morally of Broch's *Stummheit*,[35] and silence (*Schweigen*) is a constant theme in Kafka. In the novels as well as the shorter narratives, silence has meaning, often it seems to have the force of action. Here the narrator dog is clearly upset by the silence of his fellows, which is a defensive act, even though rooted in higher cognition. The feeling this conveys to the narrator and reader is often that of an aggressive act. Kafka turns the myth of Odysseus and the sirens upside down in *Das Schweigen der Sirenen,* in which their silence is a more "fearsome weapon" than their song. In *The Castle*, K. is constantly met only with silence from the inhabitants of the Castle, whose knowledge is infinite, and the boundlessness of whose knowledge is concentrated in the wordless humming of the telephone line. Kafka's use of music in his writing is related to this theme of silence. It is clear that silence is to be preferred to music. In *Description of a Struggle*, Kafka writes: "Stummheit gehört zu den Attributen der Vollkommenheit" (Muteness is one of the attributes of perfection).

This theme of silence versus music is also important in Kafka's last work, *Josephine*. The metaphor of music has often been read to mean art as a whole, and the story is read as Kafka's final critique of art, especially writing. For the interpretation of this story it is important to know that for Kafka music was a problematic area which came for him to symbolize his loneliness and isolation. The diaries repeatedly mention the emotion, or perhaps gap in emotion, which music brought about. On December 13, 1911, he attends a concert of Brahms's choral music in Prague, and writes: "the essence of my unmusicalness consists in my inability to enjoy music connectedly . . . the natural effect of music on me is to circumscribe me with a wall."[36] His love of literature, rather than music, isolates him: "There is, among the public, no such reverence for literature as there is for music." On December 16 he writes that he despises (and envies) Franz Werfel (whose book *Verdi* was Kafka's deathbed reading), in part because he is "gifted with a sense of music," as well as young, healthy and rich. "I am entirely shut off from music."[37] Writing has channeled all his talents away from the rest of life: "[Writing] . . . left empty all those abilities which were directed toward the joys of sex, eating, drinking, philosophical reflection and above all music."[38]

With Kafka's ambivalent stance toward music in his own experience, his choice of a singing mouse for his archetypal artist is freighted with irony. (This irony is tempered by Kafka's awareness of his imminent death; the reference in the story's opening paragraph to Josephine's "Hingang" (departure) must be read in this light.) This ambivalence is even reflected in the title, which although "not pretty" (nicht hübsch), as Kafka put it, is extraordinarily apt, being, as he said, "something like a scale," in that it balances off two alternative titles, "Josephine the Singer, or the

Mouse-Folk." The inability to decide (on a title, on anything) is a theme in the narrative: Is the predominant figure the artist, or the society for which she creates? Is Josephine an artist, or a charlatan? This tentativeness pervades the entire narrative: the narrator cannot state anything unequivocally, no sooner is a statement made, than it is denied or at least put in doubt. Josephine is presented as "our singer," and to hear her is to know "the power of song." But the narrator cannot even say for certain that she can sing, and if so, then perhaps no better than anyone else in the mouse-folk; perhaps her singing is just "piping," after all, an activity unconsciously performed by all mice. The hidden meaning of music, however admired as an art it may be, is subject to the doubts and reversals of Kafka's narrative perspective: music's inexpressible meaning can require faith not always available to the "unmusical":

> I have often wondered what this music of hers truly means — after all, we are entirely unmusical, so how is it that we understand Josephine's singing or, since Josephine denies that, at least believe we understand it? . . . is it really singing? Isn't it perhaps merely piping?[39] (Ist es vielleicht doch nur ein Pfeifen?)[40]

Pfeifen can mean "to whistle a tune," or "to blow a whistle," or "to play on a pipe or flute." But its most common German usage, "to whistle at," means "don't give a damn" about something. So Josefine's artistry is at least partly humorous, even ridiculous. Moreover, whistling is the European equivalent of booing; but since *pfeifen* (piping) is an unconscious habit of mice, the narrator concedes there might be the occasional *pfeifen* (whistling? booing?) from Josefine's audiences while she is performing. So what initially the narrator sees as a high art form of piping, is soon undermined by piping with overtones of a nervous habit (whistling) and a kind of booing. Indeed, some foolish youngster once started to pipe along in one of Josefine's performances, but was promptly shushed by her mouse-peers, employing yet another form of the verb *pfeifen* (niedergepfiffen), she was "piped down." In any case, the nature of Josephine's art is placed in suspicious light by Kafka's choice of the word *pfeifen*.

The highly ambivalent attitude of the mouse people toward Josephine's singing is a reflection of Kafka's own attitude toward music, and of Kafka's family's attitude toward him and his writing.[41] Kafka's distrust of music in part derives from an acute acoustic sensitivity[42] which he makes clear in conversation with Janouch, himself a composer: "with music we can achieve deep resonances in our emotions . . .";[43] but it is precisely the uncontrolled nature of the emotions loosed by music which threatened Kafka: according to Mahlendorf, "Kafka lacked the means of controlling and regulating the emotions aroused by his receptivity." Writing, on the other hand, he could use precisely for defensively controlling sensory stimulation, she continues. The narrator's attempt (ego) to tell Josephine's story, to do it in his language, is an attempt to control and censor the emotions set loose by music; he does this by narrating her story, criticising her, and finally, reporting her disappearance, that is, killing her. Josephine is the artist (the id) whose creation, music, is too threatening to the narrator to be allowed to continue.

Writing is used as a defense mechanism against unwelcome insight: the narrator keeps the reader off balance by using a dizzying technique of statement and negation, statement and retraction. The narrator's inability to determine whether Josephine's singing is really art is also a sublimation of the writer's doubts about his own writing. The second statement of the story: "Anyone who has not heard her does not know the power of song"[44] can be read to mean the narrator himself has not really heard Josephine's music: the "unmusicality" of the other mouse-folk, after all, is shared by their fellow-mouse narrator. The irony and humor in many of the narrator's descriptions of Josephine,[45] or her art, supports this view of the narrator: For example, the third sentence of the story, "There is not one among us who is not swept away by her singing" (German: Es gibt niemanden, den ihr Gesang nicht fortreißt) is ambivalent, since *fortreißen* could mean "sweep away" or "transport," but possibly also "tear away," or "drive away." The narrator admits that the mouse-folk really prefer "peace and quiet," prefer silence to music, for life is hard, and its many problems occupy their attention at the expense of an art form which seems remote from their daily lives, as it seemed "esoteric" to the dogs, and even "dangerous" and undisciplined to Kafka in his conversations with Janouch.

But the narrator's ambivalence (toward writing as well as music) produces conflicting statements: music may be "remote" from the mouse-folk's concerns, but musical occasions still play a role in their society: as art, it is a figuration of their pitiful existence as a people ("Josephine's thin piping amid grave decisions is almost like our meager existence amid the tumult of a hostile world"[46]), it has a social and political function, for her concerts are more a *Volksversammlung*, in which the people share a kind of communion together before an imminent battle. And it is a comfort in times of trouble: It gives the mice the strength to bear their misfortunes, even if it cannot stave them off.[47] But the predominant attitude of the narrator, while conceding in some instances the efficacy of Josephine and her singing, is disapproval, discredit, and disavowal. This attitude toward the artist as charlatan, as seen also in *A Hunger Artist*, complicates the interpretation of this last work of Kafka: if the artist is a charlatan, how do we appropriately evaluate this artist's writing?

Perhaps the most remarkable thing about this story is Kafka's using his own musical blind spot convincingly to portray an attitude toward (an) art, an attitude which was reflected in his own personal family history.[48] The zigzagging statements and inability of the narrator to make final judgments on Josephine's art reflect Kafka's own concerns, but they reflect real societal attitudes toward art: here and in *A Hunger Artist* Kafka has anticipated today's performance art, and the debate as to whether it is genuine art. Art is a negotiation: Josephine is an artist because society, at least sometimes, agrees that she is. The narrator alludes to this in his comparison of her singing to cracking a nut: "Here is someone creating a solemn spectacle of the everyday."[49] Like performance art, her physical presence is required: you must see her as well as hear her to understand (or believe you understand) her art. But this agreement is tentative, and ultimately dissolves into indifference. Kafka uses the lens of his own unmusicality to focus on the hostility of a public toward an art form; the constantly reversing, negating style of the narration, like a switchback road on a mountainside, consumes much time and verbiage to proceed what in reality is a very short distance. In fact, the story really does not "progress" at all; the entire story is contained in essence in the first paragraph. Under the magnifying glass of Kafka's narrative style, we examine closely and get more detail about the relationship of the mouse people to Josephine, but the narrator does not move from any of the statements made at the outset.

One commentator has noted that the opening paragraph is like an overture containing all the themes of the work to come.[50] (The only important fact missing from this exposition is Josephine's demands and their rejection.) We learn the singer's name: Josephine; she is uniquely female among Kafka's protagonists (though only a mouse, she borrows her name from Josef K. of the *Trial,* who did end up "like a dog"). Here are the other facts presented in this first paragraph: her song has power; there is no one not moved by her song; the people are unmusical in general, preferring quiet; their lives are hard, music is remote from their concerns; the mouse folk are cunning and practical, which is their greatest asset; they take comfort from this asset, more than they would from any possible "happiness" which music might provide. Josephine is the sole exception to this: she loves music and knows how to communicate with it; with her departure music will disappear from the lives of the mouse folk, for an unknown period.

Do the mice actually hear music? Although the narrative continues with what appear to be contradictions, some of them are resolved if one reads the second statement literally; whoever has not heard her cannot appreciate the power of song. But the narrator does not say anyone actually does hear her. That there is "no one who is not overwhelmed" by her song is not quite the direct admission that "all the people are thrilled by her song" would be. And one looks in vain through the story for a direct statement that the mice people actually hear her music: what they hear is "piping," and, although for various social reasons they agree to call it art (at times), they do not hear it as music. Even Josephine concedes this: she sings to "tauben Ohren"[51] (deaf ears) and does not think her people understand what they hear.[52] In a typical "switch" the narrator says it is not just piping which she produces: no, if you sat far away and listened, you would hear — what? Only a kind of soft and tender . . . piping! not different from that of everyone else.[53] It is not the sound but the sight of Josephine which makes her performance special; Josephine has a suspicion (Ahnung) that all this is so; the narrator says the fact that they listen to her at all is proof that what she creates is not music:[54] why else would she deny so passionately that her audience hears her?

The mouse people are so unmusical that they would suppress or ignore a real singer;[55] Josephine is laughable[56] but the folk would never laugh at her, even though laughter is always close to the surface for the troubled mouse folk; the reason for this is that they see Josephine as their protégé, as someone they must protect; she maintains the opposite: she doesn't care a fig for their protection (Ich pfeife auf eueren Schutz) to which the mouse people respond, Ja, ja, du pfeifst. This (intentionally?) humorous response reemphasizes the disconnect between singer and people: either they do not hear, or she only pipes, and does not sing.

The mouse people stand in a parental role in relationship to Josephine, a situation which enrages Josephine, but which she is powerless to change. She has repeatedly demanded that the mouse people relieve her of the burden of earning her living; although they could easily do this, they refuse. Josephine wants this indulgence as explicit recognition of her art and it is precisely this that the mouse society will deny her. She threatens, like a child, to withhold her music, to shorten her performances, to cut out the coloratura arias in her concerts, if her demand is not met. But the mouse people simply ignore these threats, as a parent would; they ignore her words as much as they ignore her music, even while at concerts. They are impervious to these threats, neither they nor the narrator even notice the changes that she makes to her programs. Like Kafka's own parents, their response is distant, uncomprehending, "grundsätzlich wohlwollend, aber unerreichbar."[57] This describes closely Kafka's own lack of comprehension of music, and his reason for making Josephine a musician.

Josephine insists on gathering an audience about her, even in times of severe hardship and danger; the mouse folk, even under duress, grant her this, but when they do gather around to listen, the comfort she provides is a subliminal, dreamlike kind of pleasure, of which the adult mice are barely conscious.[58] This, too, may be a veiled reflection of Kafka's reaction to music in concert; his inability to enjoy it in a "connected" way, as mentioned in the diary entry above.

The mice have some stereotypically Jewish traits: the narrator remarks that they have no youth (Jews are said to be "born old"), though they have a certain weariness and hopelessness, they are tough and confident, they possess a practicality that gets them through their difficulties, they are threatened, they live in scattered communities, they have a particular kind of humor and backbiting gossipiness, and they are "unmusical," a stereotype repeated by Richard Wagner and Otto Weininger, which gained currency against the backdrop of politically and culturally "correct" anti-Semitism of Vienna. But this stereotype, like that of the Jews being the "people of the Book" (and Germans the people of music) is a subtext in the story and in Kafka's narrative stance.

One can see this story in a historical continuum: Josephine's situation is not constant: as in *Investigations of a Dog*, there was an earlier time of authentic music, the knowledge of which is traditional among the mice.[59] Both singer and public have an intuition (Ahnung) of this lost past authenticity.[60] However, this is not the end of the story: the narrator says with her departure music will disappear from their lives altogether — who knows for how long? By the story's end this predicted event has already happened: Josephine has disappeared. (Again using silence as an act, the narrator has either withheld information or has learned something in the course of the narration.) With Josephine's passage from the scene, the connection to the authentic music of the past is permanently severed; the mice have no historical record, and will forget her. The ironic last statement is a striking exponentiation of the silence that her "departure" really is; for her *Erlösung*, her redemption, intensified by the adjective "gesteigert," is not only to be silenced, but to be forgotten, "like all her brothers." It is hard to conceive of a more negative statement on her art than this.

Notes

[1] Franz Kafka, *Letters to Milena* (London: Secker & Warburg, 1953), 62.

[2] Gustav Janouch, *Gespräche mit Kafka* (Frankfurt: S. Fischer Verlag, 1951), 86. trans. JAH.

[3] Franz Kafka, *Amerika*, trans. Willa and Edwin Muir (New York: Schocken Books, 1954), 43. Further references to the English translation will be indicated by "Muir" and page reference.

[4] Muir 43.

[5] Muir 44–45.

[6] Muir 90.

[7] Muir 90.

[8] She asks Karl several times, remarking that "one hears music so seldom here that it's a pity to miss any opportunity of hearing it." Muir 90.

[9] Muir 273.

[10] "Yet Karl's assumption that if the trumpeting were stopped more people would be encouraged to apply was proved wrong, for there were now no grown-up people at all . . . only a few children fighting over a long, white feather," Muir 292.

[11] The translator Michael Hofmann sees the encampment in Clayton as a kind of afterlife, with the descriptions of an American President's theater box pointing to Lincoln's assassination, and he sees sinister implications in the special train transport for the successful candidates (i.e., all) as well as Karl's assumed surname "Negro." Franz Kafka, *The Man Who Disappeared (Amerika)* (London: Penguin Books, 1996), xi.

[12] Franz Kafka, *The Metamorphosis and Other Stories*, trans. Donna Freed (New York: Barnes and Noble, 1996), 49. (Henceforth indicated as "F" and page number.)

[13] "Ihm war, als zeige sich ihm der Weg zu der ersehnten unbekannten Nahrung," translated by Freed as "He felt as though the path to his unknown hungers was being cleared" (F, 49). (Food as a symbol of unattainable meaning: the predicament of Kafka's Hunger Artist, who could never find any food he really liked.)

[14] "Forschungen eines Hundes" (1922), first published in *Beim Bau der chinesischen Mauer, Ungedruckte Erzählungen und Prosa aus dem Nachlaß*, eds. Max Brod and Hans Joachim Schoeps (Berlin: Gustav Kiepenhauer Verlag, 1931).

[15] Franz Kafka, *Sämtliche Erzählungen,* ed. Paul Raabe (Frankfurt: Fischer Taschenbuchverlag, 1987), 327. Henceforth "SE" and page reference.

[16] Franz Kafka. *The Complete Stories,* ed. Nahum Glatzer (New York: Schocken, 1983), 283. (Henceforth "Stories" and page reference.) Translation by Willa and Edwin Muir.

[17] Stories, 278, ". . . I find on closer examination that from the very beginning I sensed some discrepancy, some little maladjustment, causing a slight feeling of discomfort . . ."

[18] "musical law." Wilhelm Emrich, *Franz Kafka* (Bonn: Athenaeum, 1958), 153.

[19] Stories, 284; SE, 328: "ein klarer, strenger, immer sich gleich bleibender, förmlich aus großer Ferne unverändert ankommender Ton, vielleicht die eigentliche Melodie inmitten des Lärms . . ."

[20] Wilhelm Emrich, *Franz Kafka* (Bonn: Athenaeum, 1958), 154.

[21] Ritchie Robertson, *Kafka: Judaism, Politics and Literature* (Oxford: Clarendon Press, 1985).

[22] SE, 326: "Alles war Musik . . ."; SE, 327: "nahm allmählich die Musik überhand . . ."; SE, 328: ". . . war es wieder der Lärm, der seine Macht über mich bekam . . ."

[23] Stories, 289; SE, 333: "Denn was gibt es außer den Hunden? Wen kann man sonst anrufen in der ganzen, leeren Welt?"

[24] Stories, 300; SE, 341: "Das wahre Wort hätte damals noch eingreifen . . . können . . . und jenes Wort war da, war zumindest nahe, schwebte auf der Zungenspitze, jeder konnte es erfahren."

[25] Stories, 304; SE, 344: "Das Volk richtet sich mit allen seinen Zeremonien in die Hohe."

[26] Stories, 312; SE, 351: "eingeborener Bürger der Lüge".

[27] Stories, 314; SE, 352.

[28] Stories, 314; SE, 353: "Immer stärker wurde sie: ihr Wachsen hatte vielleicht keine Grenzen und schon jetzt sprengte sie mir fast das Gehör."

[29] Stories, 314; SE, 353: "Später schien es mir wieder nicht mitteilbar."

[30] ". . . den Fraß vor sich zu sehen und dabei wissenschaftlich zu experimentieren, das hielt man für die Dauer nicht aus," SE, 346.

[31] Stories, 290; SE, 333.

[32] Stories, 291; SE, 334.

[33] Stories, 315; SE, 353.

[34] "Aber immerhin Freiheit, immerhin ein Besitz" (SE, 354) [But nevertheless freedom, nevertheless a possession] (Stories, 316).

[35] Cf. Broch's essay "Geist und Zeitgeist."

[36] *The Diaries of Franz Kafka*, trans. Joseph Kresh (New York: Schocken Books, 1948), 176.

[37] *Diaries*, 182.

[38] *Diaries*, 211.

[39] F, 191.

[40] SE, 172.

[41] Ursula Mahlendorf examines the story's latent psychic drama using a Freudian schema: Kafka's personality is split among the characters, the Mousefolk are the superego, and Josephine is the id, while the narrator represents Kafka's ego. But the Mousefolk can also be seen as a projection of Kafka's feelings about his parents, particularly his father. "Kafka's *Josephine the Singer or the Mousefolk*: Art at the Edge of Nothingness," in *Modern Austrian Literature* 11, no 3/4 (1978), 199–242.

[42] Mahlendorf 222.

[43] Janouch 111–12, quoted by Mahlendorf.

[44] F, 191; SE, 172: "Wer sie nicht gehört hat, kennt nicht die Macht des Gesanges."

[45] Josephine is sometimes made to seem a caricature of the diva personality.

[46] F 200; SE, 178: "das dünne Pfeifen . . . ist fast wie die armselige Existenz unseres Volkes mitten im Tumult der feindlichen Welt."

[47] SE, 177.

[48] The hostile indifference of his father towards Kafka's writing is documented in the *Brief an den Vater,* among other places.

[49] F, 193.

[50] Ruth V. Gross, "Of Mice and Women: Reflections on a Discourse in Kafka's 'Josephine, die Sängerin oder Das Volk der Mäuse,'" in: *Franz Kafka: A Study of the Short Fiction,* ed. Allen Thiher, (Boston: Twayne Publishers, 1990), 130.

[51] SE, 174.

[52] SE, 172: "Wie kommt es, daß wir Josefines Gesang verstehn oder, da Josefine unser Verständnis leugnet . . ."

[53] SE, 173: "Josefine . . . über die Grenzen des üblichen Pfeifens kaum hinauskommt"

[54] SE, 178: "Möge Josefine beschützt werden vor der Erkenntnis, daß die Tatsache, daß wir ihr zuhören, ein Beweis gegen ihren Gesang ist. Eine Ahnung dessen hat sie wohl . . ."

[55] SE, 178; SE, 180.

[56] SE, 176.

[57] SE, 184: "Well disposed at heart, but unmoved," Freed 208.

[58] SE, 180: Hier in den dürftigen Pausen zwischen den Kämpfen träumt das Volk . . .

[59] SE, 172.

[60] SE, 172: "Eine Ahnung dessen, was Gesang ist, haben wir also und dieser Ahnung entspricht Josefinens Kunst eigentlich nicht." F, 192: "We have some idea about what singing is, and Josephine's art does not correspond to these ideas."

Conclusions

THIS STUDY HAS EXAMINED IN DETAIL the works of three major figures of German modernity whose writing has concerned itself with music to varying degrees. It has been largely descriptive and speculative, rather than systematic. Nonetheless, a number of conclusions can be drawn about these writers which center about the following points:

    (a) the influence of music on the philosophy of the writer;
    (b) the influence on the writer's style of this philosophy;
    (c) the influence of music on the writer's choice of subject;
    (d) influence of the relationship of music and time on the writer;
    (e) musicality as an influence on other writers.

Influence of music on the philosophy of the writer

As distinct from the other writers, Hermann Broch explicitly addressed himself to philosophical issues concerning music in general in his discursive writings; while Thomas Mann addressed issues having to do with specific compositions and composers, as in his essay on Wagner, *Leiden und Größe Richard Wagners.* Hermann Broch, a philosopher as well as a poet, was steeped in the philosophical currents of his time, and much of his writing on culture stems from his negative reaction to the positivism which had overtaken philosophy by the late nineteenth century. Mann's confrontation with philosophy was not nearly as professional: he was spellbound by Schopenhauer in his youth, and in maturity read the music philosophy of Theodor Adorno, and he appropriated their writings as montage for *Buddenbrooks* and *Doktor Faustus,* but the philosophy of music was not generally as critical to his thought as it was to Broch. As we have seen, Broch developed a theory of ornament which derived from rhythm, then went on to develop a whole theory of style from that. Like Mann, Broch was interested in modern music, as evidenced in the essay dedicated to Schönberg, but in a much more theoretical sense, seeing in the development of music a cognitive growth which was necessary for a culture to avoid stalemate and the artistic evil of kitsch.

But even Broch and Kafka have one point of commonality in their treatment of music: it has the potential to contain and express a world of experiential content which cannot be expressed otherwise: in Kafka's Josephine we have the figure of the isolated artist whose language is ineffably greater than that of her peers and thus not understandable to her public; the dogs' lost authentic language finds an analogy in Broch's theories of music: in his translation essay Broch hinted that music may be the closest thing man has to an understanding of his own logical thinking; it is a system, open, yet signless, as empty as mathematics, and thus capable of containing any and all meaning.

As distinct from Broch, Mann finds this feature of music, its nonmimetic quality, dangerous, and this dangerous quality is one of the leitmotivs associated with the humanist Settembrini in *The Magic Mountain*: a leitmotiv which will find an echo two decades later in the music of *Doktor Faustus,* where music has become the artist's modality of accessing the world of the demonic. But Mann is not the opposite of Broch here, for Mann sits *zwischen zwei Stühlen* (on the fence) on this question; the connection to death and the human tragic condition is as much a feature of Mann's music as it is of Broch's: the *Lindenbaum* section of the *Magic Mountain,* the song's very deep and disturbing message, so subtle as to defy expression in words, makes Castorp temporarily a better human being, with greater insight into the human condition. Mann continually shifts back and forth, showing good and evil potential even within "good" music. For Broch, there is no "bad" music: there is only "good" music, and kitsch.

Influence on the writer's style of this philosophy

Because of the marked influence of philosophical considerations on Broch's style, which he called a "lyric self-commentary" in his commentaries on *Virgil,* his style is unique, and totally unlike that of either Mann or Kafka, both of whom use a fairly conventional form of narrative. Broch's musicality is not just an arbitrary style, but is based on his conviction that the aim of literature, of all art, is to convey, irrationally, the totality of the world in a single aesthetic work, and this effect must annul time, and thus temporarily suspend the human being's consciousness of death. Broch maintains that this effect is essentially musical, and tries to translate this quality into his writing. His attempts at simultaneity in literature can be seen in *The Sleepwalkers* — particularly in *Huguenau*, with its polyhistoricity — and in the *Virgil*; one could argue that the polyhistoric quality of *The Guiltless* is also aimed at the effect of timelessness, however, each individual story within the cycle is constructed sequentially. Even with the *Virgil*, however, Broch is not always successful in creating the effect of simultaneity; there are sections where the repetitive quality of the prose works against the effect of simultaneity, despite the beauty and lyricism of the writing. With Mann, even in the lengthy *Magic Mountain*, his attempt at simultaneity/musicality through the use of leitmotiv succeeds, for the technique is not as pervasive — the reader is not burdened with syntactic complications as in Broch, with the "one thought, one sentence" architecture which results in overly long sentences. Additionally, *The Magic Mountain* attains a kind of timelessness in its discussion of time itself.

Influence of music on the writer's choice of subject

In the choice of subject matter, music is important for all three writers, but most of all for Mann. Mann's interest in music as a subject pervades his writing from all periods: from the earliest stories up through late maturity, music is a constant accompaniment — it is a theme even in some less well-known stories: *Der kleine Herr Friedemann* (1894), *Luischen* (1897), as well as in *Tristan* (1902), *Tonio Kröger* (1903), *Das Wunderkind* (1903), *Wälsungenblut* (1906); the most musical of the novels being *Buddenbrooks*, *Der Zauberberg*, and *Doktor Faustus*. Mann's ambivalence about music and its demonic powers has been mentioned, but unlike Broch, Mann would not rank music as higher than the written word: the ironic stance which Mann always maintains (and which Broch never does) toward human nature as well as toward the powers of music does not permit this kind of ranking. Music masks over and attracts the decadent, weak, and ill, and in "Fullness of Harmony," Mann's most extensive treatment of specific musical works, he does not allow an exclusively positive view of the effect of music to prevail. Throughout his long career, Mann's writing shows an awareness of the historical changes which impact all art: as Broch does in his essays, Mann's characters Gerda Buddenbrook, Serenus Zeitblom, Rudi Schwertdfeger and of course Adrian Leverkühn must reckon with music's destiny: but where Broch and Adorno see the trajectory that music, and all art, must take as inevitable progress, Mann is by no means so optimistic. Broch thought music offered the best chance for *Geist* (intellect, spirit, mind) to find expression in the coming age; in the 1934 essay *Geist und Zeitgeist* he notes:

> Have Logos and the Spirit disappeared from the earth, because they can no longer have a means of expression in language? They still do have one, and it is the most audible means of all, in this world growing silent, it is become more and more audible all the time, richer: it is music . . .[1]

But Broch, at the same time, was concerned about music's mass appeal, as he was about mass psychology in general:

> for in a kind of frenzy humanity has thrown itself, insatiably, into the arms of music, and in that radical and uncompromising manner which is a basic characteristic of the age . . .[2]

This concern was demonstrated in many of the sequences involving the political or cult effect of music in public life; in *The Sleepwalkers,* many scenes reflect this aspect of Broch's music, for example the Salvation Army music, the music of most of Esch's social life, Pasenow's experience of operatic and salon music, and Huguenau's vulgar dancing: in all these scenes Broch's mistrust of kitsch in music comes through. The negative portrayal of music in *The Spell* has political implications which are clear enough. But contrast this with other scenes from *Sleepwalkers:* for example, Pasenow's visionary experiences with Elisabeth, in the chapel and in the hunting box, and Alfons's insights which are only possible because he has a musical nature: in these instances, it is not music as a manifest work of art, specifically, but rather the idea of music which Broch uses as a kind of abbreviation, or "integral," of the cognition which his characters come to. It is evident that for Broch music, that is, "real" music, which is not kitsch but serious in its ambition and intention, is always absolutely positive.

In Kafka's case, though there are few works, it is clear that music represents the opposite of what it does for Broch. Whether this is a result of Kafka's innate unmusicality, or, more likely, the deliberate choice resulting from it, is unimportant: in any event the negativity and blindness (or deafness) which is usually associated with music as it is perceived by Kafka's characters is emphatically drawn in his final work, *Josephine*. Its ending, this forgetting and silencing of the heroine, is in the most profound contrast to the ending of Broch's *Virgil*. Like Virgil, Broch nonetheless has serious doubts about the efficacy of art, and eventually abandoned it for sociological and political studies, and in *Virgil* he expressed the gravest doubts. But the ending of the novel is a great paean to sound, and of sound. This optimistic, chiliastic ending fairly roars its announcement of a new age — it is a stark contrast to the cacophony which the hapless dog experiences in Kafka's *Investigations of a Dog*. The Word that is beyond speech, Broch's symbol for the Logos which orders and defines existence, though unknowable to human cognition, is that knowledge, that perfect *Erkenntnis*, which for Broch music comes closest to approaching. This is a thoroughgoing contrast to the dismissive, pessimistic sentence of silence and oblivion spoken by history on Kafka's singer Josephine. It is also a stark contrast to the silent, hopelessly pessimistic ending of Mann's artist novel, *Doktor Faustus*. Germany's political abyss, its final hopelessness, finds its appropriate expression in the silence almost beyond all hope which characterizes the final bars of Leverkühn's *Lamentation of Doctor Faustus*. While this work is in effect the "retraction" of the hope and optimism of Beethoven's Ninth Symphony, Broch's musical rendering of the death of a great artist is ultimately and fittingly a renunciation of the nihilism and despair of Kafka's negative view of music and of the utility of art.

Influence of the relationship of music and time on the writer

This study has demonstrated at length the important relationship between music and time on Broch's work, in particular the *Death of Virgil*. While for Mann, as for many writers, time is the great subject, for Broch it is the force which it is art's function to work against. Time's connection to death makes it the great nonvalue in Broch's system; since music, uniquely among the arts, can seem to defeat time, it is the art which other arts aspire to. With Kafka, time is present as history only; time appears to be cyclic, as in Broch and in Mann, but it is not expressly made a central topic, and music is consequently of little value.

Musicality as an influence on other writers

While the work of all three writers is unique, it may at first seem safe to say that Kafka and Mann have had more influence, if not on writer's styles, then on readers' expectations, than has Broch in the modernist and postmodern periods. Kafka and Mann are of course far better known to the public than Hermann Broch, now as ever. So it may be inappropriate to speak of the "influence," on the writing which came after him, of a writer who is so relatively un-derappreciated as Broch. It may well be, however, that an age which has grown away from the conventional sequential narrative style has inadvertently come to appreciate narrations which, while not as complex as Broch's, nonetheless have a similar polyhistoric quality, and where the musical values of words are given more play and status than the semantic ones.

Of course, many writers have used musical themes since Broch's time; here one cannot speak of influence or even "reso-nance." The fact that a writer such as Hans Henny Jahnn com-posed novels of undeniable "musicality" in another form, such as *Perrudja* (1958) in no way attests to an influence from Hermann Broch. This organ-builder/novelist was as unique, if not as well known, as Broch. An even more recent writer, born ten years after Broch's death, also Austrian, is Robert Schneider, whose *Schlafes Bruder*, a best selling novel of 1992, is also concerned with an or-ganist, who is also an idiot-savant. Here one might see a more likely influence coming from Günter Grass's Oskar Mazerath in *Die Blechtrommel* (1959), or even from Jean-Baptiste Grenouille, the genius of one sense, smell, in Patrick Süskind's *Das Parfum* (1985). But in Schneider's work, there are several Brochian ele-ments, even if the work itself is pedestrian, manipulative, and filled with gratuitious violence: the spatialization of music in the percep-tion of the protagonist Johannes Elias Alder[3] and the backward flow of time, as in *Der Tod des Vergil*.[4] The peasant village of the novel, and its tendency toward hysteria and mass violence, is also reminiscent of Broch's *Verzauberung*, but this does not bespeak influence. Even in the work of Ernst-Wilhelm Händler, who has been compared in some ways to Broch by the literary press, and whose work *Kongreß* might recall to some the coldness and amo-rality of certain characters in Broch's *Schlafwandler*, there is certainly no attempt at narration via nonsemantic techniques such as in Broch.

In fact, the more one looks the more it seems clear that the musicality of Hermann Broch's writing is unique in literature; not every idea or style in literature or the arts must result in an influence or stream of work carrying on that idea. Some artists, like Schönberg, create an entirely new idea, and nurture and promote it, giving rise to a "school," although now this school, and this entire musical movement, has all but disappeared. Others, like Scriabin, whose origins were clearly rooted in what came before him (Chopin, for one), wrote music which has had no echo on any composer since, despite its undeniable greatness. Finally, it may be the measure of Broch's greatness that no writer since has been able or willing to try to create, through music realized in words, a work of literature which despite its difficulty, succeeds so well both on an ethical and an aesthetic level, that is, both in its aim, and in its effect, as his.

Notes

[1] KW 10/2, 199 (trans. JAH).

[2] KW 10/2, 200 (trans. JAH).

[3] Robert Schneider, Schlafes Bruder (Leipzig: Reclam, 1992), 33–34.

[4] Schneider 36.

Works Cited

Primary Literature

Works by Hermann Broch

Broch, Hermann. *Kommentierte Werkausgabe*. Edited by Paul Michael Lützeler. Frankfurt: Suhrkamp Verlag

Vol. 1. *Die Schlafwandler. Eine Romantrilogie*. 1978.

Vol. 2. *Die Unbekannte Größe. Roman*. 1977.

Vol. 3. *Die Verzauberung. Roman*. 1976.

Vol. 4. *Der Tod des Vergil. Roman*. 1976.

Vol. 5. *Die Schuldlosen. Roman in elf Erzählungen*. 1974.

Vol. 6. *Novellen, Prosa, Fragmente*. 1980.

Vol. 7. *Dramen*. 1979.

Vol. 8. *Gedichte*. 1980.

Vol. 9/1. *Schriften zur Literatur/Kritik*. 1975.

Vol. 9/2. *Schriften zur Literatur/Theorie*.1975.

Vol. 10/1. *Philosophische Schriften/Kritik*. 1977.

Vol. 10/2. *Philosophische Schriften/Theorie*. 1977.

Vol. 11. *Politische Schriften*. 1978.

Vol. 12. *Massenwahntheorie*. 1979.

Vol. 13/1. *Briefe 1913–1938*. 1981.

Vol. 13/2. *Briefe 1938–1945*. 1981.

Vol. 13/3. *Briefe 1945–1951*. 1981.

———. *Bergroman. Die drei Originalfassungen textkritisch herausgegeben von Frank Kress und Hans Albert Maier*, Fassungen I, II, III, 4 volumes. Frankfurt: Suhrkamp Verlag, 1969.

Broch, Hermann and Daniel Brody. *Briefwechsel, 1930–1951*. Edited by Bertold Hack and Marietta Kleiß. Frankfurt: Buchhändler-Vereinigung, 1971.

English Translations of Broch's Works

The Death of Virgil. Translated by Jean Starr Untermeyer. San Francisco: North Point Press, 1945.

The Guiltless. Translated by Ralph Manheim. San Francisco: North Point Press, 1987.

Hugo von Hofmannsthal and His Time. Translated by Michael Steinberg. Chicago: U of Chicago P, 1984.

"Joyce and the Present Age." Translated by Eugene Jolas. *Transition.* Paris: Transition Press, 1949.

The Sleepwalkers. Translated by Willa and Edwin Muir. San Francisco: North Point Press, 1985.

The Spell. Translated by H. F. Broch de Rothermann. San Francisco: North Point Press, 1989.

Works by Thomas Mann

Mann, Thomas. *Buddenbrooks.* Frankfurt: Fischer Bücherei, 1960.

———. *Doctor Faustus.* Translated by John E. Woods. New York: Alfred A. Knopf, 1977.

———. *Doktor Faustus.* Frankfurt: S. Fischer Verlag, 1967.

———. *Die Entstehung des Doktor Faustus.* In *Schriften und Reden zur Literatur, Kunst und Philsophie,* vol. 3. Moderne Klassiker, Fischer Bücherei. Edited by Hans Bürgin. Frankfurt: S. Fischer Verlag, 1968.

———. *The Magic Mountain.* Translated by John E. Woods. New York: Alfred A. Knopf, 1995.

———. *The Magic Mountain.* Translated by H. T. Lowe-Porter. New York: Alfred A. Knopf, 1964.

———. *Rede über Deutschland und die Deutschen.* Berlin: Suhrkamp Verlag (formerly S. Fischer Verlag) Sonderdruck, 1945.

———. *Der Tod in Venedig.* Frankfurt: Fischer Bücherei, 1954.

———. *Der Zauberberg.* Frankfurt: Fischer Bücherei, 1967.

———. *Der Zauberberg.* Stockholm: Bermann Fischer Verlag, 1946.

Works by Franz Kafka

Kafka, Franz. *Amerika.* Translated by Willa and Edwin Muir. New York: Schocken Books, 1954.

———. *Complete Stories.* Edited by Nahum Glatzer. New York: Schocken, 1983.

———. *The Diaries of Franz Kafka.* Translated by Joseph Kresh. New York: Schocken Books, 1948.

———. *Letters to Milena.* London: Secker & Warburg, 1953.

———. *The Man Who Disappeared (Amerika).* London: Penguin Books, 1996.

———. *The Metamorphosis and Other Stories.* Translated by Donna Freed. New York: Barnes and Noble, 1996.

———. *Sämtliche Erzählungen.* Edited by Paul Raabe. Frankfurt: Fischer Taschenbuchverlag, 1987.

Other Primary Literature

Adorno, Theodor W. *Gesammelte Schriften,* Bd. 16. Frankfurt: Suhrkamp Verlag, 1978.

———. *Philosophie der neuen Musik.* Frankfurt: Suhrkamp Verlag, 1976.

Hofmannsthal, Hugo von. *Buch der Freunde: Tagebuch-Aufzeichnungen.* Leipzig: Insel-Verlag, 1929.

Kierkegaard, Søren. "Immediate Stages of the Erotic." In *Either/Or.* Vol. 1. Princeton: Princeton UP, 1971.

Kleist, Heinrich v. "Die heilige Cäcilie oder die Gewalt der Musik," 1810.

Nietzsche, Friedrich. *Basic Writings of Nietzsche.* Translated by Walter Kaufmann. New York: Modern Library, 1968, 37.

———. *Die Geburt der Tragödie aus dem Geiste der Musik.* In *Werke 3/1.* Berlin: de Gruyter, 1972.

Proust, Marcel. *Remembrance of Things Past,* Translated by C. K. Scott Moncrieff. New York: Random House, 1981.

Schopenhauer, Arthur. *Die Welt als Wille und Vorstellung.* Zurich: Diogenes, 1977, book 1, 327.

Wackenroder, Wilhelm. *Herzensergießungen eines kunstliebenden Klosterbruders (1797).* Stuttgart: Reklam, 1979.

———. *Die Wunder der Tonkunst.* In *Phantasien über die Kunst / von einem kunstliebenden Klosterbruder; herausgegeben von Ludwig Tieck.* Vienna: L. Grund, 1819.

Secondary Literature

Abrams, M. H. *The Mirror and the Lamp. Romantic Theory and the Critical Tradition.* New York: Oxford UP, 1953.

Adrian, Jack. "Counterpoint." In *Music and Musicians* (London: Hanson Books) 21, no. 244 (December 1972): 6–7.

Amman, Klaus and Grote, Helmut. *Die Wiener Bibliothek Hermann Brochs. Kommentiertes Verzeichnis des rekonstruierten Bestandes.* Cologne: Böhlau, 1990.

Anonymous. Article on Barraqué. In *Music and Musicians* 21 (December 1972): 6–7.

Arendt, Hannah. *Dichter wider Willen: Einführung in das Werk von Hermann Broch.* Zurich: Rhein-Verlag, 1958, 41.

Apostle, Hippocrates G., trans. *Aristotle's Physics, Translated with Commentaries and Glossary.* Bloomington, IN: Indiana UP, 81.

Barraqué, Jean. "Propos impromptu." In *Le courrier musical de France* 26 (1969), 75–80.

Barry, Kevin. *Language, Music and the Sign: A Study in Aesthetics, Poetics and Poetic Practice from Collins to Coleridge.* Cambridge: Cambridge UP, 1987.

Bergston, Gunilla. *Thomas Manns Doktor Faustus: Untersuchungen zu den Quellen und zur Struktur des Romans.* Tübingen: Niemeyer, 1974.

Boyer, Jean Paul. "Bemerkungen zum Problem der Musik bei Hermann Broch." In *Hermann Broch und seine Zeit: Akten des Internationalen Broch-Symposiums Nice 1979,* edited by Richard Theiberger. Bern: Peter Lang, 1980, 161–68.

———. "Hermann Broch: auch ein Wagnerianer wider Willen?" In *Hermann Broch: Das dichterische Werk,* edited by Michael Kessler and Paul Michael Lützeler. Tübingen: Stauffenburg Verlag, 1987, 231–38.

Brude-Firnau, Gisela, ed. *Materialien zu Hermann Brochs "Die Schlafwandler."* Frankfurt: Suhrkamp, 1972.

Buhlhof, Francis. *Wortindex zu Thomas Mann: Der Zauberberg.* Austin: Xerox University Microfilms, 1976.

Charriére-Jacquin, Marianne. "Harmonie und Kontrapunktik als Strukturprinzip im *Tod des Vergil.*" In *Hermann Broch und seine Zeit. Akten des Internationalen Broch-Symposiums Nice 1979,* edited by Richard Thieberger. Bern: Peter Lang, 1980, 169–82.

————. "Zum Verhältnis Musik — Literatur im *Tod des Vergil.*" In *Hermann Broch: Das dichterische Werk,* edited by Michael Kessler and Paul Michael Lützeler. Tübingen: Stauffenburg Verlag, 1987, 7–18.

Cohen, Hermann. *Die dramatische Idee in Mozarts Operntexten.* Berlin: Cassirer, 1915.

Cohn, Dorrit. *The Sleepwalkers: Elucidations of Hermann Broch's Trilogy.* The Hague: Mouton & Co., 1966.

Dörr, Hansjörg. "Thomas Mann und Adorno. Ein Eintrag zur Entstehung des 'Doktor Faustus.'" In *Literaturwissenschaftliches Jahrbuch* 11. Neue Folge, 1970, 295.

Dowden, Stephen, ed. *Hermann Broch: Literature, Philosophy, Politics.* Columbia, SC: Camden House, 1988.

Duebbert, Carole. "Brochs *Verzauberung* als 'Anti-Heimat Roman.'" In *Brochs Verzauberung: Materialien,* edited by P. M. Lützeler. Frankfurt: Suhrkamp, 1983, 226–36.

Durzak, Manfred. *Hermann Broch: Der Dichter und seine Zeit.* Stuttgart: Kohlhammer Verlag, 1968.

————. "Hermann Brochs Auffassung des Lyrischen." In *Hermann Broch: Perspektiven der Forschung,* edited by Manfred Durzak. Munich: Wilhelm Fink Verlag, 1972, 293–313.

Eckermann, Johann Peter. *Gespräche mit Goethe in den letzten Jahren seines Lebens,* edited by Fritz Bergemann. Baden-Baden: Insel Taschenbuch Verlag, 1981.

Emrich, Wilhelm. *Franz Kafka.* Bonn: Athenaeum, 1958.

Frank, Joseph. *The Widening Gyre: Crisis and Mastery in Modern Literature.* New Brunswick: Rutgers UP, 1963.

Frye, Northrop, ed. *Sound and Poetry: English Institute Essays.* New York: Columbia UP, 1956.

Georgiades, Thrasybulos G. *Nennen und Erklingen: Die Zeit als Logos.* Göttingen: Vandenboeck & Ruprecht, 1985.

Gross, Ruth V. "Of Mice and Women: Reflections on a Discourse in Kafka's 'Josephine, die Sängerin oder Das Volk der Mäuse.'" In *Franz Kafka: A Study of the Short Fiction,* edited by Allen Thiher. Boston: Twayne Publishers, 1990, 129–35.

Harries, Karsten. *The Meaning of Modern Art.* Evanston: Northwestern UP, 1968.

Heftrich, Eckhard. *Zauberbergmusik: Über Thomas Mann.* Frankfurt: Klostermann, 1975.

Hodeir, André. *Since Debussy.* Translated by Noel Burch. New York: Grove Press, 1961.

Hopkins, G. W. "Barraqué and the Serial Idea." In *Proceedings of the Royal Musical Academy* (London) 105 (1978/79): 13–24.

———. Broch Biography. In *Musical Times* 107 (November 4, 1966): 952.

Janouch, Gustav. *Gespräche mit Kafka.* Frankfurt: S. Fischer Verlag, 1951.

Janzen, Rose-Marie. "L'inachévement sans cesse. Essai de chronobiographie de Jean Barraqué." In *Entretemps* (Paris) 5 (1987): 119–30.

Kessler, Michael, and Paul Michael Lützeler, eds. *Hermann Broch: Das dichterische Werk.* Tübingen: Stauffenburg Verlag, 1987.

Kotlan-Werner, Henriette. *Kunst und Volk. David Bach.* Vienna: Europaverlag, 1973.

Loos, Adolf. "Ornament und Verbrechen." In *Trotzdem (Essays 1900–1930).* Innsbruck: Brenner-Verlag, 1931, 79–92.

Lukács, Georg. *Essays on Thomas Mann.* London: Merlin Press, 1964.

Lützeler, Paul Michael. *Hermann Broch: Eine Biographie.* Frankfurt: Suhrkamp Verlag, 1985.

———, ed. *Brochs Verzauberung: Materialien.* Frankfurt: Suhrkamp, 1983.

———, ed. *Hermann Broch: Materialien.* Frankfurt: Suhrkamp Verlag, 1986.

Lützeler, Paul Michael, and Michael Kessler. *Brochs theoretisches Werk: Materialien.* Frankfurt: Suhrkamp Verlag, 1988.

Mahlendorf, Ursula. "Kafka's *Josephine the Singer or the Mousefolk*: Art at the Edge of Nothingness." In *Modern Austrian Literature* 11, no. 3/4 (1978): 199–242.

Mayer, Hans. *Ein Denkmal für Johannes Brahms.* Frankfurt: Suhrkamp, 1983.

McGlathery, James M., ed. *Music and German Literature: Their Relationship since the Middle Ages.* Columbia, SC: Camden House, 1992.

Miller, James. *The Passion of Michel Foucault.* New York: Simon and Schuster, 1993.

Mozart, W. A., and Lorenzo DaPonte. *Don Giovanni ossia Il dissoluto punito.* Deutsche Grammophon, 419181 1–6, 1985., Libretto.

Naumann, Barbara. *"Musikalisches Ideen-Instrument."* Das Musikalische in Poetik und Sprachtheorie der Frühromantik. Stuttgart: Metzler Verlag, 1990.

Ozzard-Lowe, Patrick. "Barraqué Broch Heidegger." In *Entretemps.* Paris: 5, 1987.

Pfaffenzeller, Harald. Article on Barraqué. In *Neue Zeitschrift für Musik* 152 (July/August 1991): 89.

Reschke, Claus, and Howard Pollack, eds. *German Literature and Music: an Aesthetic Fusion: 1890–1989.* Houston German Studies, vol. 8. Munich: Wilhelm Fink, 1992.

Robertson, Ritchie. *Kafka: Judaism, Politics and Literature.* Oxford: Clarendon Press, 1985.

Scaff, Susan von Rohr. *History, Myth and Music: Thomas Mann's Timely Fiction.* Columbia, SC: Camden House, 1998.

Scher, Steven Paul. *Verbal Music in German Literature.* New Haven: Yale UP, 1968.

Schlant, Ernestine. *Die Philosophie Hermann Brochs.* Bern: Francke Verlag, 1971.

Schoolfield, George. *The Figure of the Musician in German Literature.* New York: AMS Press, 1966.

———. "Notes on Broch's *Der Versucher.*" *Monatshefte* 48 (1956): 2–5.

Simmel, Georg. *Schopenhauer and Nietzsche.* Translated by Helmut Loiskandl, Deena Weinstein, and Michael Weinstein, Amherst: U of Massachusetts P, 1986, 92.

Steiner, George. *Martin Heidegger.* Chicago: U of Chicago P, 1989.

Stephan, Doris. "Thomas Manns *Der Tod in Venedig* und Brochs *Der Tod des Vergil.*" *Schweizer Monatshefte.* April 1960, Heft 1, 76–83.

Symington, Rodney. "Music on Mann's *Magic Mountain*: 'Fülle des Wohllauts' and Hans Castorp's 'Selbstüberwindung.'" In *Echoes and Influences of German Romanticism: Essays in Honor of Hans Eichner.* New York: Peter Lang, 1987, 155–82.

Thieberger, Richard. *Der Begriff der Zeit bei Thomas Mann.* Baden-Baden: Verlag für Kunst und Wissenschaft, 1952.

Vietta, Silvio and Kemper, H.-G. *Expressionismus.* Munich: Wilhelm Fink Verlag, 1975.

Vollhardt, Friedrich. *Hermann Brochs geschichtliche Stellung.* Tübingen: Max Niemeyer, 1984.

Wagner, Richard. *Das Kunstwerk der Zukunft.* In *Wagners Gesammelte Schriften,* vol. 10. Leipzig: Hesse und Becker, 1914.

———. *Parsifal.* Deutsche Grammophon, 2561 090–2561 094, 1970. Libretto.

Warnaby, John. "Festival Reviews." In *Musical Opinion* (London) 112, no. 1341 (September 1989): 314–15.

Weigand, Hermann J. "Broch's *Death of Vergil*: Program Notes." In *Publications of the Modern Language Association of America* 62/2, 1947, 525–54.

———. *Thomas Mann's Novel "Der Zauberberg."* New York: D. Appleton-Century Co., 1933.

Weininger, Otto. *Geschlecht und Charakter.* Vienna: Wilhelm Braumüller, 1904.

———. *Über die letzten Dinge.* Vienna: Wilhelm Braumüller, 1930.

White, John J. "The Identity and Function of Bertrand in Hermann Broch's *Die Schlafwandler.*" In *German Life and Letters,* New Series, vol. 24, no. 2, January 1971, 135–44.

Wisskirchen, Hans. "Die ästhetische Bewältigung des Faschismus im *Doktor Faustus.*" In *Zeitgeschichte im Roman: zu Thomas Manns Zauberberg und Doktor Faustus.* Bern: Francke Verlag, 1986, 160–95.

Worringer, Wilhelm. *Abstraktion und Einfühlung.* Munich: Piper, 1976.

Wysling, Hans, ed. *Dichter über ihre Dichtungen.* Vol. 14/III. Munich: E. Heimeran, 1975.

Yamaguchi, Koichi. "Das Seelenproblem und der Mythos in Hermann Brochs *Der Tod des Vergil.*" In *Hermann Broch: Das dichterische Werk,* edited by Michael Kessler and Paul Michael Lützeler. Tübingen: Stauffenburg Verlag, 1987, 201–7.

Index

Broch de Rothermann,
  Hermann Friedrich, 3
Bruckner, Anton, 53

Charriére-Jacquin, Marianne,
  xviii n. 9, 86, 102 n. 5
Chopin, Frederic, 188
Clementi, Muzio, 67, 70
cognition: artistic vs. scientific,
  13; emotion in, 10; fragmentary nature of, in Schubert, 4;
  irrational, of music, 151;
  rational, 9. *See also* musical
  cognition
cognitive unit (as equivalent of
  sentence), 84; example of, in
  Vergil, 85–91; musical structure of, 86; musical analysis
  of, 87
Cohen, Hermann, 31, 33
conservatism: innate, of
  language, 59; of literature of
  James, Mann, Proust, 60

Danse macabre (Saint-Saëns;
  Liszt), 122, 124
Debussy, Claude, 91, 140;
  *Prelude to the Afternoon of a
  Faun,* 132, 134
dialectic: of Barraqué's work,
  92–93; of creation, 100; of
  freedom, 142; of history, 142,
  146, 149–50; of music, 35; of
  rationalizing, 10; of rhythm, 8
disintegration of values, 33, 71,
  74
Don Juan, 31–34
Durzak, Manfred, xix n. 22, 103
  nn. 15, 21

"everlasting now" (also "eternal
  now" and "*ewigwährendes
  Jetzt*): in Barraqué's music,

92, 95, 97; of *Vergil,* 94, 97;
  in *Der Zauberberg,* 117. *See
  also* time, as stasis

Faust (Goethe): parody of, 35;
  echoes of, 40, 113, 125, 129,
  133, 137, 145
Foucault, Michel, 91
Der Freischütz (Weber), 122–23

Georgiades, Thrasybulos:
  similarities to Broch, 97; view
  of time, and *Vergil,* 95, 96
Georgiades, Thrasybulos, works
  by: *Nennen und Erklingen:*
  95–97
"Germanness": of Leverkühn's
  music, 141; and musicality,
  119, 139, 152
Gesamtkunstwerk: and value
  vacuum, 53–54, 56; Wagnerian, 52; post-Wagnerian, 57
Gleichgewicht (balance), 5;
  ethical behavior and, 11; and
  the Logos, 11; relationship to
  respiratory cycle, 7
Goethe, Johann Wolfgang von,
  ix, xiii, 7, 26, 37, 51, 128
Gounod, Charles: *Faust,* 68–69,
  83, 126, 133
Grass, Günter, 187; *Die
  Blechtrommel,* 187
Grieg, Edvard, 2, 3
Grillparzer, Franz, 51; *Der arme
  Spielmann,* 161

Hegel, Friedrich, xi; on
  evolution of arts, 22 n. 53
Heidegger, Martin: echoes of, in
  Barraqué, 93
Heller, Stephen, 67, 70
Hesse, Hermann: *Das
  Glasperlenspiel,* ix, xii

Weininger, Otto, xiii, xix n. 22
Weininger, Otto, works by:
  Geschlecht und Charakter, 84
Wellesz, Egon, 1
Wesendonck, Mathilde, 1
Wolf, Hugo, 53
Worringer, Wilhelm, 6, 7, 20 n.
  29

Ziehrer, Carl Michael, 19 n. 15
Zuckerkandl, Viktor, 4